Beating the Odds

Getting Published
in the Field
of Literacy

Shelley B. Wepner
Linda B. Gambrell

EDITORS

INTERNATIONAL
Reading Association
800 BARKSDALE ROAD, PO BOX 8139
NEWARK, DE 19714-8139, USA
www.reading.org

The International Reading Association attempts, through its publications, to provide a forum for a wide spectrum of opinions on reading. This policy permits divergent viewpoints without implying the endorsement of the Association.

Executive Editor, Books   Corinne M. Mooney
Developmental Editor   Charlene M. Nichols
Developmental Editor   Tori Mello Bachman
Developmental Editor   Stacey Lynn Sharp
Editorial Production Manager   Shannon T. Fortner
Production Manager   Iona Muscella
Supervisor, Electronic Publishing   Anette Schuetz

Project Editor   Shannon T. Fortner

Cover   Design, Linda Steere; Photo © Wonderfile

Web addresses in this book were correct as of the publication date but may have become inactive or otherwise modified since that time. If you notice a deactivated or changed Web address, please e-mail books@reading.org with the words "Website Update" in the subject line. In your message, specify the Web link, the book title, and the page number on which the link appears.

Library of Congress Cataloging-in-Publication Data

Beating the odds : getting published in the field of literacy / Shelley B. Wepner, Linda B. Gambrell, editors.
      p. cm.
   Includes bibliographical references and index.
   ISBN-13: 978-0-87207-589-4
   1. Authorship--Marketing. 2. Authorship. 3. Literacy. I. Wepner, Shelley B., 1951- II. Gambrell, Linda B.
   PN161.B43 2006
   808'.0663726--dc22

                                                                                      2006020857

A candle loses none of its light by sharing its flame.
—author unknown

Thank you to four special mentors in our lives who shared the joy of literacy and the power of writing with us early in our careers when they invited us to join them in a collaborative writing project. They inspired us and nurtured our professional development as writers.

- Joan T. Feeley and Dorothy S. Strickland for Shelley B. Wepner
- Bob Wilson and MaryAnne Hall for Linda B. Gambrell

To the memory of Michael Pressley, who passed away during the editing phase of this book. A gifted teacher, researcher, and prolific writer, Michael enjoyed his role as a mentor to emerging literacy scholars and colleagues. His chapter on overcoming rejection represents so poignantly his optimism and perseverance.

Finally, eternal love to our families who will always be the light of our lives.

- Roy, Leslie, and Meredith Wepner
- Larry and Brook Gambrell

CONTENTS

ABOUT THE EDITORS

 **SHELLEY B. WEPNER** is Professor and Dean of the School of Education at Manhattanville College, Purchase, New York, USA. She was a reading teacher/specialist and administrator in K–12 education before moving into higher education. She has published more than 105 articles and book chapters and has either coedited or coauthored 7 books relating to literacy and technology, connections between K–12 education and higher education, and leadership skills for effectively supporting teacher education and literacy development.

Shelley served as editor of *The Reading Instruction Journal* of the New Jersey Reading Association, as a column coeditor for *Reading Today*, and as a column editor for *The Reading Teacher*. She served on the editorial boards of the *Journal of Adolescent & Adult Literacy* and *Reading Research and Instruction*, and is currently serving on the editorial boards of *The Reading Teacher* and the *Journal of Teacher Education*. She is the author/coauthor of three award-winning software packages for elementary and adolescent literacy development: Read-A-Logo (Teacher Support Software, 1991), Reading Realities (Teacher Support Software, 1994, and Siboney Learning Group, 2001), and Reading Realities Elementary Series (Teacher Support Software, 1994, and Siboney Learning Group, 2001). Her most recent book publications are *The Administration and Supervision of Reading Programs* (3rd edition, Teachers College Press, 2002) and *Linking Literacy and Technology: A Guide for K–8 Classrooms* (International Reading Association, 2000). Shelley is working on a fourth edition of *The Administration and Supervision of Reading Programs*.

 **LINDA B. GAMBRELL**, Professor of Teacher Education at Clemson University, Clemson, South Carolina, USA, was formerly an elementary classroom teacher and reading specialist. She has coauthored and coedited 12 books on reading instruction including *Best Practices in Literacy Instruction* (Guilford Press, 2006) and *Using Children's Literature in Preschool* (International Reading Association, 2004), and has published articles in journals such as *Reading Research Quarterly*, *The Reading Teacher*, *Educational Psychologist*, and *Journal of Educational Research*. She is coeditor of *Literacy Teaching and Learning* and serves on the editorial advisory boards of *Reading Research Quarterly*, *Journal of Literacy Research*, and *Reading Research and Instruction*.

Linda served on the IRA Board of Directors (1992–1995), received the IRA Outstanding Teacher Educator in Reading Award, and in 2004 was elected to the Reading Hall of Fame. She also served as president of the College Reading Association and the National Reading Conference, and in 2007–2008 will serve as president of IRA. Her current research interests include reading comprehension strategy instruction, literacy motivation, and the role of discussion in teaching and learning.

CONTRIBUTORS

Donna E. Alvermann
UGA Distinguished Research
    Professor of Language and Literacy
    Education
University of Georgia
Athens, Georgia, USA

Cathy Collins Block
Professor of Education
Texas Christian University
Fort Worth, Texas, USA

James Flood
Distinguished Professor of Education
San Diego State University
San Diego, California, USA

Linda B. Gambrell
Professor of Teacher Education
Clemson University
Clemson, South Carolina, USA

William A. Henk
Professor and Dean, School
    of Education
Marquette University
Milwaukee, Wisconsin, USA

Diane Lapp
Distinguished Professor of Education
San Diego State University
San Diego, California, USA

Jacquelynn A. Malloy
Doctoral Candidate
Clemson University
Clemson, South Carolina, USA

John N. Mangieri
Executive Director, Institute
    for Literacy Enhancement
Charlotte, North Carolina, USA

John Micklos, Jr.
Editor-in-Chief, *Reading Today*
International Reading Association
Newark, Delaware, USA

Judith P. Mitchell
Professor of Education and Director,
    Master of Education Program
Weber State University
Ogden, Utah, USA

Lesley Mandel Morrow
Professor of Literacy and Chair,
    Department of Learning
    and Teaching
Rutgers University
New Brunswick, New Jersey, USA

Nancy D. Padak
Distinguished Professor of Education
Kent State University
Kent, Ohio, USA

Michael Pressley
Professor of Teacher Education,
    Counseling, Educational Psychology,
    and Special Education; Director,
    Doctoral Program in Teacher
    Education; Director, Literacy
    Achievement Research Center
Michigan State University
East Lansing, Michigan, USA
(Deceased)

Timothy Rasinski
Professor of Literacy Education
Kent State University
Kent, Ohio, USA

David Reinking
Eugene T. Moore Professor of Teacher
  Education
Clemson University
Clemson, South Carolina, USA

D. Ray Reutzel
Emma Eccles Jones Professor of Early
  Childhood Education
Utah State University
Logan, Utah, USA

Shelley B. Wepner
Professor and Dean, School
  of Education
Manhattanville College
Purchase, New York, USA

FOREWORD

This book may save me hundreds of hours over the rest of my career. Instead of attempting to sit and explain the ins and outs of academic publishing with advanced graduate students, I can now simply pass on a copy of this very practical book. Of course, I probably will still sit and discuss with them the chapters they have read. But the nature of the conversations will likely change. I can imagine the question about this book that is soon to be asked of faculty advisors: "Is it really true that...?"

My experience as an author suggests that the advice and information provided in this book are both valid and vital, and some of the advice is actually entertaining. For instance, in chapter 2, the authors list one of my articles as having one of their favorite titles ("If They Don't Read Much, How They Ever Gonna Get Good?"). But they do not know the whole story behind that article and title.

It is this particular article that I often discuss with my students and other would-be first-time authors. I discuss this article because it was a "failure," as described in an anecdote in chapter 4 of this book, an article rejected five times! I do not know that the title had much to do with these rejections (from *The Reading Teacher*, *Elementary English* [now *Language Arts*], *The Elementary School Journal*, *Educational Leadership*, and *Journal of Learning Disabilities*, in that order). Actually, it was also rejected, initially, by the editor of the journal in which it finally appeared (*Journal of Reading* [now *Journal of Adolescent & Adult Literacy*]). But after almost three years of rejections, I wrote to the editor and suggested that the reviewers did not seem to be suggesting rejection of the article and asked for clarification, for a fuller description of the reason for rejection. Back came a letter noting that I had used only examples from elementary-grade classrooms but that the journal's focus was on older students. So I revised and added two examples from the middle grades and resubmitted. That revision was accepted for publication.

Finally, my paper was to appear in print. But when I received the galley proofs for review, I found that a new title had replaced the one I submitted (the one the authors of chapter 2 found so interesting). The new title was "A Rationale for Increasing the Amount of Contextualized Reading Experiences in the Middle Grades."

I objected. When the editor noted that my original title was not grammatical, I told her I knew that. Besides, she argued, the new title will make the paper easier to find in an ERIC search. I agreed but suggested that even once it was located, no one would want to read it with that title. Ultimately, I got my original title back.

That oft-rejected paper is one of the most frequently cited papers in reading education literature. I think it gained popularity because of the title, not in spite of it.

I wish I could say that that article is the only one I have ever had trouble getting published. Another of my most frequently cited articles, a research paper, was rejected by *Reading Research Quarterly*, *Journal of Reading Behavior* (now *Journal of Literacy Research*), *American Educational Research Journal*, and *Harvard Educational Review* before being given a "revise-and-resubmit" classification by the *Journal of Educational Psychology*. The associate editor basically wrote that there was an article buried in the manuscript, but the problem was finding that article. Although each of the reviewers had suggested rejection, this editor provided detailed advice (e.g., delete everything after page 31), arguing one of the principles developed in chapter 5: Do not go beyond your data. Four revisions later, "Teacher Interruption Behaviors During Primary Grade Oral Reading" was published in the *Journal of Educational Psychology*. So much for the myth about knocking out articles in an evening.

I often use these two articles as examples of the fundamental guidelines that no one ever tells you about—until now, until this book.

As I said, all the advice offered in this book rings true to me. Maybe now I will not end up telling about my publishing travails every semester because the chapters (and vignettes from an array of literacy writers) in this book provide comprehensive guidelines for writers to consider when developing a manuscript for publication.

So read it and weep! None of the authors in this book finds writing for publication "easy." Not one. But every chapter offers powerful anecdotes and guidelines that will elicit your sympathy while providing clear advice on writing for publication. It is fortunate that such a resource is finally available.

—*Richard L. Allington*
University of Tennessee, Knoxville

PREFACE

eating the Odds: Getting Published in the Field of Literacy grew out of our work as members of a panel for *The Reading Teacher* (*RT*) at the International Reading Association (IRA) conventions in Orlando, Florida, in 2003 and Reno, Nevada, in 2004. The *RT* editors at the time, D. Ray Reutzel and Judith P. Mitchell, developed a new session—a writers' conference for aspiring writers—to cultivate greater authorship for *RT* among classroom teachers and university personnel. The editors brought together a panel of individuals who had written and reviewed for *RT* and other journals to provide "tips on preparing a manuscript for success." Participants then were paired with a member of the *RT* Review Board to get feedback on manuscripts that they had written.

As we listened to one another present tips to the audience, we found that we were nodding in agreement about similar experiences and challenges and acknowledging with appreciation the many different ideas that we, too, were gathering. Bill Henk, one of the original panelists and a contributor to this book, suggested that we record our ideas in a book for the IRA readership because so many of us seemed to suffer the same anxieties about writing for publication.

This book is written for novice, developing, and experienced writers who can benefit by hearing from more experienced authors in writing for publication. It is written for faculty and administrators in university settings who have some affiliation with literacy programs and who need and want to get published. It is written for classroom teachers, reading specialists, curriculum specialists, and administrators who have ideas to share with a broader audience and are interested in getting published. It also is written for professors to use as a guide for helping undergraduate and graduate students learn how to write for publication. It can be especially helpful for graduate programs that require a piece of writing for publication.

Our intent is to help those who have tried but have not yet been successful; those who need some tips as fledgling, developing authors or as experienced authors; and those who simply are curious about the art and science of getting published. We offer the individual and collective wisdom of 17 contributors who have experienced both success and failure in writing for publication. As the authors of these chapters have discovered about writing for publication, the ratio of acceptances to rejections is approximately one to four, with three of every four articles rejected wholesale by peers. Each contributor, although writing about a specific topic, also has had experience with the other topics in the book.

Collectively, these 17 contributors have had the following published in the last 35 years: 1,235 articles in print journals, 40 articles in electronic journals, 262 books, 460 book chapters, 90 newsletter or newspaper articles, 93 booklets or technical reports, 7 software packages, 12 videotapes, 1 audiotape, and 38 book reviews. The contributors also have served or are currently serving as editors, associate editors, or coeditors of 46 international, national, or state peer-reviewed periodicals. Some of these include *The Reading Teacher*, *Reading Research Quarterly*, *Journal of Educational Psychology*, *Reading Research and Instruction*, *Journal of Reading Behavior*, *Journal of Language Experience*, *Journal of Literacy Research*, *Literacy Teaching and Learning: An International Journal*, *The California Reader*, *The Reading Instruction Journal*, and *Ohio Journal of English Language Arts*. All contributors but one have served as reviewers for at least 2 journals and as many as 10. They have published in 136 different journals, indicating the wide array of journals available to get ideas in print.

Even with the contributors' many successes in getting published, they nevertheless have had their failures. It is this combined history of success and failure that enables these authors to reflect on their own experiences as they share their ideas and stories with you. In addition, we have included author reflections from a diverse group of developing and prolific authors to help you learn from their strategies, struggles, and successes with writing.

For those who are experienced at writing, we hope that you will discover at least one new idea that can help you with your next writing project. For those new to writing for publication, we hope that you will come to appreciate new ways of thinking about writing and that you will be encouraged to try for the first time or try again to get your ideas in print.

Beating the Odds: Getting Published in the Field of Literacy contains four sections and 10 chapters. Each chapter offers guidelines for a specific topic related to writing that emerged from the contributors' firsthand experiences and their research of other authors. Each chapter also includes an advanced organizer that provides the chapter highlights and closing thoughts to recap the major themes.

Section I provides an overview of ways to get started with the publishing process in the field of literacy. Chapter 1 helps you to develop a mindset for writing, chapter 2 prepares you to begin writing, and chapter 3 encourages you to think about and pursue the idea of collaborating with others.

Section II offers specific ideas on ways to write for journals and other publication outlets. Chapter 4 presents ideas for writing for professional journals, chapter 5 describes what is needed for writing for research journals, and chapter 6 provides ideas for writing for other outlets such as newspapers and magazines.

Section III focuses on writing and editing books. Chapter 7 focuses primarily on writing books, whereas chapter 8 offers guidelines for editing books.

Section IV addresses ways to respond to reviewers' comments. Chapter 9 offers ideas for working and coping with editorial decisions that require you to revise and resubmit, and chapter 10 helps you to figure out ways to overcome rejection of your manuscript.

The author reflections across the 10 chapters demonstrate the unique and common feelings and patterns that emerge as one writes for publication. Photographs are included to provide you with images of the authors. Quotes from authors—both literacy professionals and well-known authors—also highlight the challenges that all types of writers have at every stage of the process. An epilogue highlights the top 10 guidelines that appear most frequently throughout the book for you to consider as you move forward with your own writing projects.

An important assumption of this book is that you already know how to write and have had experience with or intend to seek assistance with the writing process. Although tips are provided throughout about writing, revising, and editing, this book is not intended to show you how to write. Rather, it is offered as a comprehensive and useful guide for dealing with the oftentimes puzzling and harrowing experiences of the publishing process. We hope that, as we came to discover, you, too, will realize or remember that you are not alone in the pain and pleasure that writing for publication brings.

Acknowledgments

We appreciate and admire the many people who contributed to the publication of this book. We recognize D. Ray Reutzel and Judith P. Mitchell for inviting us to serve as panelists for an IRA symposium on writing for *The Reading Teacher*. We thank Bill Henk for thinking that what we had to say should be recorded for others to read, and Matt Baker, former editorial director of the books program at IRA, for encouraging us to move forward with this book.

We are grateful to the chapter authors for sharing their stories, ideas, advice, and wisdom. We could not have asked for a better team because of their expert handling of their assignments. We express thanks to the many literacy professionals who shared their insights about their own writing experience. In particular, we are especially grateful to the literacy authors who wrote the author reflections and to those who allowed us to use comments shared in personal conversations: Patricia Alexander, Patricia Anders, Rita M. Bean, Irene H. Blum, Patricia Cunningham, Gerald G. Duffy, Nell K. Duke, Zhihui Fang, Edward Fry, Ken Goodman, Yetta Goodman, John Guthrie, Douglas Hartman, Gay Ivey, Riitta-Liisa Korkeamaki, Patricia S. Koskinen, Jonda C. McNair, David Moore, Susan Neuman, P. David Pearson, Sharon M. Peck, Gay Su Pinnell, Rebecca Rogers, Timothy Shanahan, Lawrence Sipe, Laura Smolkin, Keith Stanovich,

William H. Teale, and Arlette Ingram Willis. Their willingness to share their personal experiences added immeasurably to the book's value.

We thank the many editors and reviewers who have helped us learn numerous different ways to strengthen our own writing. Although we unwittingly persist with our own idiosyncratic writing styles, we have developed a repertoire of alternative ways to record information and express ourselves for different audiences.

To the editorial and production team at the International Reading Association—Corinne Mooney, Elizabeth Hunt, and Shannon Fortner—we thank you for your willingness to support the idea of having writers speak to other writers about ways to succeed in publishing. We marveled at your system for reviewing, editing, and preparing our manuscript for publication. To our many assistants and helpers—Jacquelynn A. Malloy, Mary Ann DeCurtis, Deborah Tacon, Amy Bova, Paige Cohen, and Ariel Lev—we know that we could not have succeeded in completing this book without you. Your ability to find and synthesize information, prepare documents, and edit our writing gave us the gift of time to pursue other responsibilities for the book.

We also thank our colleagues who at least pretended to understand why we were glued to the keyboard at the oddest times. Finally, we thank our families—the Wepners and the Gambrells—for tolerating yet again our lack of attention to all other parts of our lives so that we could meet at a feverish pace another writing deadline. We know that we could not persist with our writing ventures without your love and patience.

—SBW & LBG

Beginning the Publishing Process

H OW DO YOU get started when trying to get published? What should you do to prepare yourself from this point forward? Although there are no correct answers, gold standards, or magical formulas for answering these questions, there are general guidelines to consider as you begin to think about writing for publication. This section helps you to develop a mindset for professional writing, get ready to write, reflect on your own skills as a writer, and consider the advantages and disadvantages of collaborative writing.

These first three chapters challenge and guide you to develop your ideas for writing, create the right writing environment for yourself, communicate effectively so that your ideas are accepted by reviewers, find appropriate publication outlets, understand the process of and rules for getting published, and become aware of your own writing needs.

Chapter 1, "Establishing a Mindset to Write for Publication," focuses on developing ideas that are publishable, learning about the publishing process, and developing skills to help write for publication.

Chapter 2, "Write From the Start," provides concrete suggestions for getting started with writing, ideas for succeeding with the writing process, and recommendations for working through your own writing challenges.

Chapter 3, "'Always Stick With Your Buddy': Collaboration and Writing for Publication," helps you to decide if collaboration is right for you, explains why collaboration works for many authors, and offers suggestions for collaborating with other writers.

Together, these three chapters provide essential considerations for getting published.

CHAPTER 1

*Shelley B.
Wepner*

Establishing
a Mindset
to Write for Publication

This chapter focuses on
- developing an idea that is publishable
- learning about the process of getting published
- developing skills to help you write for publication

W HY WRITE for publication? Various reasons drive literacy educators to write, ranging from a "publish or perish" position in an academic setting to a natural inclination to record and share our ideas and observations. Many who work at colleges and universities need to write for publication to keep their jobs, get promoted to the next level, receive performance merit raises, or maintain credibility with their peers. Those working in pre-K–12 schools, administrative offices, community agencies, publishing companies, businesses, or the medical field write for different reasons. Although probably not threatened by the Damocles sword of job loss, these individuals find that they have ideas, research, products, and new initiatives to promote in formalized venues. Then there are those who are students who need to write for publication to fulfill a course or program requirement or want to share a new idea or study that began as a course assignment.

Getting work published symbolizes acceptance of the work by others in the field. But as many contributors to this book can attest, the desire to get published is sometimes thwarted by a mismatch between what authors provide and what publication outlets expect or need. At the heart of a manuscript's acceptability is the idea put forward that comes from observations, research, or theories. Identifying ways to develop ideas that will be well received requires a keen ability to communicate thoughts for a specific type of readership. While the authors in this book do not pretend to offer ways this can be accomplished consistently and systematically, we do offer individual experiences and insights that have helped us get our work into print. To that end, this first chapter provides nine guidelines for developing a mindset for successful writing and publication.

GUIDELINE 1

Share Something Unique, Interesting, and Realistic

Literacy educators work in a field in which our ideas bring about small and sometimes significant changes in children and teachers. When unique and novel approaches are created that can benefit students or their teachers, they should be developed for a broader audience. Writing for literacy publication is about sharing ideas, experiences, and research that are unique, interesting, and realistic. Pick up any journal, book, or newsletter and you will discover that there is something unique about what is written.

The following scenarios describe how two different literacy specialists turned their unique ideas into publications.

One reading specialist working in an elementary school developed a set of game-like methods for developing students' word-reading fluency. Teachers at her school complimented her regularly on her students' success when using these methods, and one teacher suggested that she try to publish her approach. Intrigued by this idea, the reading specialist developed a pre–post assessment system to measure student achievement. She then wrote and submitted a manuscript to a state literacy journal. The reviewers replied that they were impressed with her contribution and recommended her manuscript for publication.

A young scholar in his first year of teaching literacy courses was using a unique way to encourage undergraduate students to test their theories about literacy. Although he thought that his approach was commonplace, his mentor recognized that his field-based, reflective protocol was different from what was typically expected of teacher candidates and encouraged this young scholar to investigate the value of the protocol further. The mentor suggested that he first do some reading to find out if the technique already existed in the literature and, if not, to pursue it as a line of research. The young scholar spent the next several years researching, revising, and writing about this protocol and found that he was able to get three different manuscripts published from his research.

The reading specialist and the young scholar were successful because they had developed an idea that had worked for them, had not been used before in their immediate environments, and had intrigued their colleagues. Those who reviewed their manuscripts agreed that the work was unique and relevant, and, therefore, these researchers were successful in getting published. However, it is not always that easy. What you consider unique, interesting, and realistic might not similarly impress a reviewer. How do you know that what you have to share will be considered valuable? There are some things you can and should do to test the value of your ideas.

Conduct Literature Searches

In order to develop ideas of value, adopt a mindset of becoming very knowledgeable about your specific area of interest. For example, my particular interest area, technology and literacy, is broad. Countless publications provide specific ways to use technology to promote literacy development. Software applications, the Internet, multimedia and hypermedia productions, writing projects, keyboarding, professional development, and teacher education are just some of the topics explored in the literature. However, I have a special interest in helping teachers and teacher educators become sufficiently comfortable with technology to want to use it regularly in their classrooms.

> "Writing crystallizes thought, and thought produces action."
> —PAUL MEYER

A colleague and I decided that we needed to learn from those who use technology regularly in order to know how to advise others to use these skills in the classroom. When we conducted a literature search, we found that admonishments about what teachers should know and be able to do dominated the research and that very little attention was given to the actual changes in responsibilities that teachers must realize in order to truly succeed with technology instruction. We also found that, although individual successes were reported, the teachers who were using technology were not being provided the kind of information that would guide them toward achieving the level of technology integration we envisioned, nor were they being asked about their individual experiences with technology. The results of this literature search reassured us that we should proceed with our specific line of questioning. Once we concluded our study, we again searched for any new literature on the topic in order to assure ourselves about the uniqueness of our claims. We believe that by checking the literature again and again, we saved ourselves a great deal of grief and frustration.

Talk to Others

The idea that my colleague and I developed did not just appear. Both of us had been conducting various types of technology-based studies with teachers, and because of our interest in this area, we used every opportunity to talk to others with similar interests. I spent much of my time talking to both novice and expert teachers who shared their positive and negative technology-related experiences with me. Their openness helped me realize that teaching with technology is a more complicated process than I had appreciated and that the additional responsibilities required to use technology effectively needed to be exposed and addressed.

My colleague spent a great deal of time talking to colleagues at his university about the issues related to using technology in college classrooms. His conversations with others, when combined with his own experiences, led him to hypothesize that environmental issues affected a teacher's use of technology. Our conversations with others served as a catalyst for expanding our ideas to include an interrelationship between what teachers are expected to do and how the environment does or does not support these responsibilities.

Even if it means paying for a lunch or dinner, it helps to "pick the brain" of someone who shares your area of interest. The conversation could be face to face, by telephone, through e-mail, or in a chat room. Look for listservs of individuals who are interested in your topic area and who would be willing to discuss your ideas with you. Consider using social networks outside of work as a place to test ideas. I once found myself writing feverishly on napkins at a Sunday brunch when I discovered that a friend of a friend had conducted some interesting research connected to my area of interest. He was kind enough to take the time to share with me names of people to contact and articles to read. Remember that people networks beget people networks. Once you allow yourself to open up to others about your writing and research, you will discover others who are willing to share with you in untold ways.

Read, Read, Read

Although it goes without saying that reading published work related to a topic of interest contributes to knowledge of new and historically significant ideas, it is important to realize that reading of the literature also stimulates new thought, solidifies beliefs about specific ideas, and expands horizons about research, theories, and practices. Timothy Rasinski, one of the authors in this book, shared with a group of budding authors at a conference that reading helps to generate new ideas and ways to express them. The late children's author Paula Danziger explained in a one-on-one interview (personal communication, May 31, 1992) that her voracious reading habits were the key to her success. As the contributors to this book know from their own understanding about the connection between reading and writing, those inclined to read widely are more likely to write well.

> "My advice to would-be young authors is to read a lot, write a lot, and not worry about creating a finished product."
> —KEVIN HENKES

As an avid reader of the relevant literature in your field, you come to know what is already in print regarding your topic area. Only then are you able to

Patricia Cunningham, Wake Forest University

Be an Optimist

I wrote my first pieces while a graduate student at the University of Georgia. For a research course, my colleague students and I had to conduct a research study, write it up, and submit it to a journal. My study on dialect influences on reading got published in *Reading Research Quarterly*. I wrote another article, which also got accepted. This second article, unfortunately, got returned to me when a new editor took over the journal. The editor explained that the previous editor had accepted too many articles. By the time I got this rejection, however, I was hooked. Success is a strong motivator! Because I started with two acceptances, I just assumed what I wrote would get published.

Since then, I have had many rejections, often worded "a good article but just does not meet our needs." Being an optimist, I chose to believe this and sent that piece to another journal. Soon, I was making a list of journals to which I would send an article before I even sent it to the first journal. When an article was rejected, I sent it to the next journal on my list.

For me, writing is always the last step in thinking. Mostly, I write about practical teaching strategies, and by the time I write about them, I have tried them out with lots of children and talked about them with many teachers. Writing gives me closure. When I sit down to write something, it is almost like I have no choice about writing it. It needs to be written and haunts me until I finally give in and get to work and write it.

The best example of this was *Phonics They Use* (4th edition, Allyn & Bacon, 2003). I have always loved words and loved coming up with activities that actively engaged children with words. In the summer of 1989, I read Marilyn Jager Adams' *Beginning to Read: Thinking and Learning About Print* (MIT Press, 1990) and realized that there was a whole body of research to support the kinds of phonics activities I had found to be successful with struggling readers. "I have to write a book on practical, successful phonics activities," said the persistent voice in my head. I tried to resist. "I can't write a book now. We are just about to head out for the Oregon coast for the summer. Besides, who would read it? No one thinks phonics matters anymore."

On our Oregon trip, my husband carried a "nonportable" Mac computer on and off airplanes and into and out of motels all along that beautiful coast. Being an early riser and not adjusting well to the time difference, I wrote for several hours every morning before the rest of the family awoke. *Phonics They Use* was inside me and insisted on coming out. I have not felt so absolutely compelled to write anything since then, but I have learned not to argue with the "you have to write this" voice inside my head.

---

synthesize the knowledge that exists, identify topics that need further exploration, and develop projects that address these areas of need.

Attend Conferences, Symposia, and Workshops

Make use of every opportunity to attend conferences, symposia, and workshops to listen to what others are doing in the field but have not yet published. This approach to gathering information can stimulate ideas or confirm whether your idea is unique or that it has already been explored, saving you valuable time. In addition, such forums also provide opportunities to check out the latest books and products on the market that may reveal current and upcoming trends in literacy.

At the 2004 Annual Convention of the International Reading Association, Jack Cassidy's session on "What's Hot and What's Not in Reading" indicated that the hot topic for that year centered on literacy coaches, especially with regard to the No Child Left Behind Act of 2001 (2002) Reading First initiative. While I heard conferees buzzing about the topic of literacy coaches in their attempts to find answers to the many questions they had about the effectiveness of this role, I realized that their answers could not be found yet because longitudinal data were still needed about the impact of literacy coaching on the standardized test scores of first graders. This is an example of how "hot" topics can have subtle and complicated facets that need to be explored.

See Your Ideas Written Down

The clarity of an idea that is solely in your mind can fade in and out of focus. When you venture to write the idea down and then read it silently or aloud, you can better determine if it makes sense. Although it is difficult at times to actually sit down and set your ideas to paper (I need food and decaf coffee by my side before I can focus), a quick and dirty summary—even just a listing of your ideas—can save time in the long run. The idea can become something to be researched further or become the core idea of an opinion piece.

Once you have something—anything—recorded, it is much easier to return to it than to start from scratch because you can move immediately into revising and expanding your thoughts. This also helps to avoid the "blank page (or screen) syndrome" in which, when faced with an empty page or screen, you panic at the thought of having to write. As reading researcher Edward Fry said, "You just need to sit down and do it" (personal communication, December 4, 2004). If you find that even with the best intentions you still cannot get yourself to write down your thoughts, find a friend who will transcribe for you. Have that person ask you questions such as, What is it you are trying to say? Tell me more. Why is it important for others to know this? What makes it unique, interesting, and realistic? Who are you writing for? What do you want others to know? As you share your responses, have that person record your ideas. You will be amazed by what you already know, and you will have a record for moving forward with your idea.

Communicate the Theory Behind Your Idea

Make a habit of asking yourself about the theory behind the topic of a paper you are about to write. Why are you researching the topic? What is the theory that supports your research question? I remember that when I was first asked these questions, I did not think I had a theory. I immediately thought of famous theories such as Einstein's theory of relativity and Newton's theory of gravity. I also thought of renowned educational theories such as Dewey's (1916, 1923, 1938) theory of "learning by doing" and Vygotsky's (1934/1978, 1993) theory of socially shared cognition.

I came to realize that a theory is simply a set of beliefs about an idea, issue, or phenomenon. Theories are formed through study of research and reading on a topic that usually leads to further study. Even though you might not have years of research to support your theories, you nevertheless have conceptions and views about different areas of literacy because of your unique sets of experiences. Following are two examples that demonstrate how experience can serve as a catalyst for developing and revising theories and research practices.

A former doctoral student was exploring the topic of how reading specialists are prepared for their jobs at the graduate level. Carol developed a survey to investigate what faculty and administrators of graduate reading programs across the United States do in their programs to prepare these professionals. Her survey reflected her belief that reading specialists should be prepared to serve as both leaders of literacy programs and instructors of reading in order for them to truly have an impact on literacy instruction in the schools. Her belief about the importance of their leadership role came from her own experiences as a reading specialist, her work with other reading specialists, and her research on their role in the schools. This belief or theory was reflected in the majority of her survey questions because she asked respondents to describe what their programs were doing to prepare reading specialists for a leadership role. If she had had a different theory or set of beliefs, the survey questions would have been different.

After years of experience as a high school remedial reading specialist, Chester decided that he wanted to work directly with teachers to help them consider alternative approaches to instruction and promote congruence between content area instruction and remedial reading instruction. Chester began by offering demonstration lessons in English classes and then expanded his demonstrations to social studies classes. He established an electronic feedback system for each of his students so that he knew how they were performing in the various content area classes. This system also provided information about the teachers' instructional and assessment strategies.

Chester found that his students were performing differently with him than they were in their classrooms and developed a theory about the way in which the resource role could be developed in high school settings. His review of the research led him to conclude that his specific theory had not been discussed and that he needed to conduct his own survey of high school reading specialists to test his ideas. His survey findings revealed only a lukewarm interest in his ideas due to the respondents' own situational challenges. These findings helped him understand reasons for the lack of material on this topic and motivated him to search for more realistic expectations for serving in the resource role. Currently, Chester is field-testing his theory in different high schools and has a contract to write a book on the topic.

The examples of Carol and Chester demonstrate that theories can emerge at different times in your research as a result of your own experiences and the experiences of others. Although you might approach your research with one set of beliefs, you may soon come to realize that your developing theories need to be adjusted to reflect your research findings. I have come to appreciate that the most credible theories have years of research to support them.

How can you justify your theory? The first step is to record the reasons behind your beliefs. These reasons could include your own experiences as a teacher, parent, child, administrator, staff member, spouse, or friend. The theory should include findings from the reading that you have done plus any formal or informal research that you have conducted. For example, as a parent of twins, I came to believe that preschoolers can learn to read words before they learn phonics. The second step is to chronicle the evolution of your idea. In my case, I recorded the many things that I observed or did with my own children that led me to my theory. The third step is to test your theory. After you have conducted searches, talked to others, and attended conferences (see guideline 1), collect as much data as possible to support your theory. Guideline 3 describes what this means and how it is done.

GUIDELINE 3

Provide Data Through Sound Methodology to Support Your Theory

Data—information, facts, or statistics—are needed to put forward a unique idea that is grounded in theory and worthy of publication. For instance, I have heard the claim over and over that No Child Left Behind has a history of bipartisan support that dates back to Ronald Reagan's presidency. To make that claim, information *has* to be made available to show that Democrats and Republicans have been promoting standards and testing since the early 1980s. Otherwise, the claim would not be valid.

The methodology—or process for gathering data or information to support your theory or claim—should be sensible and convincing. I recently read a manuscript submitted for publication to a reading journal about the usefulness of a particular grouping configuration for students in elementary school. I was excited about the topic because of its potential insights on how to best organize groups of students for learning. As the authors described the methodology, I discovered

Timothy Shanahan,
University of Illinois
at Chicago

Quacking Like a Duck Does Not Make You a Duck: Finding Your Own Voice

When I was a graduate student, I wanted to become a researcher and publish my ideas. I did not understand how contradictory those goals were. It took years of writing experience to figure it out.

Successful writing depends on being able to clearly communicate ideas in an interesting way that allows others to understand what you are trying to say. That is the crux of writing—trying to find appropriate ways to communicate valuable ideas. However, writers do not write to communicate message content alone. A writer creates a persona. Writing reveals a person behind the text. This implied author can seem friendly or distant, authoritative or uncertain, no matter what the human author is really like.

Unfortunately, when trying to be somebody new—in this case, I wanted to go from being a first-grade teacher to a university researcher—people tend to mimic the voices of those in the group they want to join. To be accepted as a researcher, I tried to sound like a researcher, and that meant my writing had to reveal the new me. Unfortunately, establishing a new identity usually includes bad impressions of who writers want to become, which can be the enemy of clear communication.

I hoped to be a scholar, so I tried to sound scholarly. But quacking like a duck does not make you a duck. There is almost always something missing in such mimicry. I thought scholars wrote boring, highly complicated, abstract prose, so I emulated their style to show my new identity. Fortunately, I eventually came to understand what scholarship actually was and why it had seemed too dry to me before, and I became confident in my new identity. An experience that crystallized this for me arose when I dared to relax my formal pretend-researcher voice just once and published something in a more personal style. I was surprised at the positive response from readers, and this changed my writing from then on. Writers have to find their own voice, a voice that conveys who they are, and the confidence to share that voice with others.

that the distinction between the experimental and control groups was so vastly different, and the unique aspects of the treatment were so muddled, that any conclusions drawn could not be attributed to the treatment.

Upon reading another study, I found that the author did not really know how to translate a hunch about the usefulness of a science literacy program into a viable and convincing study. The author did not explain why the program would work (the theory behind the program) and did not attempt to test its usefulness. The author should have simply reported on previous research studies conducted with children using qualitative or quantitative methods, or a combination of both.

As stated earlier, the most credible theories come from research findings. This research could include information from the literature, observations, or anecdotes.

If I use a method with children that seems to motivate them to succeed, I need to find similar examples from the literature that will help me to convince others of the value of my approach. These examples are the methods used to validate or investigate the theory's value. The theory could be a description of one or more types of data, such as observations of students' time on task, the nature of student interactions, the accuracy of student responses on worksheets, the quality of projects, or the percentage of correct answers on informal or standardized tests.

My first bona fide research project was an extension of Ken and Yetta Goodman's work with environmental logos and their theory that young children come to school already reading (Goodman & Altwerger, 1981; Goodman & Goodman, 1981). I tested their theory with my own two children, and then accidentally discovered a technique that extended the Goodmans' theory. After working with my own children for nearly a year to support the idea that children can learn to read words and sentences with logos before they learn phonics, I realized that I needed to move beyond my data set of two offspring. I went to a local nursery school to gather data from two sets of classes over a six-month period. By extending and objectifying my research, I contributed to the credibility of my theory.

Not all ideas require formalized quantitative or qualitative research. It really depends on the publication outlet. Yet, and as stated earlier, the more information and data there are to support a claim, the more receptive reviewers will be of your work. In my experience, most of the manuscripts rejected for publication do not have a sound process for collecting data. The claims are quite intriguing, but the authors do not adequately determine how best to study the importance of their idea.

To develop a sound method for gathering data, ask yourself the following: What do I need to do to best support my theory? How should I go about doing it? What help do I need for this to happen? Can I realistically accomplish what I need to accomplish? If you cannot accomplish all that is needed, that is OK, too. You may be able to narrow or reformulate your idea, postpone testing your theory until you have the appropriate context and resources, or determine a different outlet that would be more suitable. The process that you use—whether it is reading different types of material, conducting case studies, interviewing or surveying a specific group of individuals, or conducting pre–post test analyses—should contribute to the strength of your conviction and will be evident in your writing.

Convey That You Are Passionate and Knowledgeable About Your Idea

The more involved you are with an idea, the more passionate you become about it. For example, a reading supervisor named Bonita who was newly hired by an impoverished school district was convinced that if a school district wants to change teachers' beliefs and practices, teachers need professional development opportunities for extended periods of time that include training, modeling, and mentoring. Having worked successfully at another school district in a similar capacity for more than 25 years, Bonita observed that the teachers who really evolved were those who had frequent, varied, and individualized help by mentors. Bonita decided to begin her doctoral dissertation to study the use of professional development to change teachers' beliefs and practices about reading instruction. She was so pleased with her findings that she presented the results at state and national conferences and was encouraged by a journal editor to develop a manuscript about her work.

> "Never write anything that does not give you great pleasure. Emotion is easily transferred from the writer to the reader."
>
> —JOSEPH JOUBERT

Even if your work does not attract journal editors immediately, you may make discoveries that will have a lasting impact on instruction. Take, for example, Nancy Atwell's (1985) work with eighth-grade students that explored the use of writing workshop. She wanted her students to use written language naturally, and she wanted to break away from her own stereotype as a grammar teacher. Her work was especially important for middle school teachers who used her framework as the impetus for their own transformations.

Sometimes when I am reviewing a manuscript, I suspect that it may be a term paper from a graduate course rather than an enduring passion. A term paper, although probably "A" work for a professor, does not have that special spark that speaks to the author's long-term investment in an idea. Manuscripts that are alive with examples and anecdotes and clearly supported by data communicate immediately to me the author's ongoing and steadfast work in an area.

You do not have to be 50 years old with 25 years' experience in the field to claim that you are an expert on a topic. You need to embrace an idea and test it over time. Your experiences with the idea can be real or vicarious, in which others in the field are conducting work that supports or complements your ideas. Staying focused on an idea helps you to remain abreast of the most current related research and aware of other professionals who are closely aligned with and interested in your work. After a while, you know who shares your passion for a specific topic, and you can network with them to exchange ideas.

The more involved you become, the more obvious it will be to those who review your work. It will be apparent in your observations and anecdotes, your mention of previous research, and your style of communicating that you, indeed, own your work.

GUIDELINE 5

Stay Focused on Your Main Idea

Good writing remains focused. Years ago, my supervisor told me that she lived by the motto "Keep your eye on the ball." She explained that when we stop focus-

What Drives Your Passion?

Arlette Ingram Willis, University of Illinois at Urbana-Champaign

My writing joins the writing of a multitude of scholars of color who have questioned, critiqued, and challenged inequities in U.S. public education. Literacy—when conceptualized as abilities to communicate, to be understood, and to understand others—is a human right, one that automatically belongs to everyone, not one that needs to be legislated. I support and encourage the exploration of multiple ideologies to better understand the literacies of all learners.

In my writing, I critique the presumptuousness that reveres science (scientific methods and interpretations) above humanity—the qualities and characteristics and the compassion of human beings—and frames literacy as primarily cognitive. My critique focuses on research that continues to paint, with broad, uneven strokes, educationally underserved children of color, children living in poverty, and multilingual children as problematic, struggling learners and biological aberrations of white, middle- to upper-class English speakers. The essentialist traditions within literacy research that permit unchecked and unchallenged stereotyping continue to do so by ignoring or marginalizing the literacy histories of people of color as the status quo is reproduced. To counter the disinformation surrounding children of color and their literate abilities, I use multiple frameworks for understanding and grounding reading research and instruction, frameworks that document and illustrate the shortcomings of the past while suggesting reforms for present and future initiatives.

To strengthen and improve literacy research, we must begin by theoretically conceding, first, to the humanness within all children; second, to their individual uniqueness; third, to their richly complex lives, language, and experiences; and, fourth, to their abilities as learners to negotiate daily among multiple epistemologies, languages, and contexts. I believe that literacy researchers should welcome multiple ideologies, histories, definitions, theories, methods, analyses, and interpretations from a range of scholars, especially scholars of color, with a commitment to action, social justice, and equality for all literacy learners.

ing on what we believe is important, we lose momentum in achieving our goal. Hard as it is, we need to develop tunnel-like vision to maintain our focus on the light at the end. This is also true of writing. We need to clearly determine what we are trying to share and to let go of other—albeit equally interesting—thoughts to communicate our main message.

This is not as easy as it sounds. How many times has someone reviewed what you wrote and asked, "What does this have to do with...?" Even though you knew that your digression did not really relate directly to what you wrote, you thought it was too interesting to eliminate. Think of the people you know who start telling you one story and digress to three other stories that are not even remotely connected to the original tale. Our multipronged storyteller friends usually lose us somewhere in the process.

I reviewed one article on the ABCs of reading instruction that led me in so many directions that, by the time I came to the end of the manuscript, I had no idea of its purpose. It did not provide an ABC list of anything or offer any type of focused message. I reviewed another manuscript that attempted to show how two different reading programs could coexist within the same classroom. The author was caught up in presenting extensive cases of teachers' uses of each program and never really demonstrated how the two program models worked together. The effect was that the manuscript seemed directionless and pointless.

Many writers have difficulty giving up those sections of a manuscript that take the reader away from its central focus. This is where outlines can help to shape the direction of your writing. Graphic organizers, such as semantic mapping and webbing, can be used to provide a visual structure for organizing ideas. Software programs such as Inspiration 7.5 (2003) and Kidspiration 2.0 (2004) make the process of sorting and resorting ideas much easier. (Chapter 2 provides additional information about how outlines can help with writing.)

If you are someone who does not function well with outlines or graphic organizers, but you need to record all of your thoughts before you feel ready to prepare a piece for publication, keep in mind the art of pruning. Ask yourself, What do I want to communicate? Does this paragraph contribute or detract from my main thesis? What information, ideas, or stories can be eliminated without compromising my message?

Use page limits as a helpful guide to pruning. Although you might find it annoying that editors will not accept manuscripts over a specific page limit, the editors know what they are doing. Page limits actually help you to say more in fewer pages. Do not make the mistake that a colleague and I made in submitting a manuscript that exceeded the page limit. The editors returned our manuscript so we could shorten it before they would even review it. We lost time in getting our manuscript reviewed and subsequently rejected by that journal.

If you find it difficult to cut material because of an emotional attachment to your thoughts, turn your work over to someone who is more objective about the message and less sympathetic about your feelings. A strong, powerful message penetrates the mind and heart much more quickly than a loosely connected set of ideas.

GUIDELINE 6

Think About an Outlet for Your Work

Usually, writers develop ideas and then search for an outlet for their work. This outlet could be a journal, a book or software, or a newspaper. Every so often, writers fantasize about getting something published in a particular publication because of its specific appeal or reputation and then write the manuscript to fit the specifications for that outlet.

However, your goal is to identify the publication outlet that will publish your work. This goal sounds easier to meet than it is. Consider the rejection rates of three major journals in the literacy field: *The Reading Teacher* of the International Reading Association rejects up to 90% of the manuscripts submitted in a given month, *Reading Research and Instruction* of the College Reading Association rejects approximately 90% of the manuscripts submitted, and the *Journal of Adolescent & Adult Literacy* of the International Reading Association rejects up to 70% of manuscripts submitted. It becomes clear that many writers experience rejection far more than they want to admit. Every one of the contributors to this book has had manuscripts rejected and has been critiqued for not living up to editors' expectations. And we are not alone. Famous writers from all professions admit the same thing. English novelist John Creasey received 753 rejection slips before his 564 books were published. Fear of rejection cannot stop us from trying. Canfield and Hansen (1993) found a message from a 1981 issue of *The Wall Street Journal* noting that writers should worry about the chances they miss when they don't even try. As Edward Fry said, "there is only one kind of author who never gets rejections: the author who doesn't submit anything" (personal communication, December 4, 2004).

My experience as a reviewer and an editor has taught me that many authors who get their manuscripts rejected are not attuned to a journal's content focus, philosophy, level of discourse, or audience. For instance, as a reviewer for *The Reading Teacher*, I have read articles that run the gamut from having very little to do with literacy to being too inconsequential for an international publication.

Here are five questions to consider when choosing a publication outlet:

1. How would you characterize the scope of your work?

2. Is your idea best communicated as a 25-page article or a 250-page book?

3. Do you have enough material for a journal article, or is it more suitable as a column in a journal, magazine, or newsletter?

4. Do you have enough material of your own to share, or do you need others equally immersed in your topic to share their work in an edited volume?

5. Have you engaged in formal research, or are you more prepared to share intriguing practices and ideas?

Once you know the size and scope of your project, identify possible publication outlets. If you are pursuing a journal publication, familiarize yourself with the different types of journals. Become aware of the following:

• national and international organizations that have literacy publications, such as the International Reading Association, National Reading

Conference, National Council of Teachers of English, and College Reading Association;

- national and international affiliate organizations that include articles related to literacy in their publications, such as the American Educational Research Association; and
- statewide literacy organizations that publish their own journals.

(See Appendixes A and B for examples of these organizations and their respective journal publications.)

In addition, you can work with a librarian to identify promising organizations and journals. Use the Internet to search for journals that include topics related to your area of interest. Read the purpose statement of these journals and the types of manuscripts the editors are seeking. Read some of the articles to get a sense of the type of information shared and the style and tone of the writing. Check for the frequency of the publication of journal issues. A journal published monthly will require more articles than a journal that is published on a quarterly basis.

One budding author shared with me the lesson he learned the hard way. He could not understand why he kept getting rejections for what he believed to be cutting-edge research. It turned out that he did not take the time to read any articles from the journals to which he submitted his work and discovered that he was submitting to journals that had no interest in his research area.

Because my colleagues and I have had some negative experiences with the more obscure journals, I caution you to check carefully the quality of the publication and the stability of the publisher. Once my colleagues and I submitted an article to an online journal to later find out that the one-person publisher and editor had retired from his post immediately after the article was published. We discovered this when we tried to contact him to ask him to include many sections of the article that he had omitted. Although he responded to our e-mail, he told us that he would not make any changes to the article. To this day, the article contains substantial omissions and obvious errors. Another set of colleagues report that a manuscript accepted for publication did not get published until three years later because it had been lost by the publisher. It took almost two years to get the article back in the queue for publication.

If you are pursuing publication of a book, inquire about the publishers' interests and writing guidelines. For example, Linda Gambrell and I got the idea for this book from a conference we attended. Because we had published previously with the International Reading Association, we felt comfortable in approaching the editorial director of the books department personally to see if there was any interest. Once he expressed enthusiasm for the idea, we studied the guidelines for submission to best understand how to proceed. (See Appendix C for a list of educational book publishers interested in publishing books related to literacy.)

Whether you want to publish a column in a journal, magazine, newspaper, or newsletter, contact the editor to see if there is interest in your idea. As with journals, there are many statewide newsletters in literacy. One colleague who wanted to have a column published about at-home reading techniques sent letters of inquiry to many newspapers before an editor showed interest. This contact led to a two-year stint as a regular columnist with the newspaper. (Appendixes A and B list organizations that have newsletters.)

As S. Jay Samuels said 20 years ago at a workshop on getting published, there is a home for every manuscript. It is simply a matter of searching and persevering until you find a match between what the editors are looking for and what you can provide.

Learn About the Process for Getting Published

Getting published in the field of literacy requires that you understand the way in which manuscripts are reviewed, how to submit manuscripts for review, and the rules of etiquette that need to be followed. Although much of this guideline relates to things you should do once your manuscript is complete, the following should be considered before you lay your hands on a pen or keyboard.

Types of Review Processes

There is a difference between peer-reviewed (or refereed) and non–peer-reviewed publications. *Peer review* means that colleagues read your work to make a judgment about its value. Often, colleagues in a particular field serve on the editorial review boards of publications and come to those boards with a history of involvement in their specific field—in this case, literacy. Peer-review purists believe that a level of anonymity must be observed between reviewer and author in order to allow a manuscript to be judged without any bias toward the author. This is often called double-blind peer review. There also are gradations of peer review that allow for a reviewer to know the author, and vice versa. Variations occur according to the nature of the publisher (academic versus commercial), the type of association hosting the publication, and the philosophy of the publishers and the editors. Manuscripts submitted to non–peer-reviewed publications are accepted or rejected by an editor or publisher without any type of review by experts in a specific field.

An understanding of the review process used by the publications to which you plan to submit your manuscript helps you to gauge the level of rigor for the review, the time involved in having your manuscript reviewed, and the value of the review to your peers. At one university, only double-blind peer-reviewed publications may be respected, whereas at another university, any type of peer-review process may be valued.

Guidelines for Submitting Manuscripts

Guidelines for submitting manuscripts vary among publications. Journal manuscripts need to follow rules for writing and formatting, such as those described in the *Publication Manual of the American Psychological Association* (2001). Editors specify the types of manuscripts they are seeking, the way in which they want the manuscript and title page to be formatted, their guidelines for abstracts and references, the maximum page length of the manuscript, the number of copies that must be submitted, and the method for submission. *The Reading Teacher* and the *Journal of Adolescent & Adult Literacy* provide specific instructions (see www.reading.org/publications/for_authors/rt_jaal.html) explaining the type of manuscripts sought, suggestions for preparing and submitting the manuscripts, and how decisions regarding acceptance are made. The journal *Reading Research and Instruction* includes guidelines on the inside front cover that describe its submission procedures, manuscript format and style requirements, and the review process. (See chapters 4 and 5 of this book for specific guidelines about submitting manuscripts to journals.)

Because there is a significant investment of money in publishing a book, educational publishers usually ask prospective authors to address the major thrust or purpose of the book and evidence of need in their proposals. They also ask authors to provide an outline of the book, plans for its format and length, and specifics about the intended audience, as well as information about competing publications. The proposal also should include a few sample chapters to assure the publisher of the authors' ability to write as promised. (See chapters 7 and 8 for specific guidelines about submitting book proposals.)

Publishing Etiquette

When submitting a manuscript, there are certain rules of etiquette that should be followed. Unlike other professions, such as the field of law, where one manuscript can be sent to multiple journals for review at the same time, manuscripts in the field of literacy can be sent only to one journal at a time. Do not send a manuscript to multiple journals, wait for one or more to accept it, and then withdraw it from those that still have it under review or are considered to be less prestigious. Work with one journal at a time, go through the review process, and if the manuscript is rejected, it can then be sent to another publisher. Obviously, this rule of etiquette considerably lengthens the publishing process; consequently, because the review process can take up to a year at some of the larger journals, it behooves you to aim appropriately.

A second rule of etiquette relates to the way you communicate with the publisher or editor. Cover letters and their tone are important considerations. Cover letters should communicate an interest in publishing in that specific journal and provide contact information. Any communication with the editor should follow the editor's lead. Take it seriously when the editor responds to your submission with "We will get back to you in three to six months." Do not contact the editor beforehand, as the editor does not have any information to share with you about your manuscript until the review is complete. Some editors might be kind enough to talk to you about a rejected manuscript, but usually they are more interested in talking to you about a manuscript with a positive or quasi-positive review. When you are invited to revise and resubmit, follow the directions precisely and always submit any revisions by the due date. A cover letter describing in detail the changes you made to the manuscript assists the editor in deciding how to proceed. (See chapter 9 for more information about the revision process.)

However, if the editor is delinquent in communicating to you as promised, do whatever is needed through e-mail, letters, fax, and telephone to ascertain the disposition of your manuscript. Sometimes, and unfortunately, manuscripts do get lost in the process, and you need to remind them about your submission.

A third rule of etiquette relates to the anonymity of manuscripts. When a manuscript undergoes blind peer review, it should not contain any information that could reveal the identity of the author(s). Any references to yourself should be substituted with fictional or generic names and places and the words *anonymous* or *author* should be used when referencing your prior work.

In general, know the rules, follow them, and be patient. As John Steinbeck said, "The profession of book-writing makes horseracing seem like a solid, stable business." Unless you own your own publishing company, writing for other editors and publishers requires true grit.

GUIDELINE 8

Offer Recommendations to Your Readers From the Material That You Share

"So what?" is one legendary question posed to doctoral students who are defending their dissertations. A professor might follow with, "Why is what you are sharing any more valuable than the unnoticeable, muted paint on this wall?" or "Why do you think that anyone who reads this will benefit in any way?" Doctoral students usually are so traumatized at this point that they cannot imagine why a professor would even ask those questions—especially when considering that the student has just spent years researching and writing about a topic that a group of colleague professors had approved. This line of questioning, although harsh, helps provide doctoral students with a rationale for their work so that other readers can understand its significance.

In addition to asking yourself, So what? ask yourself as a writer, What are the applications of my work? This question will lead to writing recommendations about ways others can use your ideas in their own situations. Ask yourself,

What do I want my readers to do with the information and ideas that I have shared? What would I want my readers to do that I still have not been able to do? Recommendations to readers provide an impetus for changing the way something is done or inspiring readers to try something different. Recommendations could also point to new directions in research; a change in teaching, administrative, or parental behavior; or a new approach to product development. Recommendations can be a powerful springboard to new beginnings.

The way in which recommendations are presented depends on the purpose of the writing and the type of publication. Even a straightforward review of a new legislative policy usually includes the author's opinions embedded in the text, which are essentially recommendations about what the readers might consider doing. It may be helpful to know, however, that specific ideas are better than admonishments. For example, one author submitted a manuscript for review encouraging teachers to use their imaginations when voicing their opinions on literacy policy. It would have been better if the author had explained how to do this and what the impact might be on the policy. Another author submitted a manuscript that described research about a professional development plan for teachers. The manuscript would have been more valuable if it had offered recommendations about how to replicate successful elements and avoid unsuccessful ones.

Use the following ideas to help you make sound, helpful recommendations:

- Think of your potential readers and imagine yourself in their situations. If they are practitioners, think about how they could apply your findings in their classrooms. If they are researchers, think about questions to pose that would help them frame additional research.

- Be as specific, creative, and realistic as possible. Although creativity and realism seem to be competing forces, it helps to brainstorm several possibilities for applications and then to assess their practicality.

- Be sure to connect your recommendations to your work so that the readers understand how your ideas emerged. For example, in *Leave No Child Behind: Preparing Today's Youth for Tomorrow's World* (Comer, 2004), the author criticizes standardized testing and recommends a shift in teachers' focus that is more psychologically and whole-child oriented (Kirp, 2004). However, his recommendation is not only an attack on the essence of No Child Left Behind Act of 2001 (2002), but also an outgrowth of a series of studies of 600 schools. He had information about pupil learning from 600 schools that he used to make recommendations about the teacher's role in the classroom.

In general, when you write recommendations, you must think critically and creatively about ways that your thoughts and ideas can apply to others. You are helping readers to connect their own situations and experiences with your ideas. Thoughtful and relevant recommendations can help readers take action in their own environments, which, in a sense, is a primary reason for writing in the literacy field.

Assess Your Own Skills in Relation to the Task at Hand

Be honest with yourself about the skills that you bring to the task. What are your strengths? Generating ideas? Conducting the research? Writing? Editing? Grammar and spelling? Formatting for specific publication guidelines? Your skill set can range from a robust knowledge base about a topic to strong editing skills. It is important to assess your abilities so that you know what you can do alone and the areas in which you need some help.

E.B. White said, "Writing is an act of faith, not a trick of grammar." On one hand, a strong commitment to write can sometimes override worries about word-smithery when others who excel at the mechanics are available to help. On the other hand, if you know that you are not an effective writer and do not have access to others who are, you are probably better off waiting until you have developed your skills or have succeeded in developing a relationship with someone who can assist you in writing well.

For example, I read a manuscript about the impact of alternative certification on students' literacy scores—one of the best longitudinal studies that I have seen on this topic. It was so poorly written, however, that it had to be rejected outright. It did not offer a coherent description of the study and was filled with grammatical and spelling errors. Even with its potential contribution to the field, I recommended that it be returned to the authors without an invitation to revise and resubmit.

An awareness of your skills and available resources will contribute to your ability to proceed in a timely fashion. If possible, work with a mentor who will guide you through the process and even read your work. Read books about writing for publication such as *Thinking and Writing for Publication: A Guide for Teachers* (Wilcox, 2002) or *Writing for Professional Publication: Keys to Academic and Business Success* (Henson, 1999). Attend sessions at conferences on writing for publication such as the one conducted by *The Reading Teacher* at the International Reading Association annual convention. Seek out others who are willing to collaborate. Allow yourself to be the last author listed on a manuscript, and be willing to do the gofer work—for example, finding information for citations, formatting, or checking the word count for manuscripts that have word limits—for experienced authors if it means that they will include you as an author. Allow your family and friends to read your ideas and offer their professional and layperson advice on ways to improve.

Are You a Writer?

John Guthrie,
University of
Maryland–
College Park

My self-concept as a writer was formed by one event. Thirty years after earning my doctorate, I took a sabbatical. Retreating to a family cottage on a remote Bahamian island, I basked in the sea and sun. Daily I read and wrote about John Dewey for sheer joy, though no one knew at first. But around the island village, there were questions about the visitor. In Bert's Bar during the evenings, where most of the light and most of the people on the island gathered, curiosities grew. Soon they inquired, "What do you do for a living?"

Now, this island was populated with fishermen and homebuilders. Daily they put in 14 hours of labor and produced a tangible result that you could touch and smell. Those who did not fish cooked fish for those who ate fish or exported fish. Replying to this question by saying, "I do research on children's reading" would have been gibberish. So I did not say that. For the first time in my life, I conceived the phrase, uttered it, savored it, and sent it: "I'm a writer." It worked, passing the Dewey test of something true. They got the point. Just like them, I sweat, scream, and come home at night with a tasty morsel. Like them, at the end of a day, or a working life, I have a deep gratification, and a lingering restlessness.

Closing Thoughts

Writing is hard work. Ask any successful author. Writing is a commitment that demands that you forego other activities and events to share with others what is inside you. As Ernest Hemingway (as cited in Plimpton, 1963) wrote, "For a long time now I have tried to write simply the best I can. Sometimes I have good luck and write better than I can." As with Hemingway, you have the potential to surprise yourself with your abilities, to share your thoughts and experiences, and to craft language that connects powerfully with your audience.

REFERENCES

American Psychological Association. (2001). *Publication manual of the American Psychological Association* (5th ed.). Washington, DC: Author.

Atwell, N. (1985). Writing and reading from the inside out. In J. Hansen, T. Newkirk, & D. Graves (Eds.), *Breaking ground: Teachers relate reading and writing in the elementary school* (pp. 147–165). Portsmouth, NH: Heinemann.

Canfield, J., & Hansen, M.V. (Eds.). (1993). *Chicken soup for the soul: 101 stories to open the heart and rekindle the spirit.* Deerfield Beach, FL: Health Communications.

Comer, J.P. (2004). *Leave no child left behind: Preparing today's youth for tomorrow's world.* New Haven, CT: Yale University Press.

Dewey, J. (1916). *Democracy in education: An introduction to the philosophy of education.* New York: Macmillan.

Dewey, J. (1923). *The school and society*. Chicago: University of Chicago Press.

Dewey, J. (1938). *Experience and education*. New York: Macmillan.

Goodman, K.S., & Goodman, Y.M. (1981). *A whole language comprehension-centered reading program*. Tucson: University of Arizona, Arizona Center for Research and Development.

Goodman, Y.M., & Altwerger, B. (1981). A study of literacy in preschool children (Research Report No. 4). Tucson: University of Arizona, Arizona Center for Research and Development.

Henson, K.T. (1999). *Writing for professional publication: Keys to academic and business success*. Boston: Allyn & Bacon.

Inspiration (version 7.5) [Computer software]. (2003). Portland, OR: Inspiration Software.

Kidspiration (version 2.0) [Computer software]. (2004). Portland, OR: Inspiration Software.

Kirp, D.L. (2004, November 7). The whole child. [Review of the book *Leave No Child Left Behind: Preparing Today's Youth for Tomorrow's World*]. *The New York Times*, Education Life Section 4A, p. 10.

No Child Left Behind Act of 2001, Pub. L. No. 107-110, 115 Stat. 1425 (2002).

Plimpton, G. (1963). *Writers at work: The* Paris Review *interviews, second series*. New York: Viking Press.

Vygotsky, L.S. (1978). *Mind in society: The development of higher psychological processes* (M. Cole, V. John-Steiner, S. Scribner, & E. Souberman, Eds. & Trans.). Cambridge, MA: Harvard University Press. (Original work published 1934)

Vygotsky, L.S. (1993). *The collected works of L.S. Vygotsky* (Vols. 1–2). New York: Plenum Press.

Wilcox, B.L. (2002). *Thinking and writing for publication: A guide for teachers*. Newark, DE: International Reading Association.

CHAPTER 2

Linda B.
Gambrell

Lesley
Mandel
Morrow

Jacquelynn A.
Malloy

Write From the Start

This chapter focuses on

- understanding your writing style and writing needs
- assembling the background knowledge and tools you will need to get started
- developing writing skills and habits that will see you through and keep you inspired

Most writers, if they are really honest, will tell you that writing is not easy—some may even describe it as a painful process. Yet most writers also agree that writing can be enjoyable, challenging, and fulfilling. As introduced in chapter 1, there are many reasons for writing: to clarify thoughts and ideas, to share thinking and expertise with others, to publish, and, as most in academia would admit, because it is linked to promotion and tenure. We would like to think, however, that our professional writing in some way contributes to our profession, expands the knowledge base in literacy, and furthers our own professional development. We believe that in the literacy community "writers encourage other writers, share their knowledge and experiences, and read so that their voices might further develop" (Afflerbach, 1991, p. vi).

Successful writers often talk about writing as an extension of thinking. To some, putting their thoughts down in print helps them to clarify and expand their thinking. As the famous writer William Faulkner said, "I never know what I think about something until I read what I've written on it." Developing the discipline of writing on a regular basis can not only help you to clarify and expand your thinking, but it can also help you to gain power over the writing process. According to Elbow (1981), writing with power means "getting power over yourself and over the writing process; knowing what you are doing as you write; being in charge; having control; not feeling stuck or helpless or intimidated" (n.p.). Unfortunately, the discipline of writing does not develop overnight—there may be some obstacles to overcome. In response to the question, What is the most difficult thing about writing? many of the most proficient and successful writers in the field of literacy would answer, "Getting started!" In order to address this initial hurdle, the ideas presented in this chapter are designed to inspire you to get started and gain power over yourself as a writer and over the writing process.

As you begin to tackle a writing project, there are some things that you can do to assure success. As you face that first blank page on your next writing project, consider the following guidelines to help you start writing and write from the start.

GUIDELINE 1

Decide What Kind of Writer You Are

There are two kinds of writers: those who love to write and those who hate to write. Interestingly, prolific and influential writers can be found in both categories. What they share in common is that they like having accomplished a writing project. Some people only begin to like the process once they have a first draft completed. Others find great pleasure in the entire writing process.

There are some people who write best when they are in a quiet and private place, free from any outside distraction. Others are at their writing best over a cup of coffee at the local coffee shop, where the hustle and bustle create just the right environment. Some people are able to write at home. They can block out the temptation to watch television, unload the dishwasher, do the laundry, or wash the car. Others are so distracted by all the things that need to be done around the house that focusing attention on any writing project is impossible. Some people are able to write at the office. They can shut their door for periods of time and focus only on their writing. Others find it impossible to write at work due to other obligations or the pull of social engagement with students or colleagues.

Deciding what kind of writer you are can facilitate your productiveness. What is it that supports your engagement with writing? Some people work best in a rather sterile environment—a computer and a printer will do. Others need the

Writing Is a Frame of Mind

Patricia Anders,
University of
Arizona

I absolutely love to write. That is not to say that it is easy or that I always do it well—the blank page is always daunting, but when I am really into it, I cannot stop. Over the years, I have found some circumstances and conditions that are helpful. The ones that seem most important include colleagues, space, time, and literature.

For a time, my productivity was limited due to my teaching load and parenting. It is just plain hard to concentrate with three kids to raise and oodles of students. I did find some shortcuts. One strategy was to carry a notebook and scholarly journals with me. I was not too sociable at soccer games, but at least I kept up with reading and recorded my ideas.

Now life is simpler, and my writing life has improved. I have a room that is just for writing. The important things about this room are my books, my computer, plenty of scrap paper, and, in addition to my desk chair, a comfortable reading chair. When I am stuck, I peruse bookshelves or dig in files. I almost always find just what I need to get over a rough spot. By the time I draft a piece, all those sources are scattered and piled around me. I find great satisfaction in putting them back. Next, I take the piece someplace different, like the backyard or a coffee shop, to read it with a new perspective. Then I rewrite.

For me, writing is a frame of mind. I find that I am at my best when I am writing every day. It is a zone that is like nothing else. When I do that, whether the writing is personal or professional, I am a much better scholar, teacher, and colleague—maybe a better mom and friend, too.

comfort of their things around them—a desk covered with mementos, special pencils, and paperweights. Some writers need absolute quiet, some like soft jazz in the background, and we even know someone who likes the blaring beat of hard rock in the background. The author Joseph Conrad is reported to have had a sure-fire technique for being a productive writer: He had his housekeeper chain him by the ankle to his desk at an appointed time every morning. She was not to unlock him before the designated hour—no matter how hard he begged and pleaded, whether he wrote or not. It is doubtful that many of us take such extreme measures, but knowing what works best for you can help you become a more productive and efficient writer. Lesley Morrow, for example, has this advice:

> Don't answer the phone. Don't answer the door. Don't do your e-mail. Don't get a snack. Just sit down and start writing—at the start, try to write down a lot of your ideas so you feel you have accomplished something...just free flow at the beginning...and then it gets easier.

Thinking about what kind of writer you are also can help you be more productive. We agree with Douglas Hartman (personal communication, March 15, 2005) that what works for one writer may not work for another. What works for one purpose may not work for another. And what works for one genre may not work for another...people, purposes and genres are not very normative. They're idiosyncratic.

Writers are certainly idiosyncratic, so your job is to figure out what works best for you.

I Enjoy the Act of Writing

**David Moore,
Arizona State
University–West**

Years ago a fellow dissertation writer at the University of Georgia complained to me that he needed to play the "publish or perish" game. However, his writing difficulties were causing him to worry about his ability to get his work published. That day, I realized how fortunate I am because I enjoy the act of writing. I realized then that some enjoy only having written; I take pleasure in the entire writing process.

Over the years I have gathered dictums about the writer's craft and posted them by my computer. Some sayings that I have taken to heart include these:

- Do less, more thoroughly. (Harry Wolcott)
- The first rule of style is to have something to say. The second rule is to control yourself when, by chance, you have two things to say. Say the first one, then the other, not both at the same time. (George Polya)
- Easy reading is damned hard writing. (Nathaniel Hawthorne)

My favorite guidebooks for writing are Barzun's *Simple & Direct: A Rhetoric for Writers* (Harper Perennial, 2001) and Strunk and White's *The Elements of Style* (3rd edition, Allyn & Bacon, 2000), which provides compelling advice such as

- Use active voice.
- Omit needless words.
- Make paragraphs the building blocks of ideas.

Collaborating with those who write well and whose work styles are complementary is a certain aid for emerging writers. I have been fortunate to write frequently with my wife, Sharon Arthur Moore, as well as with colleagues and friends such as Donna Alvermann, Pat and Jim Cunningham, and John Readence. Collaborators support writing projects immeasurably by helping to generate ideas, enforce deadlines, and suggest needed revisions. I recall comments such as "This is brilliant—in places"; "Why don't you reduce it by 10 pages and get to the point quicker"; and "Just say aloud to me what you're trying to say in print, and perhaps it will come out better." Hearing these comments from insiders generally is preferable to hearing them from outsiders!

Environment Matters

Creating a special place for your writing can go a long way toward getting those creative juices flowing. Once you know what your writing needs and preferences are, tailor your work environment to what will help you to be at your writing best. There are writing rituals that help us settle into our writing. Having a place for the coffee cup, tissues, sticky notes, or whatever makes a comfortable writing environment is very important. For most writers, spending time organizing a place for writing will pay off in the long run. Devote some time and energy to identifying and creating a place where you can get the writing job done—a place that works for you.

The author of *The House of Sand and Fog* (1999), Andre Dubus III, has small children at home, so he created a space for writing in his car. While writing *The House of Sand and Fog*, he would get up early every morning, fill a thermos with coffee, and grab his writing materials—a yellow-lined notepad and a few pencils. Before going to work, he would drive to a local cemetery where he wrote in his car for an hour or so every day. This environment worked for him. What matters is that you create a place where you can concentrate on your writing. For most of us, it will probably be home or office; however, many authors also find other places and spaces for writing. For example, the three of us agree that writing at home is most efficient. However, all three of us write, and especially edit, in a variety of settings—at the airport, while waiting for doctor appointments, even at soccer games. Printing a copy of your work and tucking it in your bag or briefcase gives you the opportunity to write and edit on the run.

Tools Matter

As mundane as it seems, getting ready to write requires certain tools for the job. These tools will depend on many factors. For some writers, the only tools needed are a computer or pen and pad. For others, there are many necessary tools. The three of us agree on the following tools for successful writing:

- word processor
- spell checker on word-processing software
- dictionary
- thesaurus (the one included on word-processing software is a must)
- style manuals (e.g., *Publication Manual of the American Psychological Association*, *The Chicago Manual of Style*)
- writing handbooks (e.g., *The Elements of Style* by William Strunk, Jr., & E.B. White; *Eats, Shoots & Leaves* by Lynne Truss)

- lined notepad
- sticky notes
- scissors
- tape
- correction fluid (for editing printed drafts)

The Sweetness and Fulsome Character of the Writing Experience

P. David Pearson,
University of
California
at Berkeley

It has been more than 35 years since my first article appeared in print. I was the *al* in *et al.* in a 1970 publication in the *Journal of Educational Psychology* entitled "Children's Comprehension of Within and Between-Sentence Syntactic Structures." (John Bormuth was the first author and I was the last of four, after John Manning and Jay Carr.) One of the expectations that I held (in retrospect, all too naively) was that over time, the whole publication process would get easier. I expected that my hit rate would increase and that I would not have to go through as many revisions as I did on my first four or five published pieces in the archival, juried journals. I also expected that I would get better at writing eloquent, elegant prose—prose so compelling that a developmental or copy editor working for a journal would not have to touch it or, better yet, would consider it sacrilege to touch it.

Well, here it is 35 years later, and I am here to tell you all that any illusions I had about improving my hit rate or writing rhetorically untouchable prose have been shattered—and thankfully so! I say thankfully so because I have become convinced that participating fully in the entire research and publication cycle—from question formation to data collection and analysis to early, later, and final drafts—is good for all of us, irrespective of how long we have been playing the game. My work, both the work I do on my own and the work I do collaboratively, is the better for the collegial review, the rejections, the revise and resubmits, and the friendly tussles with editors that I experience anew with each manuscript I develop and submit.

In fact, I have become convinced that the sweat equity that I pour into my work makes the outcome all the more satisfying. And speaking of outcomes, the article I have in the first number of the 2005 volume of *Reading Research Quarterly* marks the publication of my 170th article. Most significant about number 170 is this: I can tell you that the rush I got when I saw the actual material copy of the journal with that article included was as sweet and fulfilling as the day in 1970 when I got the copy of *Journal of Educational Psychology* containing my first article. Part of the sweetness and fulsome character of the experience is seeing one's name and one's work in print, but a part of it is feeling the cover, turning the pages, and, yes, even smelling the mix of ink on paper (and every book and every journal is slightly different). When I am writing, I leave a little of my soul on every page, but I get a little of it back when I can see, and touch, and smell its reality. And then the cycle begins anew, for there is always another article out there (or in there—I am never sure where they start) waiting for its realization.

In addition, having the books, articles, and notes that are specific to your writing task is essential. If you are writing for a specific journal, newspaper, or book publishing house, having the publishing guidelines at hand will be most helpful.

Not All Publishing Outlets Are Created Equal

As chapter 1 advises, think about an outlet for your work, and do your homework before you begin to craft your journal article, book chapter, or book. Pay attention to the topics of articles that are published in the potential publication outlets as well as their format, length, tone, and the format used for citations and references. If you are editing or writing a book, look at the various publishing houses to determine the types of books they publish. Sending a manuscript or book prospectus that does not fit a particular publication outlet is likely to result in having your work returned to you, unread. As reviewers of journal articles and books, we can tell you that it is disappointing to receive a manuscript or book prospectus from an author who appears to be totally unfamiliar with the journal or type of book that is published by a particular publishing house.

Publishing Outlets for Journal Articles

If you want your work to receive the recognition it deserves, you should consider the citation impact rating of various journals in the field of literacy and education. *Journal Citation Reports* is compiled by Thomson Scientific (formerly the Institute for Scientific Information; Philadelphia, Pennsylvania, USA) each year (see www.isinet.com/products/evaltools/jcr for more information). Thomson Scientific has a selected group of journals in the areas of education and educational research for which it has calculated an "Impact Factor." The Impact Factor measures the average number of times recently published articles have been cited in a given year. For example, a 2005 Impact Factor of 2.0 means that, on average, articles published in a given journal in 2003 and 2004 were cited two times in 2005. At the end of each calendar year, that year's data are compiled, and the Impact Factors and other citation metrics are published in early summer of the following year.

If you want to increase the probability that your work will receive wide recognition, aim for publication in a journal with a high impact rating. Table 2.1 provides the 2005 ratings of selected journals, reflecting citations of articles published in 2003 and 2004 in the category Education and Educational Research.

Publishing Outlets for Books and Edited Volumes

Before you put a great deal of time and effort in an edited volume or book, you should consider the type of publication house that would be appropriate for your book and contact a representative to discuss the publisher's interest in a publication

Gambrell, Malloy, & Morrow

Table 2.1.   Impact Factors From *Journal Citation Reports*–2005 Social Sciences Edition

Category: Education and Educational Research
Selected* Literacy and Literacy-Related Journals Ranked by Impact Factor

Journal	Impact Factor
1. *Journal of the Learning Sciences*	2.79
2. *Review of Educational Research*	1.76
4. *Learning and Instruction*	1.55
5. *Scientific Studies of Reading*	1.53
6. *American Educational Research Journal*	1.38
15. *Language Learning*	0.98
17. *The Elementary School Journal*	0.91
18. *Harvard Educational Review*	0.86
19. *Reading Research Quarterly*	0.86
22. *Early Childhood Research Quarterly*	0.70
24. *TESOL Quarterly*	0.70
29. *Journal of Experimental Education*	0.65
39. *British Educational Research Journal*	0.53
42. *Journal of Teacher Education*	0.50
54. *School Effectiveness & School Improvement*	0.41
55. *Journal of Research in Reading*	0.41
56. *Journal of Adolescent & Adult Literacy*	0.39
57. *Educational Review*	0.39
59. *Journal of Literacy Research*	0.38
61. *Journal of Educational Research*	0.38
62. *Research in the Teaching of English*	0.38
67. *The Reading Teacher*	0.34
70. *Theory Into Practice*	0.34
77. *Phi Delta Kappan*	0.28
80. *British Journal of Educational Studies*	0.26
84. *International Journal of Educational Development*	0.23
86. *Young Children*	0.21
88. *Innovations in Education and Teaching International*	0.20

Note. Thomson Scientific, Inc., is the publisher of *Journal Citation Reports.* Permission has been granted to reprint selected data for illustrative purposes only. This permission is not extended to any other use of the Impact Factor.
* Journals that are not broadly based on education or literacy have been omitted from the listing.

on your topic. There are some publishing houses that do intense national and international marketing whereas others market more regionally, and there are smaller publishing houses that do little in the way of marketing other than distributing a catalog listing of their publications. Some publishing houses have established a reputation for more scholarly publications, whereas others target practitioners. However, before you start contacting publishing house representatives, do your homework and get to know the mission and focus of the publishing house.

Doing Your Homework—Being Informed About Journals and Publishing Houses

The most obvious way to become informed about journals and publishing houses and more familiar with the kind of material they are interested in receiving is to read widely. Another good idea is to attend conference sessions on how to publish—especially those presented at national conferences. Almost every international and national professional organization in education has a number of sessions at their annual conference devoted to how to write for their publications (e.g., International Reading Association, National Council of Teachers of English, American Educational Research Association, National Reading Conference, College Reading Association). These sessions usually are conducted by the editors of the journals and may include recent authors who have published in the journals.

Attend these sessions and introduce yourself to the editors—talk with them about the topics you are writing about. Editors are always interested in receiving good manuscripts and are willing to talk with prospective authors. Authors frequently can gain insights about topics of importance by talking with journal editors. One experienced and well-published writer attended a session for emerging writers during which the editors provided tips on how to get published in their peer-reviewed journal. During the presentation, one of the editors was asked, "What are the hot topics in literacy right now?" The editor replied, "Well, there is always room in the journal for research that provides insights about effective literacy instruction, but I can tell you that we don't need another manuscript right now on the topic of reader response." That was exactly the topic the writer was working on, so this was a worthwhile session—the manuscript did not get sent to that particular journal.

GUIDELINE

Engage in Prewriting Oral Language

It is our belief that you should talk a great deal about your ideas for a journal article or book before you begin writing it. Diane Lapp and James Flood (personal communication, June 21, 2005) call this stage the Prewriting Oral Language Stage, during which ideas are freely exchanged, all audiences are possible, and the structure of a particular format is not yet constricting your presentation. By talking through your big idea with others, many smaller ideas will naturally fall into place. In our experience as journal and book authors, we find that this initial stage of writing helps to establish the tone, determine real audiences, refine choice of style, and even occasionally to change the topic or content completely. During the process, it may seem that you have said all that you can about your ideas, and yet some areas still need clarity. When this occurs, allow yourself pause to read a little more and then return to the conversation.

GUIDELINE

The Title—First Impressions Are Important

Sometimes the title of an article or a book comes to you at the beginning of a project, and sometimes it is the very last thing you think about. Whether a title comes first or last, it is quite literally the first, and perhaps most important, impression the reader has of your message.

Some writers mull over an idea or problem and begin to think about the most important message they wish to share with the reader. This message becomes the focus of the article or book, and all of the other ideas begin to form around this central theme. For others, the idea must be fully developed before the right title emerges. All three of us agree that it is the title that often grabs the reader's attention. The following are some of our favorite titles from literacy publications:

- "If They Don't Read Much, How They Ever Gonna Get Good?" (Allington, 1977)

- "Mental Imagery Helps Eight-Year-Olds Remember What They Read" (Pressley, 1976)

- "But *The Five Chinese Brothers* Is One of My Favorite Books! Conducting Sociopolitical Critiques of Children's Literature With Preservice Teachers" (McNair, 2003)

- "Matthew Effects in Reading: Some Consequences of Individual Differences in the Acquisition of Literacy" (Stanovich, 1986)

- "3.6 Minutes per Day: The Scarcity of Informational Texts in First Grade" (Duke, 2000)

The reason these titles are among our favorites is that they give the reader a good idea of the major message and pique the reader's curiosity. When reading titles such as these, you want to know more about what the author has to say.

A good title can serve other purposes as well. For instance, when trying to locate information on a specific topic, such as direct instruction, it is wonderful to find a title such as *Direct Instruction Reading* (Carnine, Silbert, Kame'enui, & Tarver, 2004). On the other hand, readers are intrigued by titles such as *No Quick Fix: Rethinking Literacy Programs in America's Elementary Schools* (Allington & Walmsley, 1995). This title is catchy, makes us curious, and the part after the colon draws us in and gives focus to the content of the book. And there is nothing more irresistible than a title about a hot, current, and controversial issue such as *Bridging the Literacy Achievement Gap: Grades 4–12* (Strickland & Alvermann, 2004).

> "A good title should be like a good metaphor; it should intrigue without being too baffling or too obvious."
>
> —WALKER PERCY

The topic and purpose of a book, as well as the audience for which it is intended, all play an important role in selecting a title for your work. So whether the title is the first thing that emerges in the writing process or the last, it is important that the title convey the major message and grab the reader's attention.

Just Start Writing

Sit down and write the first sentence. Then write the second sentence, and then the third. Most successful writers will tell you that *if* you just sit down and write those first three sentences, the process will begin to jell. A well-known quote from Mary Heaton Vorse—journalist, novelist, suffragist, and labor activist who wrote 16 books, 2 plays, and hundreds of newspaper articles—makes this very important point: "The art of writing is the art of applying the seat of the pants to the seat of the chair." What Leonard Bernstein said about composing music is true of writing as well—his words were something to this effect:

> The first moments are critical. You can sit there, tense and worried, freezing the creative energies, or you can start writing *something*, perhaps something silly. It simply doesn't matter *what* you write; it only matters *that* you write. In 5 or 10 minutes the imagination will heat, the tightness will fade, and a certain spirit and rhythm will take over.

> "I'm writing a book.
> I've got the page
> numbers done."
> —STEPHEN WRIGHT

In order to become a successful writer and enjoy the process of writing, as mentioned in chapter 1, you must begin by getting your thinking down on paper (or on the computer). One thing is certain: Just thinking about writing will not get you published. Some writers find it helpful to set writing goals such as, "I will write for two hours Monday, Wednesday, and Friday," or "I will write three pages every day." While these goals may seem to be trivial, many successful writers are able to accomplish their writing objectives by making a commitment to write on a consistent basis and by striving to accomplish small goals each day or each week.

Outline: At the Beginning, During, or After?

If the thought of outlining triggers horrible flashbacks of "Roman Numeral I, Section A, Subsection 1" as you may have learned it in your elementary years, then relax. The outline is your friend, and it comes in many disguises. Even those who swear they never outline a paper or writing project actually *do* have a road map in mind at some point in their project. Some writers have a very clear idea of where they are going with each section of their paper, and others wait for their writing to settle into obvious sections and then organize it at the end. But as all writing must have a form, which necessarily differs according to the type of writing project, the outline essentially directs your writing.

For example, journal articles written to report quantitative research will have the following sections: abstract, introduction, review of literature, methods section, results, and discussion. You will need to address each of these topics in your article at some point, so at the "just get started" stage, you might want to make headings for each of these sections and then fill in bits of information, citations, or random thoughts under each one as they come to you. This is a great way to begin and can really help you to focus your thoughts on the whole picture—how it all needs to come together. You do not have to use everything you list under each section—you can separate the chaff from the grain later.

Because qualitative and mixed methods research have very different narrative formats, it is important to read a few of these types of articles in top-tier research journals before you start writing to get a sense of how they can be effectively structured. For example, some forms of qualitative research highlight theory at the end of an article rather than the beginning, and the review of literature can play a very different role in qualitative research than in quantitative reporting. You may want to consult some specialized reference books for writing qualitative and mixed methods reports. John Creswell's recent books on qualitative and mixed methods designs (1998, 2003) clearly address writing style and format for these types of research and are wonderful references to have on hand.

A theoretical piece or commentary will need to be written quite differently than research reports, but it still must have a form or a flow that leads the reader to come to the same conclusion as you have regarding your topic. You will want to hook the reader's interest in the title and the first paragraph and to lay out the rest of the paper in a clear and convincing manner that allows the reader to follow with indisputable clarity from one point to the next. In these types of articles, you may want to answer three important questions: What? So what? and Now what? You will need to clearly state the topic, the significant issues that make the topic important and relevant, and your assertions or ideas on the topic. With this type of article, your outline may look more like a concept map or a trail of sticky notes that begins with your introduction and continues to each point or piece of evidence and ends with your conclusion.

Another effective outlining technique for writing articles, book chapters, and whole books is the pile or folder method. As you read articles and chapters that pertain to your topic or take notes on discussions with others about thoughts you have been developing, group the articles and notes into piles or folders that seem to make sense. When you feel you have read sufficiently and that your thoughts are converging on themes and ideas you feel passionate about, begin to lay the piles or folders out on the floor or a tabletop in a manner that reflects a coherent flow of ideas and supporting evidence. Use sticky notes to label each pile, such as Introduction; The Problem; Related Work; New Idea; Supporting Evidence 1, 2, 3, etc.; and Concluding Remarks. When you are ready to write, simply begin with the first pile, look through its contents, and write some summative remarks about what is important in that group of papers. Continue in this manner to the last pile and then read what you have written to see if it makes sense and flows well. If so, you can make another pass through the folders and fill in your ideas, adding citations and building your reference section as you go.

It does not matter whether your infrastructure for building your paper consists of sticky notes on poster board or labeled piles of articles on the floor; what matters is the framework, which will guide you from a stirring introduction to a compelling conclusion and ensure that you have adhered to a form that is recognizable and acceptable to the publisher to which you wish to send your work. When you use an outline as your road map, you can be assured of including everything you want—or need—to include without veering off course and missing the target altogether. A good outline makes a great writing companion.

Write Clearly and Coherently

Writing clearly and coherently requires effort and consistent monitoring. Authors who have something worth sharing need to be able to present their message in a way that is clearly understood. The following are three basic suggestions that will aid you in writing clearly and coherently:

1. Use appropriate headings, subheadings, and signal words to guide the reader.

2. Avoid clutter, jargon, and clichés.

3. Edit by rereading drafts to remove redundant or unimportant information.

Use Appropriate Headings, Subheadings, and Signal Words

Clarity and coherence are greatly increased when you make use of appropriate headings, subheadings, and signal words. The process of outlining provides exactly the sort of information that is useful in developing headings and subheadings to guide the reader. Headings should provide an infrastructure that, when read alone, affords the reader a good idea of what the article is about. Be sure to consult the appropriate style guide, such as the *Publication Manual of the American Psychological Association*, to help ensure that you are including all the needed headings in the correct format.

> "Good writing is clear thinking made visible."
> —BILL WHEELER

Signal words are other markers used in the body of the text to guide the reader's thinking and that help to make writing more comprehensible. The chart in Table 2.2 provides suggestions for signal words and how to use them appropriately.

Avoid Clutter, Jargon, and Clichés

Henson (2005) identifies cluttered writing as a major obstacle to developing a clear message. Cluttered writing can be avoided by replacing long expressions

Table 2.2. Signal Words

Enumeration	Time Order	Comparison/Contrast	Cause/Effect	Problem/Solution
To begin with	on (date)	however	for this reason	because
First	not long after	but	in order to	since
Second	now	as well as	since	therefore
Next	as	then	because	consequently
Then	before	not only...but also	so	as a result
Finally	after	either...or	therefore	this led to
Most important	when	while	it follows that	so
In fact	at last	unless	thus	accordingly
For instance	immediately	similarly	accordingly	if...then
For example	ago	yet	as a result	thus
The following	at that time	however	hence	nevertheless
Another	until	otherwise		
Moreover	while	despite		
Besides	already	still		
In addition	during	in spite of		
And	afterward	nevertheless		
As well as	in the meantime	rather		
Last		although		
Also				

Adapted with permission from a handout distributed by William Henk (Writing for *The Reading Teacher*, International Reading Association Annual Convention, 2003).

with fewer words. Table 2.3 lists some of the most common examples of bulky expressions that muddle writing, along with Henson's suggestions for more concise wording.

Word choice is another important consideration for expressing ideas clearly. As Mark Twain said, "The difference between the right and the not-so-right word is like the difference between lightning and the lightning bug." Look for word choices that will make your meaning apparent to a wide audience. The use of jargon and clichés should be avoided. They do not enhance the quality of a manuscript and may identify you as a weak or inexperienced author. According to Henson (2005),

> it is difficult to shed the pedagogical jargon that we have learned to use so effectively to cloud our meanings. For most of us, developing a good, simple writing style requires *unlearning* years of poor word selection and complicated sentence structure. (p. 46, emphasis in original)

Table 2.3. Replacing Bulky Language With More Concise Wording

Bulky	Concise
Until such time as	until
A high rate of speed	fast
On account of	because
In the event that	if
Provides information	tells
In the majority of cases	usually
Each and every one	each
Has to do with	concerns
Has the capability of	can
In spite of the fact that	although
Cancel out	cancel
Mandatory requirement	requirement
At that point in time	then
At this point in time	now
In attendance	there
Improve the quality of	improve
A new innovation	an innovation
In short supply	scarce
In the final analysis	finally
Continues to occur	reoccurs
In the foreseeable future	soon
She is a woman who	she
In the majority of instances	usually
In view of the fact that	since
On a daily basis	daily
In a hasty manner	hastily
In close proximity	near
There is no doubt that	undoubtedly
Administrate	administer
A large percentage of	most
Once upon a time	once
During the past year	last year
Can't help but think	think
Almost everyone	most
Need to be established	needed
Filled to capacity	full
Give consideration to	consider
As to the question as to why	why
Rank order	rank
As to whether or not	whether
Put in an appearance	attend
Revert back to	revert to
A great deal of	much
With the exception of	except
In the amount of	of
To have to tell you	to say
Have no other choice	must

Edit Your Work by Rereading Drafts to Remove Redundant or Unimportant Information

The best time to verify the clarity and coherence of your writing is after you have finished the rough draft and can put the piece to rest for a day or so. What we write makes perfect sense to us as we are writing—we know exactly what we are saying. But if we let our writing sit for a while and then come back to it, we may see where a sentence or paragraph needs to be added or rearranged in order to unify ideas or to bridge a giant chasm in our thinking. It is also a good idea to allow a trusted colleague or friend to look it over to see if the piece flows well. Allow time to take several passes at your writing in this manner—it is amazing what you will find.

The goal is to have a polished piece of writing that represents your ideas in the most comprehensible manner possible. Striving for clear and coherent writing will make your name at the top of an article something readers will anticipate and trust.

GUIDELINE 10

Turn Professional Activities and Assignments Into Writing Projects

Successful writers are adept at turning real-life experiences into writing projects. Classroom teachers often write about the results of action research conducted in their own classrooms. Professors who are invited to give presentations at conferences decide that their topics are sufficiently important to develop for publication. Researchers frequently publish work conducted as a part of a funded grant. Graduate students, and sometimes undergraduates, publish a paper that was written for a class assignment. Successful authors write about what they know and take advantage of these real-life opportunities to publish.

For example, a university professor who was writing a book about literacy in the kindergarten classroom invited a graduate student to participate as part of an independent study. After their research was concluded, the student collaborated with the professor on writing a chapter for the book that described a week in the life of a kindergarten child. This collaboration resulted in the student completing an independent study and coauthoring a chapter with the professor, and the professor's book benefited from the real-life experiences of a kindergarten teacher.

The work that you conduct as a member of a committee for a professional organization can also result in a publication in the form of a position statement, an article, or a book. So, too, can that presentation that you gave at your local, state, or national conference. Committees and conferences offer great opportunities to connect with others who are interested in your topic area. The common work on a committee or sharing of information as a presenter or participant at a workshop provides you and your colleagues an opportunity to discuss needs for research or to exchange ideas about an article that really needs to be written—perhaps leading to a fruitful collaboration.

The possibilities for making new contacts and the inspiration for new thoughts and ideas are present in nearly all working environments—in schools, at institutions of higher learning, and in professional transactions. It is important to be aware of—and open to—these opportunities as they present themselves to make the best use of our professional activities and assignments.

Closing Thoughts

Writing is not easy, but it is rewarding. There is nothing quite like seeing your name in print for the first time. In the field of literacy there are many important reasons for writing. As literacy researchers, we wish to disseminate the results of our studies, and as literacy professionals, we endeavor to present the "how to" articles that translate research into practical classroom applications. We write because we have something important to say.

Most of us would agree that one of the hardest things about writing is getting started. Our best advice here is to write something—anything! Even a sketch or a brief outline of your main points will do. At least you will see something on the page and have some sense of satisfaction. Remember, too, that in good writing, less is more. Your writing needs to be succinct and clear—not long and drawn out. Have someone read your work before submitting it. It is hard to objectively evaluate your own writing for clarity and coherence. But don't get stuck in a cycle of unending revision; you could edit forever. There comes a time to say, "This baby is done!" and send it off to a publisher.

Master the art of using professional activities and collegial experiences for your writing. Write about issues that make you passionate and about topics you enjoy. Most important, do not get discouraged. Good writing takes commitment and practice, perseverance and patience. We hope that these 10 guidelines will prepare you to write from the start, to write often, and to write well.

REFERENCES

Afflerbach, P. (1991). Foreword. In J.F. Baumann & D.D. Johnson (Eds.), *Writing for publication in reading and language arts* (pp. v–vi). Newark, DE: International Reading Association.

Allington, R.L. (1977). If they don't read much, how they ever gonna get good? *Journal of Reading, 21*, 57–61.

Allington, R.L., & Walmsley, S.A. (Eds.). (1995). *No quick fix: Rethinking literacy programs in America's elementary schools*. New York: Teachers College Press.

American Psychological Association. (2001). *Publication manual of the American Psychological Association* (5th ed.). Washington, DC: Author.

Carnine, D.W., Silbert, J., Kame'enui, E.J., & Tarver, S.G. (2004). *Direct instruction reading* (4th ed.). Upper Saddle River, NJ: Pearson/Merrill/Prentice Hall.

Creswell, J.W. (1998). *Qualitative inquiry and research design: Choosing among five traditions.* Thousand Oaks, CA: Sage.

Creswell, J.W. (2003). *Research design: Qualitative, quantitative, and mixed methods approaches* (2nd ed.). Thousand Oaks, CA: Sage.

Dubus, A., III. (1999). *The house of sand and fog.* New York: W.W. Norton.

Duke, N. (2000). 3.6 minutes per day: The scarcity of informational texts in first grade. *Reading Research Quarterly, 35*(2), 202–224.

Elbow, P. (1981). *Writing with power: Techniques for mastering the writing process.* New York: Oxford University Press.

Henson, K. (2005). *Writing for publication.* Boston: Allyn & Bacon.

McNair, J.C. (2003). But *The Five Chinese Brothers* is one of my favorite books! Conducting sociopolitical critiques of children's literature with preservice teachers. *Journal of Children's Literature, 29*(1), 46–54.

Pressley, M. (1976). Mental imagery helps eight-year-olds remember what they read. *Journal of Educational Psychology, 68,* 355–359.

Stanovich, K. (1986). Matthew effects in reading: Some consequences of individual differences in the acquisition of literacy. *Reading Research Quarterly, 21,* 360–406.

Strickland, D.S., & Alvermann, D.E. (2004). *Bridging the literacy achievement gap: Grades 4–12.* New York: Teachers College Press.

Strunk, W., Jr., & White, E.B. (2000). *The elements of style* (4th ed.). New York: Longman.

Truss, L. (2004). *Eats, shoots & leaves: The zero tolerance approach to punctuation.* New York: Gotham Books.

University of Chicago Press. (2003). *Chicago manual of style: The essential guide for writers, editors, and publishers* (15th ed.). Chicago: Author.

CHAPTER 3

"Always Stick With Your Buddy": Collaboration and Writing for Publication

Nancy D. Padak

Timothy Rasinski

This chapter focuses on
- deciding if collaboration is right for you
- why collaboration works well for many authors
- how to collaborate with others in writing

D o you recognize part of our title as Officer Buckle's Safety Tip #101? In *Officer Buckle and Gloria* (Rathman, 1995), neither Officer Buckle nor Gloria the dog was as successful alone as they were as a team. By the end of the story, theirs was a true collaboration: "a cooperative endeavor that involves common goals, coordinated efforts, and outcomes or products for which the collaborators share responsibility and credit" (Austin & Baldwin, 1991, p. 7). Officer Buckle and Gloria collaborated on lectures about safety; many educators collaborate instead with writing. Like Officer Buckle and Gloria, we are more successful and productive if we work together than if we work alone.

In the spirit of our title, we organized this chapter around tips that underscore, we believe, important considerations related to collaboration in writing. Rather than Officer Buckle's Safety Tips, we offer several guidelines. The ideas we share come from our own collaborative efforts, both together and with other writing partners. In addition, we introduce you to three other "characters" whose ideas about collaborative writing we will share with you. Bill Bintz is a literacy colleague of ours at Kent State University, Kent, Ohio, USA. He frequently collaborates with Sara Moore, a teacher educator whose areas of expertise are in mathematics and science education. Melody Tankersley is a special education professor, also a colleague at Kent State and also an active and productive collaborator.

Bill, Sara, and Melody shared their experiences and suggestions with us so that we can, in turn, share them with you. Now that you know the "cast of characters," let us begin to think about if, why, and how to collaborate.

GUIDELINE 1

Decide if Collaboration Is Right for You

Not everyone likes to collaborate. We have colleagues who are more like the Lone Ranger (without Tonto) than Lucy and Ethel, Thelma and Louise, Rogers and Hammerstein, or Amos and Boris. Yet if you are reading this, you are probably at least somewhat inclined to consider collaborative writing. So we begin with some advantages of collaboration, specifically the rewards of working together.

Writing together is more enjoyable. We are more productive. The cross-fertilization of ideas that results from collaboration improves the quality of our writing. Bill says, "The borders or parameters of what I could do expanded. [Because Sara is a math and science educator] I can now talk to teachers from more than just a reading perspective."

Collaboration allows partners to learn from each other and to complement each other's strengths. Although we share interests in and are passionate about all aspects of instruction and developing readers, Tim tends to focus on word decoding and reading fluency in his scholarly efforts; Nancy shares these interests but regularly reminds Tim that all instruction in literacy must focus ultimately on comprehension through authentic experiences with texts. Through our own collaboration we have strengthened and deepened each other's understandings about our own areas of interest, and this has resulted in a synthesis of instructional approaches and ideas that we believe are, to some extent, novel, effective, and theoretically valid.

Research about collaborations underscores these points. Katz and Martin (1997), for example, found that those who collaborate tend to be more productive. They also found that articles with multiple authors have a higher acceptance rate than those with single authors. They speculate that the reason for this may be the built-in opportunities for "presubmission refereeing" (p. 6) available when members of an authoring team critique the work before it is submitted for editorial review. In other words, when it comes to multiple authorship, two heads may really be better than one.

Kochan and Mullen (2003) interviewed several highly productive scholars who regularly collaborate. Two of them offered additional advantages of collaboration: "A partner can lift you when you need a lift." "Collaboration pushes my thinking. It's never boring" (p. 160). Bill puts it this way: "I've spent too much time with myself. I can't learn much from myself anymore." Instead, he and Sara ask themselves, How can we make each other smarter?

GUIDELINE 2

Look for Collaborators Everywhere

Although collaborators frequently share interests, their backgrounds may differ. For example, we are currently working on a book for elementary principals; its

---

AUTHOR REFLECTIONS

Inspiration and Collaboration

Rebecca Rogers,
Washington
University
in St. Louis

The idea that the writing demands of different institutional pressures change who we are as people and as writers has not been lost on me. As a doctoral student, I joined three other women (Haley Woodside Jiron, Stacy Leftwich, and Sharon Peck) who were working on their PhDs, and, together, we formed a collaborative writing group. These women inspired me to take risks as a thinker, pushed the boundaries of my writing, and reminded me that regardless of the audience or purpose, I am at the center of my writing and, thus, writing is always a spiritual practice. These women provided an essential network for my transition as a writer from graduate school to the academy. The academic adage of "publish or perish" is alive and well in the academy, and it can be paralyzing and soul stripping for women and people of color who often occupy the margins rather than the center of research and writing traditions. As writers, we lay ourselves on the line when we write. We bare our souls for others to see, critique, and ultimately accept or reject.

I care deeply about the people with whom I work in my research and want to represent them in the best way possible. *They* have something to say. I am constantly learning to center myself in my writing and, at the same time, detach myself from my writing. I have to remind myself that my writing is a reflection of who I am at one point in time, not my totality. I think one of the toughest challenges for me as a writer is to confront this paradox of learning how to get completely into the heart of my writing and also learn how to get completely out of it. Over the years, I have sought out people who care deeply about the practice of writing. These people have spent time modeling and talking about the craft of writing with me—Linda Bartosik, Hjess Berman, Heather Brundige, Janet DePasquale, Jay Ephraim, Ginny Goatley, Jed Ingersol, Peter Johnston, Linda Pustolka, and Lynn Rogers (my mom), among others. There are times when I forget why I ever enjoyed writing in the first place. These are the times when I turn to my writing mentors as a way to nourish myself as a writer, to remind myself why writing matters to me and why my writing could possibly matter to anyone else.

---

purpose is to provide information about school reading programs. We are collaborating with a colleague who is a pre-K–12 educational administration professor. She adds an important perspective to our work, as we do to hers.

Especially now in the computer age, you do not even need to work with (or near) your collaborators. Collaborators can be a click of the mouse away. This leads to another important reason to collaborate: Sometimes it is lonely on the job. The people who are also passionate about your interests may not work in your schools or colleges. Melody, our special education colleague, found this to be the case:

> I found it significant early in my first university job that I was the only person in my department who had...been trained in a specific area. I felt quite lonely—no one else knew who the "big names" were in my field or found it exciting when a particularly insightful (from my perspective) article was written in the lead journal in my field. Although my new colleagues were polite in their enthusiasm when I had a grant funded or an article published, their eyes kind of glazed over when I explained it in detail.... I was fortunate to have trained with several other doctoral students who were interested in behavior disorders in children. We worked together on research projects, took seminars together, and enjoyed each other's companionship outside the university.... When we graduated, we all went to different universities.... I was disappointed when my new colleagues were busy with their own scholarly interests—interests that I did not share.... Soon I realized that my colleagues for research and scholarship...were scattered across the U.S., in other institutions, making unique contributions to their departments so that their programs were comprehensive—just as I was doing at mine.

We know classroom teachers who have similar feelings. Staff colleagues do not share their professional interests or, sometimes, their enthusiasm for innovation. The feelings that result have a slightly different source than what Melody describes, but the consequences are the same: professional loneliness. The solution—finding collaborators outside of the immediate workplace—may also be the same. Establishing professional partnerships and, therefore, built-in support systems, makes a good deal of sense.

Collaboration has certain advantages—it improves what we know about literacy, our approach to studying it, how we write about it, and our motivation to be the best literacy scholars possible. Improving any single one of these areas would make collaboration well worth the effort. Improving all of them makes collaboration a wonderful tool for growth as literacy scholars.

GUIDELINE 3

Give Relationships Time to Develop, But Do Not Be Afraid to Move On

It takes time to develop effective collaborations. Although we also work alone and with others, we have been collaborating in many ways since the late 1980s. Over that period, the scope of our collaborations has increased and deepened. We write together, we conduct research together, we edit together, and we lead professional development workshops together. In our case, collaborations arose from working at the same university, sharing educational values and concerns, and developing a personal friendship.

Melody has had a similar long-term collaborative experience. In her case, the collaboration began in graduate school:

> I was fortunate to meet a fellow doctoral student with whom I shared similar research interests and professional goals. Luckier still, I really enjoyed being around this guy as he made me laugh often and I found him to be exceptionally bright. In the past eight years, Tim and I have cowritten 12 articles or chapters and presented more than 25 times at national conferences. Of course we also have other collaborators with whom we work. But I know that if I had to forge a new relationship with a colleague each time I began a project, I would not be able to accomplish nearly as much as I am able to with Tim because we have established an ongoing line of inquiry and we have experience working together. I think the first key to collaboration is to find a person with whom you share similar professional goals and scholarly interests. Just one line of inquiry with one other person can serve as a backbone to your work. Take turns supporting each other through the tasks [of a project] and learn what strengths each of you brings to the work.

Bill and Sara also speak to the importance of learning about and taking advantage of each other's strengths. Because Bill (literacy) and Sara (math and science) have the added dimension of different educational fields, they look for projects that interest them both, that have value in both fields, and to which each can contribute both content and perspective. Sara calls these instances "symbiotic."

Although it takes time to develop collaborative relationships, every active collaborator we know has also ended collaborative relationships. Reasons for this vary. Sometimes partners try to take advantage of others. Most people find this "riding on the coattails" tiresome after awhile. In other cases, people's interests diverge. Sometimes inability to meet deadlines or other procedural issues get in the way. We advise that you try to work out difficulties, but if this is not possible, then move on.

So what makes a good collaborator? Shared interests. Friendship. Perhaps similar work styles. Maybe complementary content knowledge or expertise as well. Even, perhaps, complementary ways of approaching a problem. One collaborator that Kochan and Mullen (2003) interviewed noted, "I am the kind of person who sometimes will see step 10 of a project, but I desperately need people who can do steps 8 and 9" (p. 161).

Complementary, in whatever form, seems to be an important descriptor of effective collaborations. We also suspect, however, that no firm rules for effective collaboration exist. Instead, people's working relationships develop over time. So our advice to you is to keep your mind open to possibilities.

Collaboration: A Way to Better Writing and Less Procrastination

Patricia S. Koskinen,
Reading Consultant

Irene H. Blum,
Reading Consultant

The bagels and fruit have been eaten. Politics, cultural events, and family issues have been discussed. It is time to stop procrastinating and get down to work. This is a pattern we have established over the past 20 years of collaboration (minus the bagels and fruit when we are living in different cities or countries). Although we have written many documents on a variety of topics, both individually and with other colleagues, most of our collaborative work has focused on one area: exploring the benefits of integrating reading practice into the school and home environment of young children. Together we have written more than 25 documents in this area, including articles for research and practitioner journals, proposals, and teacher resource materials.

Although our collaborative work may not rise to the standard of excellence set by Rogers and Hammerstein, we know that our final manuscripts have been improved by working together. Discussion plays an essential role in our collaboration. Talking together, whether in person or on the phone, gives us opportunities to refine and clarify thoughts, as well as to expand on each other's ideas. We find that our different work and life experiences help generate new perspectives and deepen our understanding of concepts within our shared knowledge base related to our area of research.

An important result of our collaboration is that it has made the task of professional writing more enjoyable. However, if we were going to select an ideal research and writing team, we probably would not put ourselves together. Both of us like to plan, organize, and collect and analyze data, as well as discuss a study in speeches or workshops. Writing articles for publication is our least favorite part of the process. We find it a chore. Because we recognize that publishing is important and necessary to communicate the results of our work, we have explored different ways to increase our interest in this type of writing. For us, the combination of friendship, food, and structure within a social situation both decreases procrastination and increases our motivation to write. This combination makes the task not only easier but actually pleasant.

When asked to reflect on our writing, we found that we successfully collaborate in a number of ways. We also noticed that all of our writing projects include both collaborative planning and editing. For our initial planning, we discuss the structure of the document and delineate individual sections that are needed. Although we always begin with a plan, it is flexible, and we each feel comfortable suggesting changes at any time. After the planning stage, the degree of collaboration has varied dramatically among our projects. Typically, we simply select sections to work on individually. At times, we brainstorm a list of ideas for a particular section and then one of us completes that section. If there is a question or a problem, we frequently send out an SOS and work it through together. At times, when we have been in an especially collaborative mood, we compose with a "shared pen" or, in our case, a shared keyboard, with one partner creating and the other typing.

(continued)

Collaboration: A Way to Better Writing and Less Procrastination (continued)

We then switch roles. To varying degrees, our different ways of collaborating provide opportunities to receive immediate feedback and support for decision making.

Before we jointly edit the final manuscript, we exchange individual sections for critical review and editing. Of course, reviewing each other's work does not always go smoothly. When people collaborate, they can run into a range of roadblocks. They do not always like their partner's writing style and may have ideological conflicts. Because we share a wealth of knowledge related to our research projects and have similar philosophies of teaching and learning, our disagreements are usually technical or relate to information gaps. In any case, if a difference of opinion cannot be worked out through discussion, we refer to resource manuals and research documents or consult with colleagues who may be able to help resolve our differences. We see writing as social interaction and, as such, the general rules of respect and courtesy apply as we work together.

Collaborative writing is not for everyone. However, we have found that our writing is enhanced when we build on each other's ideas. The writing process is more enjoyable, the paper gets written in a timely manner, and, when we procrastinate, at least we are doing it with a friend.

GUIDELINE

Match Working Style to the Project

Complementary working styles are important considerations in effective collaborations. Like other aspects we discuss earlier and later in this chapter, no one way of working is effective for all collaborative teams or for all projects. Instead, teams must find ways to work that are effective for them as individuals and for the projects they undertake.

With longer and more involved projects, such as those that begin with research studies, collaborative working styles may also take on added complexity. Speaking of her graduate school colleague, Melody says,

> We wrote a small grant together, it was funded, and we began our work. We corresponded daily to design and implement the study. I collected data in Ohio; he graphed it in Virginia. Tim analyzed the data and wrote the introduction to our study. I wrote up the methods section and results.

Our own research collaborations are sometimes like this: We may plan and conduct a study together, a process that often involves current doctoral students, which we have found to be an excellent way to help new scholars learn about the research process and to add publications and presentations to their résumés. When writing books together, we typically divide chapters, each taking first draft responsibility for approximately half of the chapters. The other then critiques, makes suggestions, and revises chapters for content and style.

Finding a productive working style, then, appears to be an important aspect of successful collaborations in writing. Whichever way work is divided, the resulting product seems not to be simply additive but, in reality, greater than the sum of its parts. One of the scholars interviewed by Kochan and Mullen (2003) said it this way:

> I do not think of collaboration as someone strategically dipping into my newspaper to use my comic section for his or her own purposes. It is collaboration to me when you can no longer say where an idea came from within a joint work because you could not really trace it back to one person or the other. (p. 157)

GUIDELINE 5

Find a Working Style and a Writing Voice

As all writers know, writing sometimes feels like banging one's head against the wall. Our experience has taught us that we can lessen this head-banging feeling by working through the writing process together. Not literally though—few collaborators we know literally write together, side by side in front of a computer screen. Yet finding a comfortable and productive working style is important to successful collaborations.

There are many ways to write together. With articles or chapters, we often trade first draft responsibilities. In fact, Nancy drafted much of this chapter, and Tim refined it, adding his own thoughts and examples. He also helped with places where she got stuck. For example, at the very beginning of guideline 1, the original draft said, "Not everyone likes to collaborate. We have colleagues who are more like the Lone Ranger than WHAT GOES HERE? BATMAN AND ROBIN? BUTCH AND SUNDANCE?" We use notes in capital letters to embed comments and questions to each other in our drafts. This helps to keep us going when that head-banging feeling comes over one of us.

Revision often follows the planning and drafting of collaborative writing projects. This can be a tricky aspect of working together because, somehow, authors need to ensure that the writing does not sound like it was written by committee. Here, the issue of voice is important. Although writing like yourself, or having a strong voice, is indeed one mark of a good writer, authoring teams must sometimes compromise in this aspect of their writing. Read a few articles written by author teams and see if you can discern who wrote what. We bet you will be unsuccessful, because the individual writers' styles or voices have been blended together. Like other aspects of collaboration, blending voices or styles becomes easier with experience. This process takes us much less time and effort now than it did years ago when we first began to work together. In part, this is due to added experience, but we have also found that technology assists our collaborations. We use Microsoft Word's Track Changes function, located in the Tools menu, to work with a piece. Because the original text and all changes are visible using Track Changes, we can play with the language and order of ideas without losing any of our original thoughts. This back and forth facilitates revision, usually a tricky process when two or more writers blend ideas and writing styles.

Bill and Sara also find this issue of smoothing out their writing styles to be an important aspect of their work together. In their case, keeping audiences in mind has been helpful. Each revises the other's language to ensure it will be acceptable to literacy professionals (Bill) and math and science educators (Sara).

GUIDELINE 6

Keep Lines of Communication Open

Those who write about effective collaborations note the importance of writing partners keeping one another apprised of progress and problems. In commenting on the costs of collaboration, Katz and Martin (1997) note, "Time must be spent keeping all the collaborators fully informed of progress as well as deciding who is to do what next" (p. 15). This does not seem to us to be too high a cost. Indeed, making joint decisions about next steps and keeping everyone on a writing team informed of progress seems efficient. Moreover, sharing writing problems with collaborators most likely leads to speedier solutions. Still, communication is important, and it takes time.

Communicating about authorship may be important, especially for writers who are early in their careers. Fine and Kurdek (1993) offer a discussion of the process for determining order of authorship in faculty–student collaborations. Many of their suggestions apply as well to any type of collaboration. For example, they advise making decisions about author order early in a particular project. These decisions, they suggest, should be based on scholarly contributions, not just on time and effort (although those are important, too).

GUIDELINE 7

Be Patient, Honest, and Open

Writing is time-consuming, and writers are busy. Moreover, whether we work in schools or universities, distractions abound—classes, meetings, and more. Sometimes we use these distractions as an excuse not to write. Certainly, collaboration has the potential to lessen this tendency. Knowing that we are at least partially responsible for others' progress can keep us on track. Yet collaboration may also become a distraction, for example, if one writing partner needs something from another in order to proceed. Patience with the collaborative process and careful communication can prevent this from happening.

Bill and Sara note that they frequently need patience to compromise on pace of projects and even sometimes their structure. This has been the case in our own collaborations as well, although sometimes one's spurt of productivity motivates the other. For example, Tim wrote *all* of his chapters for a jointly authored book over one winter break. To say the least, this motivated Nancy to move ahead quickly with her responsibilities. We have learned, though, to adjust to the other's writing preferences and schedules. Tim likes to write a lot at one time. This does not work well for Nancy, so she tends to write some every day. Because we know this about each other, we are able to be patient with the other's preferred paces for and ways of writing.

> "No passion is greater than the passion to alter someone else's draft."
> —H.G. Wells

Finally, honesty and openness are important to successful collaborations. We must be willing to give and receive honest feedback, to be able to say (and hear), "I don't get this part" or, in shorthand that we sometimes use, "Huh??" We have found that keeping audience in mind helps in these cases. If one of us does not understand the point the other is trying to make, the odds are good that the point also will be unclear to at least some of our audience.

Throughout this professional conversation and process, a sense of trust must permeate. Our goal in collaboration is not to outdo or upstage one another (as Gloria's tricks did with Officer Buckle) but to improve the quality of our scholarship and our writing so that I benefit, you benefit, we benefit, and the readers of our work benefit. At the risk of interjecting a song lyric, "You've got to give a little, take a little, and let your poor heart break a little" (William Hill, "The Glory of Love," 1936). A productive collaboration is a bit like a good marriage—you need to work at it, you need to nurture it, you need to know that in the end you have a common purpose and a supportive partner. And, like a good marriage, good collaboration will enrich both partners and lead to outcomes that are more than what could have been expected from each partner alone.

Closing Thoughts

Like all writing and, indeed, like all relationships, collaborative writing is not without problems. Kochan and Mullen's (2003) interviews uncovered occasional conflicts about who would get credit for ideas and some difficulties in solving problems. Bill and Sara believe that unsuccessful collaborations are characterized by professional jealousy, power differences, and competition. They advise, "Don't keep score too much."

Kochan and Mullen's (2003) conclusion in this regard is probably worth remembering: "Trusting relationships take time and energy to build" (p. 162). We

Close Collaborators

**Yetta Goodman,
Regents Professor
Emerita, and
Ken Goodman,
Professor Emeritus,
University
of Arizona**

When people visit our home, they are often surprised that we do our writing in the same room—desks and computers adjacent to each other. Some even voice surprise that a marriage like ours can survive for more than half a century, working in the same field and collaborating as we do. Some of our students wonder if we ever disagree. We do, of course, but not often in public.

Any kind of collaboration is much more complex and time-consuming than working alone. When we present together, it takes us five times as long as it does to present separately. We are selective in doing joint presentations, particularly if either of us could handle the topic and the time is short. It is a waste of other people's money and our time to travel halfway across the country—or the world—to do a joint 30-minute talk, even if our audience thinks we are cute presenting together. But we do longer presentations together because then we can combine our interests. Oral presentations often grow out of work we have published, but just as often our presentations are on topics we are exploring currently and intend to write about. That makes us think through our ideas and how we want to express them.

We have been amused when someone congratulates us for something the other one wrote. Those who have read what we have written know that though we are often lumped together as "the Goodmans," we most often write separately. We each have our own expertise and research interests. We have done research together and separately. And each of us has collaborated with many others in research and writing.

When we write it is because we have something we need and want to say to a particular audience. Whether we collaborate with each other or others depends on whether our message is a shared one, whether collaboration will reach the intended audience more effectively, and whether we can divide the aspects of a publication in efficient and effective ways. Each collaboration is different, and, to be honest, they do not always work.

Because the two of us have a long history of collaborations, we know each other's work routines, writing styles, strengths, and weaknesses. Even when we are not collaborating, we bounce ideas off each other. We usually read each other's work as it develops and often help in editing and revision. Even there, we bring different styles to what we do. Yetta is a patient, fine-tuned editor who can catch missing commas and attend to close detail, as well as revise structure and organization. Ken is good at looking at overall coherence and working out the right turn of phrase. And he comes up with great titles.

Both of us work hard at involving our graduate students in our writing. That works like an apprenticeship. They begin assisting in researching and editing and eventually become coauthors. One or both of us will invite a current or former student to coauthor an article or book chapter we have been invited to write. That helps us, but it also provides a sheltered opportunity for new voices to get into publication.

(continued)

Close Collaborators (continued)

We have learned to accommodate our collaborations for our different work habits and writing styles. Yetta begins with very rough drafts, which she then revises repeatedly, rewriting and reorganizing. Ken, until the advent of word processing, was a one-draft writer. He hated to rewrite and revise. Fortunately, he was able to get a lot of his first drafts published with recommended revisions made by editors. With word processors, however, there is no first or last draft, and Ken finds it easier to revise as he goes.

We are also different in the ways we use time. Yetta can stay with a piece she starts in short periods of available time until it is done. Ken needs large blocks of time, and it takes him a while to get into a piece each time he picks it up. Though we know each other well, these differences can lead to tensions—particularly as deadlines near and Ken is not done with his part or Yetta wants to do one more revision and Ken thinks the piece is done.

All writing is a somewhat lonely experience—just you and your pencil or computer. Perhaps that is the best part of our close collaboration—it is not so lonely.

agree, as do Melody, Bill, and Sara. Collaborations cannot be imposed or mandated. They need time to grow, and they need to be nurtured. But true collaborators are willing to persist beyond whatever glitches they may encounter. As Bill says, "I value that way of working. Together we have a whole that neither has alone." Just like Officer Buckle and Gloria.

REFERENCES

Austin, A., & Baldwin, R. (1991). *Faculty collaboration: Enhancing the quality of scholarship and teaching. ASHE-ERIC Higher Education Report.* Washington, DC: George Washington University School of Education and Human Development.

Fine, M., & Kurdek, L. (1993). Reflections on determining authorship credit and authorship order on faculty–student collaborations. *American Psychologist, 48,* 1141–1147. Retrieved November 22, 2004, from http://www.apastyle.org/authorship.html

Katz, J., & Martin, B. (1997). What is research collaboration? *Research Policy, 36,* 1–18.

Kochan, F., & Mullen, C. (2003). An exploratory study of collaboration in higher education from women's perspectives. *Teaching Education, 14,* 153–167.

Rathman, P. (1995). *Officer Buckle and Gloria.* New York: Scholastic.

SECTION II

Writing for Journals and Other Outlets

W HERE SHOULD I send my manuscript? Where will my manuscript have the greatest chance of getting accepted? These two questions are asked by beginning, developing, and experienced writers alike because of the need for any author to be accepted in the most appropriate publication. Given that not all publication outlets are equal, it is important to understand the different missions of these outlets and in which your work could possibly fit.

This section describes what you should consider when you write for different types of journals and other outlets such as newspapers and magazines. The more knowledge you have about the different outlets, the easier it will be to determine the best places to submit your writing. The three chapters in this section offer general and specific guidelines for writing for professional journals, research journals, newspapers, magazines, and other outlets.

Chapter 4, "Publishing in Professional Journals," discusses the process of writing for professional journals, describes different types of professional journals, and explains how to prepare a manuscript for publication.

Chapter 5, "Writing for Research Journals," discusses writing for research journals as a unique genre and the process for writing for this genre, including general and specific guidelines.

Chapter 6, "Writing for Other Outlets," focuses on writing for nonjournal outlets, preparing articles in the proper style and format, and following specific guidelines and needs of outlets such as newspapers and magazines.

Together, these three chapters prepare you for writing self-contained pieces that are included in issues with other writers' work.

CHAPTER 4

Judith P.
Mitchell

Publishing in Professional Journals

D. Ray
Reutzel

This chapter focuses on:
- the process for writing for professional journals
- different types of professional journals
- ways to prepare a manuscript for publication

PUBLISH OR PERISH! This oft-repeated maxim is the nemesis of many a higher education faculty member, particularly those who work in institutions not classified as research intensive or extensive universities. We have a dear colleague, a wonderful and experienced literacy educator, who has maintained that she would perish long before she would ever publish. When she joined the faculty of a large private university as a clinical professor, she was not expected to publish, but much to our delight and her astonishment, she accepted the assignment to write and edit a monthly column on a topic she is exceedingly well versed in for *The Reading Teacher*. On the other end of the spectrum is the reading educator who has published widely but finds professional journals to be the outlet of choice to share knowledge, applications of research, and experiences.

This chapter explores some of the unique aspects of writing for professional journals, as well as many aspects involved in getting published generally in any scholarly journal, be it research or professional.

Professional journals are scholarly in nature. However, they are published primarily to assist those in the profession in improving their practice. Likewise, the target audience for professional literacy journals is composed of (a) educators in the field, (b) teacher educators (faculty in colleges and universities), and (c) undergraduate and graduate students. Although literacy research journals publish manuscripts that report original and rigorously conducted studies that advance the knowledge of the literacy field, professional journals often publish original manuscripts that translate research into practice for application in the classroom by detailing strategies and classroom activities that teachers or researchers have tried out in classrooms and found to be effective with students. Most top-ranked literacy professional journals utilize a review board of experts who blind review manuscripts and a staff of editors who make the decisions about the value of articles and whether they should be published. Other educational publications and magazines, such as *The Kappan*, *Educational Leadership*, *The Instructor*, or *Teaching K–12*, follow a journalistic tradition, but the contents are not blind reviewed by experts in the field but rather are often solicited and published at the discretion of a sole editor with full knowledge of the author's identity. Although these periodicals offer timely and high-quality information to their readers, these educational publications and magazines, unlike peer-reviewed professional journals, contain primarily invited articles intended to either invite debate and dialogue around a topic or simply represent the views of the editor.

> "You don't write because you want to say something; you write because you've got something to say."
> —F. SCOTT FITZGERALD

In this chapter, we share information and ideas for authors about how to prepare for, engage in, understand, and hopefully succeed in writing for and publishing in professional literacy journals. We have structured the chapter's content around nine guidelines we believe will be helpful for those whose work and interests are best suited for writing for professional journals.

GUIDELINE 1

Develop Ideas and Plans for Publishing in Professional Journals

Writers who are alert to problems, misunderstandings, and unmet needs as they talk with colleagues, teachers, and students often discover interesting subjects for their writing. Unanswered research questions reflected in theses, dissertations, and journal publications often provide a jumping-off point for additional research. These publications also reflect rich research that could be studied and adapted for classroom applications.

> "Starting something is easier than finishing it. You must have discipline to go from a few sentences, to a few paragraphs, to a piece of writing that has a beginning, a middle, and an end. Finishing something bridges the difference between someone who has talent and one who does not."
>
> —E.L. KONIGSBURG

Think about your own classroom practices as well as the practices observed in other classrooms. What areas seem to need attention in order to enhance literacy learning? Or what practices are being observed in classrooms that seem to encourage and enhance the literacy development of students? What instructional issues are teachers facing? How are the student demographics changing and how do those changes affect reading and writing instruction? Many of the current practices need to be examined for effectiveness and then shared with a professional audience.

For some of us who write and publish, doing things totally unrelated to our professional lives, relaxing, listening to music, cross-country skiing, or planting flowers invite thoughts and applications of knowledge that we have not considered previously. We often find in the middle of the night we will have an insight about a practice we have seen or experienced that might make an interesting article.

As you think about your topic, make a plan for the writing, considering the organization and the audience for whom you want to write. With professional journals, such as *The Reading Teacher* and the *Journal of Adolescent & Adult Literacy*, the primary audience is teachers, so write and organize with classroom teachers in mind.

The setting of goals and deadlines for completing writing projects is good for motivation. One goal may be to write a certain number of pages or a chapter at each sitting, or it may be to set a deadline—for example, completing the first draft by June 1. However you set your goals, stick with them, and forge ahead.

GUIDELINE 2

Know the Audience of Professional Journals

As chapter 2 began to discuss, know the audience for your work by learning about the titles, editors, reviewers, and publishers of professional journals of high quality (hint: look at which journals authors cite the most in books you have read in your undergraduate and graduate studies). Obtain copies of four to six different journals and read them carefully to get a sense of the writing style: voice, formality, first or third person, length, the organization of the articles you found most engaging as a reader, and the audience for whom the articles are written. At this point in your investigation, you may decide that a particular professional journal is not read by the right audience for your work. Keep in mind that readers of these journals are not interested in your dissertation, thesis, or other formal document on research, but pieces of your dissertation or thesis might be appropriate with some tweaking to include in an article.

Although teachers are the primary audience for practitioner journals, other important audiences are students in teacher preparation programs, faculty who teach in these programs, and graduate students. Therefore, the accuracy and examples of procedures or strategies, as well as the effects of using them, are vital. For many undergraduate students, practitioner journals are their first experience with the professional literature, and the notion of *professional* in terms of accurate representation of the research foundation, as well as the importance of the suggested teaching processes, cannot be overstressed.

University faculty often use articles in their undergraduate and graduate courses as assigned readings to bolster their students' knowledge gained from language arts textbooks. Thus, articles that deal accurately with important topics are valued. Faculty also use articles from these journals for their own research and writing endeavors.

The following describes the use of *The Reading Teacher* in an undergraduate reading methods course:

> I teach the basic reading course in our Elementary Education core. The students come into the course with little experience reading or using scholarly journals. One assignment that has proved very valuable is for students to read two literacy articles from *The Reading Teacher*. I expect students to abstract one of the articles and then complete a visual, web, map, or some type of graphic organizer of the main ideas of the second article. The students benefit in many ways from this assignment. They recognize the wealth of meaningful ideas and knowledge available to them from these journals. One student remarked, "I had no idea there were journals with such great ideas for teachers." They become acquainted with new resources for their professional work, and they view themselves as professionals as they become users of scholarly ideas and writing. Their abstracts are informative and demonstrate insightful synthesis of professional writing. Their visuals reveal creative and thoughtful extracting of key ideas that highlight and synthesize key points. I suggest to many students that they put them in poster form to use in their classrooms with students or as excellent teacher-focused reminders. This is a rewarding assignment for me to sense students' discernment as well as their new insights and perceptions gleaned from their reading and study in these journals. (C.F. Eliason, personal communication, February 15, 2005)

> "The first essential is to know what one wishes to say; the second is to decide to whom one wishes to say it."
> —HAROLD NICOLSON

It is important to engage your audience from the beginning. Your opening paragraph needs to be interesting enough to "hook" your readers. Good articles have a clear focus and stick to the topic or subject. Be sure to write so that there is a logical flow from one point to the next. Interesting examples and the avoidance of highly technical vocabulary and jargon keep your readers reading. Remember, you are writing to inform your readers, not to impress them.

Do not be afraid to send your work to the top journals. If rejected, you will learn a great deal from the review process about what to do in the future to be successful.

Know the Different Types of Professional Journals in the Field

As you prepare a manuscript for submission to a journal, take time to read carefully two or three issues of the particular journal to get a clear idea whether your work would be considered. You can either become familiar with the various journals prior to crafting your article or write your article and then find a journal that might be a good fit. We strongly suggest you consider the first option so that before writing you select the appropriate tone and subject matter for the audience you are addressing.

We have provided an annotated list of literacy and literacy-related publications based on the list of journals in Appendix A (see Table 4.1). All of these journals employ blind peer-review processes for the manuscripts selected for publication. See chapter 1 for an explanation of peer review. To obtain submission guidelines, we suggest that you either obtain a recent hard or e-copy of the journal or visit the journal's website.

A practical tip to consider is the difference between themed and nonthemed issues. On average, journals that publish both themed and nonthemed issues receive three times as many manuscripts for nonthemed issues. You can possibly increase your acceptance rate by 300% by writing for themed issues (Henson, 2005). Of course, different journals have different track records, and it would be worthwhile for you to inquire with the editor(s) about a specific journal's acceptance rate for themed issues.

Table 4.1. Literacy and Literacy-Related Journals for Practitioners

International Reading Association
- *Journal of Adolescent & Adult Literacy*, designed for teachers of adolescents and adults, is a peer-reviewed journal that serves those interested in the teaching of reading to adolescents and adults. The journal is intended to reflect current theory, research, and practice for a broad audience of reading professionals and to encourage effective instruction.
- *Lectura y Vida* is IRA's Spanish-language quarterly. The journal is of particular interest to those working in Latin America and elsewhere in the Spanish-speaking world. Each issue offers insightful articles on research, theory, and practice applicable to all teaching levels.
- *The Reading Teacher*, designed for teachers of students to age 12, is a peer-reviewed journal. It reaches a readership of 60,000 individuals and institutions in 100 countries, and is intended as a forum for current theory, research, and practice in literacy education.

National Council of Teachers of English
- *Language Arts* is a journal for elementary and middle school teachers and teacher educators dealing with the issues of teaching children in prekindergarten through the eighth grade.
- *Voices From the Middle* is a peer-reviewed journal that devotes each issue to one topic or concept related to literacy and learning at the middle school level.
- *English Journal* is a peer-reviewed journal for teachers in junior and senior high schools and middle schools that presents information on the teaching of writing and reading, literature, and language.

(continued)

Table 4.1.   Literacy and Literacy-Related Journals for Practitioners (continued)

Other Well-Respected Peer-Reviewed Journals for Professional Literacy Educators

- *Journal of Literacy Research* (JLR; previously titled the *Journal of Reading Behavior*) is an interdisciplinary journal sponsored by the National Reading Conference and one that publishes original research, critical reviews of research, conceptual analyses, and theoretical essays. *JLR* serves as a forum for sharing divergent areas of research and pedagogy and encourages manuscripts that open dialogue among professionals.
- *Journal of Educational Research* has for more than 80 years contributed to the advancement of educational practice in elementary and secondary schools.
- *Reading and Writing Quarterly* disseminates critical information to improve instruction for regular and special education students who have difficulty learning to read and write. The journal addresses the causes, prevention, evaluation, and remediation of reading and writing difficulties.
- *Reading Horizons*, published since 1960 on the campus of Western Michigan University, is an international literacy journal devoted to teaching reading and writing at all levels. It addresses theoretical and instructional issues, concerns, and trends in literacy.
- *Reading Psychology* publishes manuscripts in the fields of literacy, reading, and related psychology disciplines. Articles appear in the form of practitioner-based "experiential" methods, teacher services for guiding all levels of reading skill development, attitudes, and interests, as well as reports of completed research.
- *Reading Research and Instruction* (formerly *Reading World*), a publication of the College Reading Association, is an international, refereed professional journal that publishes articles dealing with research and instruction in reading education and allied literacy fields. Authors are encouraged to submit articles concerned with instructional practices and/or applied or basic research.

Professional Peer-Reviewed Journals That Focus on Specific Populations and Often Feature Articles on Various Aspects of Literacy

Early Childhood

- *Childhood Education*, a refereed journal of the Association for Childhood Education International, seeks to stimulate thinking rather than advocate fixed practice. It explores emerging ideas and presents conflicting opinions for those involved with the education and well-being of children from infancy through early adolescence.
- *Early Childhood Education Journal* publishes peer-reviewed articles covering curriculum, child-care programs, child development, and so on. Articles analyze issues, trends, policies, and practices as well as offer practical recommendations.
- *Young Children* is a peer-reviewed journal published by the National Association for the Education of Young Children. Issues are organized around topical clusters that devote special attention to issues in the field of early childhood education.

Special Education

- *Beyond Behavior* is a journal on practice published by the Council for Children with Behavior Disorders. The journal accepts articles on issues related to the behavior of children and adolescents, and the impact of research on practice in schools by making research more accessible across disciplinary boundaries.
- *Learning Disabilities Research and Practice* is a publication of the Division for Learning Disabilities, the Council for Exceptional Children. The purpose of the journal is to provide a forum for presentation of current research and practice in the field of learning disabilities. Articles reporting original research; articles directly related to practice in the field; and articles that describe validated practices in identification, assessment, placement, teacher education, and service delivery systems are appropriate.
- *Teaching Exceptional Children*, an official publication of the Council for Exceptional Children, is published specifically for teachers of children with disabilities and children who are gifted. It features practical articles that present methods and materials for classroom use as well as current issues in special education teaching and learning.
- *Young Exceptional Children* is a peer-reviewed publication produced by the Division for Early Childhood of the Council for Exceptional Children for teachers, early care and education personnel, and others who work with children from birth through 8 years old who have identified disabilities, developmental delays, are gifted/talented, or are at risk for future developmental problems.

ESL

- *TESOL Quarterly*, a refereed professional journal, fosters inquiry into English-language teaching and learning and provides a forum for TESOL professionals to share their research findings and applications.

Prepare a Manuscript for Publication: Characteristics of Accepted Manuscripts

Successful professional journal manuscripts differ from successful research journal manuscripts in several important ways. Because the audience for professional journals is composed largely of practicing educators, the language and style of the successful article in a professional journal is written in a voice and uses language intended to teach, inform, and clarify. Rich descriptions of the students, the classroom, and the details about a procedure or strategy encourage teachers to try the ideas in their own classrooms. Teachers need to have a sense that there is a grounding in previous research, but they also need a sense of that grounding within the realities of an actual classroom. Because teachers want to read information that they can use in their classrooms, translating research into practical applications for the classroom is one of the challenges of writing for these journals.

Although some teachers have had significant educational experience in understanding statistics and the conventions of reporting literacy research, many have not, and unless an article provides practical suggestions for the classroom as well as evidence of the effectiveness of the described procedures, the article will likely not be published in a professional journal. If the article is filled with educational jargon (explained or not) or language generally used only by statisticians and researchers, the reviewers and potential readers may well give up before they get into the article.

Another characteristic of professional journals is the abbreviated literature review. Although authors are encouraged to ground their work in theory, the literature review is generally far less extensive than one would find in a research manuscript. There are also journals that seem to require no literature review. These articles are "how to do it" pieces without a literature foundation or, for that matter, any information on the effectiveness of the strategy or procedure. Teachers often view these described practices as "fun" for the students or time fillers, and fail to reflect on whether they actually help students grow in their reading and writing capacities.

The following are reminders for you as you write, revise, and reflect on your writing efforts:

1. Write an engaging title that focuses your topic and writing around that topic (see chapter 2). Potential readers need to know what they are going to read about, and the title needs to engage them enough to choose to read the article. The following are examples of engaging titles:

   "Reading Coaches: Adapting an Intervention Model for Upper Elementary and Middle School Readers" (Bacon, 2005)

   "Words Are Wonderful: Interactive, Time-Efficient Strategies to Teach Meaning Vocabulary" (Richek, 2005)

"Proof, Practice, and Promise: Comprehension Strategy Instruction in the Primary Grades" (Stahl, 2004)

2. Write an engaging beginning that includes brief theoretical and previous research underpinnings. The beginning of the article needs to hook the reader, the reviewers, and the editors, so they are interested in reading further, such as in the following example:

> Every year thousands of U.S. students take standardized tests and state reading tests, and every year thousands fail them. With the implementation of the No Child Left Behind legislation, which mandates testing all children from grades 3 to 8 every year, these numbers will grow exponentially, and alarming numbers of schools and students will be targeted for "improvement." Whether you believe this increased focus on testing is good news or bad, if you are an educator, you are undoubtedly concerned about the children who struggle every day with reading and the implications of their test failure. (Valencia & Buly, 2004, p. 520)

3. Remember to justify your article in such as way as to convince a jury of your peers, reviewers, and editors. For example, Duke and Purcell-Gates (2003) cited supporting research and developed the rationale for their work under the major umbrella of "Rationale for the Project," and under each of the following topics:

> Children learn about literacy at home as well as at school. (p. 30)
>
> Many suggest linking home and school literacies, particularly in early schooling. (p. 30)
>
> Genre provides one powerful way to think about literacies. (p. 31)
>
> Children develop genre knowledge early. (p. 31)

4. Make sure to use accurate and current information. The readers of professional journals are sophisticated, knowledgeable educators who will be concerned about the accuracy as well as the recency of the research cited in the theoretical grounding of your article. If your citations reflect only older research, readers will wonder whether you are current in your personal knowledge and could question your credibility.

5. Use headings and subheadings to help readers follow the organization of your manuscript. Whether readers read or choose not to read an entire article, headings that divide and organize your article allow the reader to locate and select particular information or to go back and review especially interesting or useful sections.

6. Make sure that transitions between paragraphs and major ideas are clear and effective. Clear writing and careful editing help solve the problems of transitions between sections.

7. Avoid giving any clues in the manuscript that would allow identification of you, the author. This is especially important for manuscripts submitted to top-ranked professional journals that use blind review.

8. Provide clear descriptions of procedures and materials so that readers can implement an idea or strategy in the classroom. Educators who read professional journals look for details that allow them to replicate a particular procedure in the classroom. For example, a sidebar in Lubliner (2004) contained an instructional sequence that can be replicated by a teacher.

Questioning Cue Card

Building main-idea questions will help you understand what you read. Read a paragraph and follow these steps:

THINK: Think as you read each sentence. What is author saying?

BUILD: Put the ideas together and build meaning.

SUMMARIZE: What is the main idea of the text?

QUESTION: Choose a question word (who, what, when, where, why, how) and build a question about the main idea of the text.

ASK: Ask your main-idea question and consider the answer.

Modeling the cue card:

1. I gave the students the Questioning Cue Card and explained each step in the process.
2. Read aloud: I read a single paragraph of text aloud to the students and talked about the meaning of the sentences.
3. Think aloud: I verbalized the thoughts that were going through my mind as I built meaning, summarized the gist of the text, and identified the main idea.
4. Think aloud: I verbalized my thinking as I selected an appropriate question word (who, what, when, where, why, how) and formulated a main-idea question.
5. Ask for a response: I called on one of the students to answer my question. (p. 434)

9. Use rich descriptions and situated-classroom or school-based examples to enhance your article. This helps readers to see how they could use the information in their own classrooms.

10. Provide some evidence of efficacy in educational settings. Educators need to know whether the described procedures made a difference in the literacy behaviors of students in classrooms, and it is imperative for the author(s) to provide this information. See the following for an example:

The strategies presented in this article have helped my students to learn meaning vocabulary effectively and enthusiastically. They have even empowered students to seek out unknown words. My students start to see vocabulary learning as a source of enjoyment rather than as a boring or threatening burden. They look forward to learning new words because words are wonderful! (Richek, 2005, p. 422)

11. Write a strong ending by restating the purpose of the manuscript, summarize the most important aspects or points, explain again the significance of the contribution, acknowledge limitations, and point the way to future work and research. See the following example:

At the conclusion of this two-part investigation we were left with the following questions that we believe should be investigated as we move toward a fuller understanding of the power of read-alouds in literacy development: (1) Do children tend to select the books that their teachers have read to them for independent and home reading programs? (2) Do children tend to learn the vocabulary words that are included in the read-aloud books more fully than other vocabulary words that they are taught? (3) Do children exhibit traces of the writing style of the authors of their read-aloud books? (4) Do children exhibit extensions to their learning that come directly from their read-aloud books? We plan to study these questions and invite others to join us. (Fisher, Flood, Lapp, & Frey, 2004, p. 16)

12. Allow your manuscript to simmer for a while. Take a break from it. Leave it in the drawer. When you take the opportunity to distance yourself from your work, you will find ways to improve, clarify, rewrite, and ultimately strengthen your writing.

13. Ask a colleague to read your manuscript and provide feedback. This must, of course, be a trusted colleague whose work you admire. It is hard

AUTHOR REFLECTIONS

It Sometimes Takes Time—A Long Time!

**William H. Teale,
University of Illinois
at Chicago**

Let me tell you about an article I published in the September 1982 issue of *Language Arts*. It was titled "Toward a Theory of How Young Children Learn to Read and Write 'Naturally.'" The piece focused on the issue of how learning to read and write is like (and not like) learning to talk. I started writing this article in 1979, shortly after I arrived at the Laboratory of Comparative Human Cognition (LCHC) at the University of California, San Diego. Emergent literacy was just evolving at that time and was one of the hot topics that touched on issues I was interested in—the processes by which young children learn to read and write. There was a skirmish between folks who proposed that "learning to read is natural" and those who contended that it was definitely not. My work at the LCHC steeped me deeply in the theories of Vygotsky, and I felt that his ideas about cognition's being internalized social interaction fit nicely with what I saw happening as young children developed in their literacy.

I read everything I could find that related to the topic and started drafting my manuscript. I finished writing the first third or so of the article and then started outlining the remainder of my ideas while revising what I had written—a great start! Six months later, I was still revising and trying to complete a draft of the final part. Six months after that, the manila folder containing the manuscript, related notes, and new things to read was so big that I could no longer carry it around with me. Yet another six months passed with writing and thinking going on, and a few early literacy colleagues began to ask whatever happened to that interesting idea. I knew there was something still needed to make the piece work. Close to two years into the process, something clicked for some reason, and I reread the section of Edgar Rice Burroughs's *Tarzan of the Apes* in which Tarzan learns to read. I had found what I needed. I completed writing what is still one of my favorite pieces I have ever done. Moral: It may take time—a long time—and just the right element for your writing to achieve what you want.

to expose your thoughts and the competency of your writing ability to another person, but the peer-review process does get easier as you do it.

14. Ask a friend who is not an educator to read your manuscript and provide feedback. If the friend has questions and finds it full of "educationese" and jumbled writing, you will be able to address these problems before submitting the article for review.

15. Avoid the use of jargon when writing or at least be prepared to explain it when used. Don't use five-dollar words when simple language will convey your message with more clarity. Certainly, defining necessary educational words and terms is appropriate so that readers will not misunderstand or fail to understand your manuscript.

16. Follow author guidelines and style manuals. Remember, nothing is ever perfect. Let it go to review and be prepared to revise.

GUIDELINE 5

Avoid the Top 10 Fatal Mistakes of New Authors

As you prepare a manuscript for submission to the journal of your choice, a number of issues need to be considered if you expect your work to be accepted for publication. These issues apply whether you are submitting to a professional journal or a research journal. Without serious attention to these details and myriad conventions, you immediately tip the editors and the reviewers to the fact you have not done your homework prior to submission and convey the impression that you do not care about spending the time it takes to craft an interesting, considerate, and high-quality manuscript.

As you begin, take time with your writing, keeping in mind the audience, style, and tone of the journal you have chosen. If you misdirect your writing to an audience that does not read the journal, you can be virtually assured that your manuscript will not be favorably reviewed. Keep your writing simple and elegant. Stay focused on your topic and the message you want to convey. Don't be in a hurry to send it off to the journal: write, revise, edit, let the manuscript simmer, and then repeat the process. Be sure to check and double-check a journal's guidelines for authors and carefully adhere to them. Attend to the expected conventions and submission guidelines of the journal, including spelling, usage, house style (e.g., American Psychological Association, 2001), current and appropriate citations, and headings before sending the manuscript for review.

Several years ago, a colleague, William Henk (personal communication, May 5, 2001), prepared a tongue-in-cheek list of ways to tip off editors and reviewers that your paper has not been professionally prepared, and that list is presented in Table 4.2.

Table 4.2.	Ways to Tip Off Editors That the Paper Is Not Professionally Prepared

- Don't worry too much about its appearance. It's only the content that counts.
- Use a title so unique that it doesn't sound like anything else ever published in the journal.
- Use a repetitive style like in a dissertation or a thesis. Purposeful redundancy and rigid formality are welcome.
- Whatever you do, don't include a running head. Readers find them distracting.
- Follow an older version of the APA style manual to show your appreciation for history and respect for tradition.
- List sources within parentheses in chronological order, because that only makes sense.
- Throw a few references in at the end you haven't mentioned in the body of the manuscript to demonstrate how widely you've read.
- Better yet, leave a few references you've cited off the reference list to check to see if editors and reviewers are reading carefully.
- Trust your spell check to catch all of the typos.
- Neglect to mention in your cover letter that the manuscript is original, that it is not previously published, and that it is not under consideration elsewhere. (Simultaneous submission is a no-no.)
- Don't bother to make sure that you've spelled the names of any editors correctly. These are well-adjusted people with limited ego involvement, so that kind of thing really doesn't bother them.

Source: W.A. Henk (personal communication, May 5, 2001)

GUIDELINE 6

Know What Happens to Your Manuscript When It Is Submitted for Review: The Review Process

Once you have put the finishing touches on your manuscript and you are ready to submit it to the appropriate journal, there are other issues to consider. Perhaps the one most overlooked by new writers is the journal's review process turnaround time. If turnaround time is more than four months, you may want to reconsider the journal you have selected. One of the problems with a long turnaround time is that your manuscript is in limbo. You are unable to submit it to another journal that might be interested in your work until you have received word from the first submission. (And yes, as explained in previous chapters, you cannot simultaneously submit to more than one journal at a time!)

It is important to prepare a submission letter that briefly outlines your topic, the audience for your topic, and why you think the manuscript is appropriate for the journal and that contains all the contact information for the authors. It is also useful to include a statement in your letter that the material has not been previously published nor is it currently out for review.

Most professional journals employ two or three reviewers for each article. Generally, when reading a list of reviewers for a well-respected literacy journal, you will recognize many names of writers of journal articles or books that are widely used and cited or of presenters at reading and writing conferences. When manuscripts are sent to reviewers, any information identifying the author(s) is removed so that the review can really be blind and reviewers are not swayed by the recognition of the author(s).

While waiting for the reviews and the editor(s) disposition to be returned, you can pursue other writing endeavors. Productive authors report they always have more than one project going at a time. Remember that research and writing sharpen your teaching and keep you current.

Once the reviewers have written their reviews, the manuscript and the reviews are sent to the editor(s) for final disposition, which may include one of the following:

- Accept, which means that the manuscript is put in the lineup for final editing by the editorial staff for publication.

- Accept with revisions, which means the manuscript needs minor revisions to be made by either the author(s) or by the editorial staff.

- Revise and resubmit, which means the manuscript is returned to the author(s) to address the concerns of the reviewers and editor(s), to make suggested revisions, or to justify why the revisions should not be made. The author then returns the manuscript with a letter outlining the actions for another round of reviews.

- Reject, which means that the manuscript is returned to the author(s) often with suggestions from the editor(s) or reviewers about alternative outlets for the work. The author should carefully attend to these suggestions made by reviewers and editors, which may help to get the manuscript published elsewhere.

GUIDELINE 7

Know Your Options if You Receive a Rejection Letter

There are a number of good reasons that manuscripts are rejected for publication in professional journals. The following list includes reasons for receiving the oft-dreaded rejection letter:

1. The topic is inappropriate for the professional journal audience. The author failed to keep the audience in mind. Teachers want to read selections that relate directly and immediately to the classroom setting. They want suggested applications for the classroom to affect and enhance teaching and learning. Highly theoretical articles are often of little interest to a teacher-professional audience.

2. The project or idea described in the manuscript is insufficiently grounded in theory or research. Teachers are subject to a vast number of ideas

available from a never-ending array of vendors. However, the role of a professional journal is to help teachers sort through the many claims made about good reading instruction to get to reliable research or classroom-tested information that will help them to become intelligent consumers and knowledgeable practitioners.

3. The manuscript failed to provide tangible, evaluative evidence of the effectiveness of the suggested procedures or strategies. Professional journal readers need to know that procedures or strategies have been tried with real students and what the results were.

4. The manuscript contains a misuse of sources, omissions of references, and misinterpretation of the reading research, whether intentional or unintentional. Authors must be knowledgeable and informed about the appropriate research to support their work.

Occasionally manuscripts are rejected because the journal has recently published several articles on the same topic. Manuscripts are rejected if the journal publishes only topical issues, and your article does not fit the outlined topic. Manuscripts are rejected because they differ sharply from the style, voice, and organization of the journal. They also are rejected because the writing is disorganized, lacks logical sequence, and is carelessly edited. See chapter 10 for an in-depth discussion of reasons for rejection and ways to address these issues.

Keep in mind that one rejection does not mean that the manuscript is unworthy of publication. One editor of *The Reading Teacher* was told as a young author by a former editor of the journal that an article isn't a failure until it has been rejected at least five times. Persistence and careful reading and response to reviewer comments usually win the day. Margaret Mitchell's *Gone With the Wind*, for example, was rejected 37 times.

Authors can use reviewers' and editors' suggestions to revise and strengthen their manuscript for eventual submission to other international, national, regional, or state professional journals. Sometimes a rejected manuscript also can be put into a drawer for a few months, and then later substantially revised, retitled, and resubmitted as a new submission to the same journal. Chapter 10 describes other options for working with rejected manuscripts.

GUIDELINE

Know Your Options if You Receive a Revise-and-Resubmit Letter

A revise-and-resubmit (RR) letter is reason for a small celebration. It means that the reviewers and editors see value in your work, and there is a chance, with diligent work, that your manuscript will be published. Reasons for an RR letter can indicate that you need (a) to work on your writing style, voice, tone, content, detail, or organization; (b) to add key pieces of necessary information that were omitted, such as important foundational or current research on your topic; and/or (c) to correct or edit mechanics, spelling, or adherence to a style guide.

Carefully read the reviewers' and editors' comments and make a list of the suggested revisions. An editor's letter trumps the reviewers' comments, so pay close attention to this letter. Make the suggested revisions wherever possible and explain or defend any revisions not made in a letter of response. This letter should include a detailed page-by-page, line-by-line revision letter for editors and reviewers, telling where and how you made the requested revisions. See chapter 9 for a more detailed explanation of the revise-and-resubmit process.

Once a revised manuscript is received by the journal editor, it is sent to reviewers (sometimes to the same reviewers) for another round of blind reviews. Again, the same outcomes could apply: accept, accept with revisions, revise and resubmit (this is unusual), or reject.

GUIDELINE 9

Know What You Should Do If You Receive an Accept-With-Revisions Letter

When you receive an accept-with-revisions letter, you know that the manuscript will be published eventually. However, first you must make some minor changes. These changes must be made carefully and exactly and the manuscript returned as quickly as possible. At this point, revisions are reviewed only by the editors, so you will need to satisfy only them. Once you do, you will receive an accept letter. At this point, it is time for a major celebration.

Closing Thoughts

As we prepared this chapter, we drew on our experiences with writing and publishing in professional journals as well as the comments and experiences of many successfully published colleagues. We are hopeful that the result is a valuable resource for other potential future authors. Publishing in professional journals is one of the most important ways in which reading research finds practical application in classrooms for the improvement of practice, and thus reaches those with the responsibility for teaching students.

Our final advice is to remind writers and prospective writers that writing for professional journals is hard work and to do it well takes time, effort, and persistence. But when at last that acceptance letter comes, it is well worth all the effort.

REFERENCES

American Psychological Association. (2001). *Publication manual of the American Psychological Association* (5th ed.). Washington, DC: Author.

Bacon, S. (2005). Reading coaches: Adapting an intervention model for upper elementary and middle school readers. *Journal of Adolescent & Adult Literacy, 48*(5), 416–427.

Duke, N.K., & Purcell-Gates, V. (2003). Genres at home and at school: Bridging the known to the new. *The Reading Teacher, 57*(1), 30–37.

Fisher, D., Flood, J., Lapp, D., & Frey, N. (2004). Interactive read-alouds: Is there a common set of implementation practices? *The Reading Teacher, 58*(1), 8–17.

Henson, K.T. (2005, June). Writing for publication: A controlled art. *Phi Delta Kappan, 86*(10), 772–776, 781.

Lubliner, S. (2004). Help for struggling upper-grade elementary readers. *The Reading Teacher, 57*(5), 430–438.

Richek, M.A. (2005). Words are wonderful: Interactive, time-efficient strategies to teach meaning vocabulary. *The Reading Teacher, 58*(5), 414–423.

Stahl, K. (2004). Proof, practice, and promise: Comprehension strategy instruction in the primary grades. *The Reading Teacher, 57*(7), 598–609.

Valencia, S.W., & Buly, M.R. (2004). Behind test scores: What struggling readers really need. *The Reading Teacher, 57*(6), 520–531.

CHAPTER 5

Writing for Research Journals

Donna E. Alvermann

David Reinking

This chapter focuses on

- writing for research journals as a unique genre
- comparing and contrasting this genre to writing as disciplined talking
- revealing the process, but also the necessary commitment, characteristic of this genre
- providing general and specific guidelines aimed at assisting writers interested in writing for research journals

ames Boswell, the 18th-century Scottish lawyer, diarist, and biographer of Samuel Johnson, is reputed to have said that good writing is disciplined talking. We think there is merit to his observation, and we explore that idea to some extent in this chapter. At the same time, we believe that Boswell's aphorism breaks down in some forms of writing. Talking and writing, although clearly related, are not simply mirror processes. In fact, academic writing in general and writing for journals in particular is probably the least talk-like among the many genres of writing and, consequently, may be one of the most abstract and difficult genres to master, at least in the expository realm.

Beating the Odds: Getting Published in the Field of Literacy edited by Shelley B. Wepner and Linda B. Gambrell.
Copyright © 2006 by the International Reading Association.

Further, research journals represent a specialized genre with a unique discourse that requires writers to possess a high level of expertise about content. But just as important is developing an awareness and knowledge of the intricacies of academic discourse, including the vagaries of vetting manuscripts for publication and what ideas are likely to be embraced or rejected by whom. Such knowledge, which includes a nuanced awareness of many interrelated factors, is often difficult to state explicitly.

Successfully publishing work in top-notch research journals, at least in the field of education, often entails a long apprenticeship typically under the tutelage of experienced scholars and not infrequently with many false starts and recurrent rejections, from which one must also learn. In our role as editors, one of the most rewarding aspects of the work is the opportunity we have to assist inexperienced authors in their effort to turn sound research projects into equally sound research reports. This process is best described as developmental in scope, and it is in line with our approach to editing, which we describe metaphorically as a brokering process. This approach is described in detail in the inaugural issue of our editorship of *Reading Research Quarterly* (Alvermann & Reinking, 2003).

Thus, we acknowledge from the start that the complexities involved limit the likelihood that simply reading this chapter can provide the kind of advice that will result in furthering prospects for success in publishing in a research journal. What we can provide, however, is a fairly up-close look at the arduous process of writing for publication in such a journal. We hope that a glimpse into the nature of this genre may be valuable in developing an awareness of the work that is involved and the level of commitment required.

From Where We Sit as Editors

Having been engaged in one type of editing or another (research journals, books, handbooks, technical manuals, newsletters, and so forth) for over two decades now, we can say with certainty that it is easier being an editor than an author. This conclusion is especially the case when we reflect on our earlier years and the time we spent learning the trade of moving a research idea from the drawing board through to publication. Those years saw us exhilarated at times, frustrated at others, but always a bit wiser for the experiences we gained from working with editors and reviewers who were committed to publishing the best the field had to offer.

Although we do not want to oversell the difficulty of writing for research journals, we would be remiss if we failed to acknowledge the long hours, and sometimes even days or months, that go into each step of the process. Research journals, as noted earlier, represent a unique genre. However, once researchers who conduct rigorous and important studies have mastered the genre, their odds for publishing in a research journal are relatively high. At that point, it is much easier to get published than it is to convince more than a few people to read and use your ideas.

Because our objective in this chapter is to create an awareness both of the process involved when writing for research journals and the commitment demanded of authors, we begin by sharing some insights we have gained from reading the work of others who, like us, are interested in this particular genre. Whether good writing is similar to disciplined talking is a theme we examine in guidelines 1–5 that follow. Then, we move to a different level of analysis, one that explores some of the nuances of writing for research journals that we have found useful both as authors and editors that we discuss as specific advice from the editors in guidelines 6–9.

GUIDELINE 1

Understand the Nature of Academic Discourse as a Unique Genre

As with any discourse, there are certain ways of "doing" and "being" in the world—what Gee (1996) refers to as "discursive practices," or one's identity kit—that mark a person for membership (or not) in a particular group at a particular time. The same can be said for the discourse in which academics engage when writing for research journals. That discourse makes visible certain ways of behaving that are strategically sound if you want to be recognized by others as doing the work of an academic. For example, Kaufer and Carley (1993), in tracing the roots of academic journals, pointed out that many authors who have had success in writing for research journals engage in sophisticated strategies of selective citation.

Anticipating who may be reading their manuscript to judge its acceptability for publication may lead savvy authors to cite or to highlight some work that may be viewed favorably and to avoid citation of other work that may be viewed less favorably. However, returning again to Boswell's comparison, this type of enlightened self-interest is akin to taking into account the perspectives and biases of whomever you are addressing orally, especially if you wish your ideas to be well received. Thus, a highly developed sense of audience is critical for scholarly writing that is intended for a research journal.

As the previous example suggests, success in writing for a research journal means being deeply literate about the process of scholarly publication. An aspiring writer for research journals can learn much by carefully reading and analyzing articles published in leading research journals. However, as has been argued elsewhere (see Gaskins et al., 1998), the articles published in journals are only the visible tip of an enormous iceberg. More enlightening to the uninitiated is what happens below the surface. Fortunately, short of actually participating in the process by submitting a manuscript, there are sources of information about academic publishing written by those who are well familiar with the process. We include a listing of such sources in Table 5.1.

Table 5.1.   Sources of Information About Academic Publishing

Canagarajah, A.S. (2002). *A geopolitics of academic writing*. Pittsburgh, PA: University of Pittsburgh Press.
Henson, T.K. (1995). Writing for publication: Messages from editors. *Phi Delta Kappan, 76*, 801–803.
Holschuh, J.L. (1998). Why manuscripts get rejected and what can be done about it: Understanding the editorial process from an insider's perspective [editorial]. *Journal of Literacy Research, 30*, 1–7.
Readence, J.E., & Barone, D.M. (1996). What kind of manuscript draws favorable reviews [editorial]. *Reading Research Quarterly, 31*, 128–129.
Reinking, D., & Alvermann, D.E. (2003). The RRQ peer-review process [editorial]. *Reading Research Quarterly, 38*, 168–171.

AUTHOR REFLECTIONS

Read Promiscuously and Study Others

Douglas Hartman,
University of
Connecticut

I have written enough over the years to see the rough outlines of some high-utility practices. At the risk of sounding like an old Dutch uncle, I offer two of them as food for thought—read promiscuously and study others.

First, read promiscuously. Read narrowly in your specialty area and broadly in newly developing areas that could have some bearing on your specialty area. I have found that some of my best ideas have come while reading outside the literacy research arena. That is not to say that I ignore the journals, books, newspapers, and websites on literacy. I avidly scour *Reading Research Quarterly, The Reading Teacher, Australian Journal of Language & Literacy, Journal of Adolescent & Adult Literacy, Journal of Literacy Research, Literacy, Written Communication, Practically Primary, Language Arts, Reading Research & Instruction, Literacy Learning: The Middle Years, Scientific Studies of Reading, Reading & Writing Quarterly, Journal of Research in Reading, College English,* and *English Journal.* Plus, I surf a wider swath of periodicals that sometimes include literacy-related scholarship: *Social Text, History of Education Quarterly, American Educational Research Journal, American Journal of Education, Educational Researcher, The Elementary School Journal, Signs, Harvard Educational Review, Teachers College Record, Journal of Educational Psychology,* and a few others.

To keep abreast of new ideas outside the literacy research community, I employ a strategy I learned from Peter Schwartz in his book *The Art of the Long View: Planning for the Future in an Uncertain World* (Currency, 1996). I read against the grain. I make time to immerse myself in unfamiliarity. I consciously seek to encounter difference. I tune my reading attention to frequencies on the fringe (which are not really the fringe to someone else, but only seen that way if literacy research is your center). I deliberately read across disciplines, subjects, social strata, and languages. I am looking for new insights and perceptions that run counter to the intellectual current of the day.

Second, study others. Read how others put their writing together. I started my career by studying more than the ideas presented in an article, chapter, or textbook: I studied *how* they put their ideas together. I learned to do this from a course I took in graduate school from Alan Peshkin on academic writing. He had us analyze lead paragraphs, for example, across a number of genres and tease out the features and patterns that worked well across these cases. We then tried our hand at writing lead paragraphs for our own academic manuscripts that exemplified some of these features. I have been doing it ever since.

Realize That Writing for a Research Journal Is More Calculated, Planned, and Rigorous Than Other Genres

Returning to the idea of writing as disciplined talk, writing for a research journal is more calculated and rigorously planned when compared to the relative spontaneity of talk, even more so than other genres of writing. Arguably, writing for a research journal is more labor-intensive than any other genre of writing. To make our point, we offer this conjecture: If one were to create a numerical value representing the proportion of person-hours of work per word in an article published in a research journal, we believe it would be a higher number than for any other kind of academic writing. Consider, for example, the number of hours devoted to planning and conducting a study, collecting and analyzing data, writing a draft of a manuscript, and revising that draft multiple times before and after submission. Then, after submission, factor in the hours that reviewers and editors spend in reading multiple drafts and in writing their own prose (a review of a research manuscript is another genre) to provide authors with feedback. The review process points to another fairly unique dimension of academic writing: Few other genres of writing are as carefully and deeply scrutinized as a manuscript submitted to a research journal.

> "Your manuscript is both good and original. The part that is good is not original, and the part that is original is not good."
>
> —SAMUEL JOHNSON

GUIDELINE 3

Realize That Precision and Clarity Are Highly Valued and That Manuscripts Are Rigorously Scrutinized for These Qualities

Those who are most successful in having their work accepted for publication in top-notch research journals understand and accept the need for a high level of scrutiny, which has a profound effect on the way they approach and carry out their writing. Although as editors we subscribe to the notion that a highly developed sense of precision and clarity is one of the hallmarks of academic writing, some writers of academic prose question that notion and, in fact, test its limits on theoretical grounds (e.g., see Aoki, 2000; Lather, 1996). The need for precision and clarity in academic writing extends far beyond most oral communication, in which a variety of missteps or misstatements are tolerated, and it even goes beyond what is typically tolerated in most other genres of writing. From our perspective, individuals who are inexperienced in writing research reports often attempt to achieve just the opposite effect. That is, they seem to operate on the principle that writing academic prose requires inflating ordinary ideas by using esoteric prose, often laced with jargon. In the worst cases, these attempts could be interpreted as purposefully disguising a lack of substance.

The precision and clarity demanded of writing for research journals may mean adopting a writing style contrary to a style that speakers and writers in other genres employ to add variety and spice to prose. For example, speakers and writers often are advised to vary their choice of words and phrasing in order to avoid repetition and maintain their audiences' attention. However, if you followed that advice while writing for a research journal, the consequences would be less positive. Varying language in research reports more often than not leads to confusion. For example, referring in a report of a research study to a single test as alternately an "exam," "standardized test," "assessment protocol," "evaluation instrument," and a "pre- or posttest" can result in a lack of precision and clarity that are expected by a scholarly readership. In a research report, precision and clarity always trump rhetorical variety and cleverness. On the other hand, skillful writers of research reports can make their prose interesting and engaging on an intellectual, if not aesthetic, level. We would argue that a well-crafted research report can have a certain aesthetic appeal to those who understand and appreciate that genre.

When compared to speaking, scholarly writing might best be compared to a president's (more accurately a president's speech writers') composition of a State of the Union address. Every word, every line, every idea is carefully crafted to communicate a particular viewpoint, but also one that is politically astute and aimed at carrying the listener along toward an inevitable conclusion. It is also crafted with the awareness that a variety of pundits and political analysts will deconstruct every word, line, and idea to look for errors, weaknesses in logic, and so forth. Likewise, it is important for those who wish to write for scholarly journals to realize that their writing process needs to be distinctly intense and meticulously slow in attending to every word, phrase, and sentence.

GUIDELINE 4

Know Intimately the Intended Outlet for Your Work and Its Likely Audience, Including Editors, Reviewers, and Readers

As noted earlier, the parallels between good writing and disciplined talk are interesting to contemplate, though in research report writing they have limited application compared to other genres. Still, one application in particular stands out when we think of some advice we might offer individuals seeking to publish in a research journal for the first time. Just as in oral communication, it is a good idea to know your audience in terms of its background, interests, biases, and the like. It is equally a good plan to research a journal's history, goals, intended audience, and reach.

A good place to begin is to locate previously published articles in the targeted outlet for your work and to study them carefully to determine how your work compares, especially in terms of scope. For example, pilot studies, and other research efforts of limited scope or duration, are not typically considered for publication in major research journals, although sometimes research journals publish brief research reports in a separate section. But this is just one consideration. In addition, savvy authors will sometimes examine the list of members of the editorial review board of a particular journal trying to anticipate who might be selected to review a manuscript they intend to submit. Likewise, knowing the perspectives of the editors helps. In many instances editors will publish their editorial philosophies or orientations when beginning their tenure as editors. Some editors also present at conference sessions or conduct workshops aimed at providing advice about publishing in research journals.

GUIDELINE 5

Realize That Writing for Research Journals Means Carefully Managing Emotions, Biases, Interpretive Preferences, and So Forth

Like all communication, whether oral or written, there is a personal and emotional aspect to writing for scholarly journals, which may be useful for writers to acknowledge outright. In that sense, all writing, even for research journals, is rhetorical (see Cherryholmes, 1993). Everyone has pet perspectives and theories that they would like to advance, and many researchers are highly invested in certain viewpoints. These biases unavoidably enter into scholarly writing to some extent whether that is the intention or not. Various research traditions and approaches view the personal and emotional aspects of academic writing differently, but writing for research journals typically involves to some extent managing, explicitly or implicitly, your biases and preferred interpretations. If potential biases are not managed, even if not acknowledged explicitly, they are apt to be quite evident to reviewers and editors who are likely to question a writer's commitment to considering a variety of interpretations of data. Failure to take into account the possibility of more than one interpretation undermines the notion of skepticism, which is a key component of scientific research, used in the broadest sense of the term (see Robson, 2002).

> "Always make sure you are right and then—go for it."
> —DAVY CROCKETT

To summarize the preceding general guidelines, writing for research journals is similar and dissimilar in some respects to disciplined talk. It certainly is extremely disciplined even if it is not always like talk. However, in addition to the exceptional discipline required for the sake of clarity and precision and for the sake of more dispassionate interpretation, writing for research journals often entails high stakes for authors. Specifically, people interested and engaged in writing for research journals typically do so because their jobs depend on it. Publication in research journals, more than any other type of scholarly writing, paves the road to success for scholars and is typically a requirement for them to retain their place in academia, to be promoted, to obtain salary increases, or to increase their standing in the academic community. Thus, in most instances, for those who engage in writing for research journals, the enjoyment, pleasure, satisfaction, and rewards often occur late rather than early in the writing process, particularly because the earliest stages of writing can be particularly arduous.

But more specifically, what advice might be offered to an inexperienced author who is writing or considering submitting a manuscript to a rigorous, peer-reviewed research journal? That is, what might we suggest as editors that would not only help writers to achieve their goal of publishing a piece, but perhaps even to enjoy the disciplined process? That is the focus of the next set of guidelines.

GUID**6**LINE

Establish a Clear Focus

It has been our experience as editors that reviewers have little tolerance for manuscripts that clearly lack focus. Their frustration is understandable given the time that is required to review a manuscript and the irritation that inevitably develops from rereading a paper several times to infer an author's main purpose or intent. It is better to do the hard work of focusing up front so that a manuscript presents the data in the best and most interpretable light. Following this guideline is often challenging for authors because they are so immersed in the topic and methodology of their research that they fail to see where a reviewer or reader, even one familiar with their topic, might need help understanding the rationale and methodology. A good strategy for adhering to Guideline 6 is to ask colleagues (and here we include graduate students)—especially individuals who are not that familiar with your work and who will be honest—to read your manuscript before you submit it.

As a related aside, writing a good abstract, which is required for most journal articles, is critical to conveying a clear focus. In our own writing for research journals, we typically write our abstract after a first draft. If, in writing our abstract, it is difficult to write a concise summary that conveys a central focus, that probably means that we have not been successful in establishing a clear focus for our work in the body of the manuscript. We also tend to devote more time to writing the abstract than to writing any prose of comparable length in a manuscript. The reason is simple. Not only is it an intense exercise to concisely explain the focus of your work; it is the first thing that editors and reviewers typically read. For better or worse, a strong opinion is often formed about a manuscript after reading its abstract. In our experience, many abstracts, even of otherwise good manuscripts, are poorly written and often do not conform to standards such as those specified in the *Publication Manual of the American Psychological Association* (2001), a source that should be studied and used by anyone who aspires to write for research journals in the social sciences.

GUIDELINE 7

State Research Questions Clearly and Succinctly

The ability to state questions clearly and concisely is both a science and an art. Striving for clarity and conciseness, however, need not distract from the larger goal of wording questions in such a way that they are interesting to read, intellectually engaging, and memorable. To state questions at that level, adequate time must be devoted to composing questions for a research report. An author who has learned the art of crafting questions that take into account the theory behind them, while not losing sight of the study's focus, will have succeeded on two counts. First, the questions will be true to the study's theoretical framework, producing a cohesiveness that is both pleasing to read and necessary for making connections between theory and purpose. Second, the questions will serve as guides to keep the author focused while writing the paper, and just as important, these questions will keep the reviewers on track while reading a manuscript. Sustaining reviewers' attention and their sense of feeling that they know where they are going in a well-crafted manuscript can thus have many positive effects.

On the other hand, experience tells us that even the best-worded questions will not serve their purpose if authors fail to systematically state them the same way throughout the different sections of the report. A common misperception is that by changing the wording of a perfectly good question, repetition and the potential loss of audience through boredom can be avoided. Questions that are worded one way in the introduction to the manuscript, but metamorphose into something else halfway through the report, only to reappear as a new amalgam at the end of a manuscript, serve to confuse, not guide, readers. To prevent this unnecessary complication, state the questions the same way throughout the study (unless, of course, it is a qualitative study in which the questions truly did change, and a methodological note is needed to that effect).

GUIDELINE 8

Clearly Explain the Research Methodology as a Logical Extension of Your Questions and Theoretical Stance

Because the methodology section of a manuscript involves more than simply the methods used to collect and analyze the data, editors and reviewers expect to see some connection between it and the theoretical framework that situates the questions and all that follows. For example, when, as editors, we initially read a manuscript to decide whether or not it should be sent out for review, we look for a thread that connects the theoretical framework to the research questions, to the methodology, and to the interpretation of the findings. If this thread is broken or snagged at any one of those points, then the study is not cohesive. It is often useful for authors to discuss explicitly why their methodology fits the questions and issues they are addressing and why it is particularly appropriate to the theoretical stance they are taking. Of course, it is even more important to establish this logical connection and coherence before conceptualizing and conducting a study.

Appropriate methodologies are those that work with, not against, the theoretical framework and literature review that ground a study. For example, a study of adolescents' multiliteracies would make little sense if grounded in a theory that views reading as an autonomous process, or one that focuses on cognitive development to the near exclusion of the sociocultural and historical contexts that embed such development.

In regard to reports of quantitative studies, it is important to name the design and not leave it up to the reviewers and editors to infer it, which we find is a common problem. In regard to quantitative studies, well-written reports state specifically whether or not there was random assignment and a control group, as well as the effect sizes obtained for any statistically significant results. As editors, we continue to be surprised at the number of submitted manuscripts that lack both an explicitly stated research design and the effect sizes of the findings.

Any manuscript reporting the results of a research study should provide sufficient detail so that another researcher could replicate the study. This is foundational to maintaining a strong research base in any field. Good methods sections meet this standard, particularly in the most rigorous research journals. In reporting research of any kind, it is imperative that a rigorous accounting be made of how the data were collected and analyzed. Reports of qualitative research in particular must give sufficient details about the study's participants, the procedures used in collecting the data, and the role of the researcher. Without this information, editors and reviewers have little or no basis for making judgments about the authenticity of the data or the degree to which the researcher is aware of how his or her subjectivities enter into the research process and affect the trustworthiness of the data.

GUIDELINE 9

Clearly Support Your Findings, Conclusions, and Interpretations With Data (and Do Not Go Beyond Your Data)

It is important to be cognizant of the fact that meanings are made rather than found. Data do inform results, but the interpretation a researcher gives data is

Alexander's "Rules of the West"

Patricia Alexander,
University of
Maryland–
College Park

When I was a professor at Texas A&M University coming up through the ranks, there were certain personal guidelines to which I adhered—guidelines that helped me to shape my current approach to professional writing. I am never shy about sharing my thoughts with anyone in earshot and I am passionate about mentoring graduate students. I must have strongly voiced my personal guidelines on repeated occasions to aspiring Texas A&M PhDs because the students humorously christened them Alexander's "Rules of the West" for professional writing.

Even though I left Texas for the wide open spaces of Maryland in 1995, I did not fail to bring those infamous rules along with me. Even though the western moniker may not carry the same meaning to those outside Texas, the students and young faculty have acknowledged the utility and practicality of these guidelines for professional writing. Therefore, I share a few of them with the endorsement that they have served me and a generation of graduate students well.

Rule #1. Seek quality in every piece you write, but do not hold out for perfection. Quality and perfection should not be confused when it comes to writing for literacy publication. Whatever you elect to make part of the public discourse that carries your name should always be constructed with quality in mind. Care, thoughtfulness, and precision are aspects of that quality. However, no manuscript, no matter how much care, thought, and precision are involved, will ever achieve perfection. There simply are no perfect manuscripts. So abandon the quest for perfection, but never relinquish the goal of quality.

Rule #2. Get yourself in a research–writing cycle that works for you. One of the observations I have made about productive individuals is that they operate within a particular research–writing cycle. Because of that cyclical behavior, they are consistent and not sporadic in their work. Even though their rate or pace of writing can vary, they are rarely idle. For me and my graduate students, that research–writing cycle is clearly displayed on a large board in our lab. We always seek to have a study in conceptualization, another in data analysis or writing, even while other works are under review or in revision. It is rewarding for us to watch ideas take shape on the board and eventually find their way into manuscript and hopefully into publication.

Rule #3. Become known for a line of inquiry. Contrary to popular opinion, it is not the sheer number of publications that matter most in the literacy field. Rather it is the quality and significance of the ideas conveyed in those publications. From the standpoint of academic success in literacy publication, one measure of quality and significance for the individual comes in the form of a discernible line of inquiry. What is the message or related ideas that you are seeking to share with the literacy community? The leading scholars in literacy are known for those messages and ideas. They have a line of inquiry with which they are associated, and the combined weight of their related works helps to communicate that message to the broader community of educational researchers and practitioners.

Whether or not these particular rules work for you, I believe that we all benefit from well-articulated, personal guidelines to which we can turn as we grow and develop as literacy researchers and practitioners.

what determines their meaning. That is, meanings are constructed based on any number of interpretive stances a single researcher might take; they do not simply emerge, full-blown, from data. Researchers' backgrounds, theoretical perspectives, historical context, issues of power, and numerous other factors come into play when meaning is made of data. Although we often see the inappropriate use of phrases, such as "the findings emerged...," the problems and issues run deeper. Editors and reviewers want to see clear support for an author's findings and conclusions. The theoretical framework, the types of questions asked, and the methodological choices made are at stake in drawing conclusions from data, and these are much too important pieces of information to bury in jargon or to assume that readers will accept without appropriate evidence.

Likewise, it is important to limit discussion of findings and interpretation of them to the data presented. Inexperienced authors often give in to the temptation to extrapolate the meanings, interpretations, and implications of their data far beyond the data and the inherent limitations of a single study. They do so, presumably, for at least two reasons. First, they may want to emphasize the importance of their work and its far-reaching implications. Second, and this is the more deadly error, they may want to advance a preferred perspective or bias. On the other hand, the discussion section of a research report invites some reasonable speculation about and extrapolation of data. Thus, a careful balance must be sought between engaging in reasonable, moderate, data-based speculation and going too far beyond the data or even further toward risking the impression of unmitigated bias.

Closing Thoughts

Writing for research journals requires a set of well-honed skills and an overall understanding of this particular genre's intricacies. Though not for the undisciplined writer, it is at the same time a genre that is capable of providing both enjoyment and a sense of accomplishment among writers who devote the necessary time to master it, which often means dealing with rejection (see Pressley, chapter 10, this volume). For certain, our own time will have been well spent in writing this chapter about writing for research journals if it invites new writers into the field and encourages them to add to the many nuances already present in this genre.

REFERENCES

Alvermann, D.E., & Reinking, D. (2003). On metaphors and editing [editorial]. *Reading Research Quarterly, 38,* 8–11.

American Psychological Association. (2001). *Publication manual of the American Psychological Association* (5th ed.). Washington, DC: Author.

Aoki, D.S. (2000). The thing never speaks for itself: Lacan and the pedagogical politics of clarity. *Harvard Educational Review, 70,* 347–369.

Cherryholmes, C.H. (1993). Reading research. *Journal of Curriculum Studies, 25,* 1–32.

Gaskins, R.W., Kinzer, C.K., Mosenthal, P.B., Pailliotet, A.W., Reinking, D., Hynd, C., et al. (1998). Bringing scholarly dialogue to the surface: A view of the JLR review process in progress. *Journal of Literacy Research, 30,* 139–176.

Gee, J.P. (1996). *Social linguistics and literacies: Ideology in discourses* (2nd ed.). London: Taylor & Francis.

Kaufer, D.S., & Carley, K.M. (1993). *Communication at a distance: The influence of print on sociocultural organization and change.* Hillsdale, NJ: Erlbaum.

Lather, P. (1996). Troubling clarity: The politics of accessible language. *Harvard Educational Review, 66*(3), 525–545.

Robson, C. (2002). *Real world research* (2nd ed.). Malden, MA: Blackwell.

CHAPTER 6

Writing for Other Outlets

John Micklos, Jr.

This chapter focuses on
- determining appropriate nonjournal outlets for your ideas
- preparing articles in proper style and format
- understanding specific guidelines and needs for *Reading Today*

---

1. "This article on teaching comprehension was just turned down by *The Reading Teacher*, so I'm sending it to *Reading Today*. It's 3,000 words long and has 20 references. I hope you will publish it soon."

2. "I took a darling photo of my grandson reading on his potty chair. It took me 30 minutes to get the pose just right and have him smile at the camera while he's holding the book. I just love the photo, and I know you will, too."

3. "I'm a freelance writer. I see your publication is about reading. I'm sure you'll want to publish my essay telling about why I think reading is important."

WOULD LIKE to say that such submissions are rare, but they are much more common than you might think. Let me give you a quick rundown of why each of these submissions is problematic (if you have not guessed already).

Submission #1 has several glaring problems. First, *Reading Today* is a newspaper; *The Reading Teacher* is a journal. Articles that are originally written with

---

a journal in mind probably do not fit our needs or format. Second, if an article is not good enough for *The Reading Teacher*, it probably is not good enough for us either. Just because we are a newspaper does not mean we do not have the same high standards a journal does. Third, 3,000 words is about 2,000 words too long, and we do not use articles that require references.

There are multiple problems with submission #2. The first is that posed photos always look posed. We want photos that reflect a more natural depiction of reading. As before, we have high standards for both the writing and artwork that appear in *Reading Today*. Also, this is not an original concept—we get photos of toilet-sitting tykes on a fairly regular basis. (The same goes for dogs and cats "reading" and cute babies reading with their parents and grandparents.) The cute babies at least have a chance. Over the years, we have run a few of the hundreds of such photos we have received.

Well, the author of submission #3 is right; *Reading Today* covers reading. However, our audience is reading educators. Telling them that reading is important is a case of preaching to the choir.

All of this leads to the following guidelines.

Study Your Market

No matter what kind of publication you are writing for, it is important to study your market before submitting. Indeed, this may be more important when writing for trade publications and newspapers than it is for journals because audiences of trade publications and newspapers are often broader and less clearly defined than those of academic journals. Therefore, you need to carefully research the publication's audience and needs.

Every publication has its own specific guidelines and ways of doing things. Many expert freelancers recommend reading at least a year's worth of issues before submitting material. There is nothing more irritating from an editor's viewpoint than receiving a query or manuscript from a prospective writer that shows the writer has no conception of the publication or its needs. I far too often get submissions for *Reading Today* that have nothing to do with reading or reading education.

Editors also frown on getting submissions that clearly have been sent to many different publications at the same time. Even if editors like an article, they have to be concerned that someone else will publish it first. Furthermore, many of these simultaneous submissions are mailed to a wide net with little or no thought as to the specialized needs of any of the individual publications.

Another turnoff for editors is receiving articles or proposals on topics they have recently covered. I must admit I have inadvertently done this as a writer. On several occasions, I have queried a magazine or newspaper with what I thought was a great idea for them only to find out that it was indeed a great idea—so great that they had already published a similar piece a few months earlier. I could have saved both them and me some time and effort by doing better research.

This type of research is probably more important when writing for magazines and newspapers than when writing for journals. Because journals generally have fairly long lead times, even if you see an article on comprehension instruction as you are finalizing one on a similar topic, the editors will probably take into account that it may be a year or so until your article goes through the review process and, if accepted, is prepared for publication. Magazines often have a shorter lead time of several months; for newspapers the lead times may be measured in weeks or even days. Therefore, they are much less likely to repeat topics quickly, unless the second article builds on the first or takes a significantly different approach.

GUIDELINE

Conceptualize Possible Outlets

Other outlets, as mentioned in the chapter title, certainly leave open many possibilities, and it pays to think broadly.

Newspapers

Reading Today is just one of a number of newspapers that accepts articles from educators. For example, the articles in *Education Week* are written by staff writers. However, *Education Week* runs a large and active commentary section in each edition, accepting both commentaries and letters to the editor. Many of the commentary writers are well known in the literacy field, while others are relatively unknown professors or teachers.

The key to writing an effective commentary or letter to the editor, whether for *Education Week*, *Reading Today*, or your local newspaper, is to have an interesting viewpoint to share. You should make it clearly, succinctly, and with a certain amount of style. For commentaries, especially, it helps to have a certain unique "voice," for example, a touch of humor, sarcasm, or irony. And while it is all right to be controversial, it is important to back your opinions with fact. Some people believe that an opinion piece offers a venue to rant, rave, and ramble at will, but doing so will likely turn off editors and readers.

Do not limit yourself to education newspapers. Local newspapers, too, often are receptive to submissions. They, too, often use letters and commentaries. In addition, they may be open to ideas for feature articles about interesting events in the local schools. In some cases, the editors may take your idea and assign it to a staff writer, but this is still good publicity for your school. And, if you make your case strongly enough, they just might assign you to write the piece.

Newsletters

Newsletters are another publishing outlet that also may provide a stepping stone to writing articles for other outlets. Writing newsletter articles helps you to hone your writing skills as you prepare to tackle more competitive markets.

Many International Reading Association (IRA) state, provincial, and local councils publish newsletters, as do many school districts (and even schools). These outlets offer a less threatening, less competitive avenue for getting published. Indeed, many newsletters eagerly seek contributions, and the editors may be delighted to work with you.

In addition, building a stockpile of published clips from small or local publications makes it easier for you to approach larger ones. These clips provide evidence to editors that you can conceptualize and carry through on preparing an article.

Teacher Magazines

Teacher magazines are another publishing outlet. Some accept articles from freelance writers and take special interest in ideas from a teacher who can write well. The annual edition of *Writer's Market*, the preeminent guide for freelance writers, lists a dozen or so trade magazines in the "Education & Counseling" section, ranging from *Early Childhood News* to *Teacher Magazine*. Furthermore, *Writer's Market* lists specific submission guidelines and contact information for each publication.

Many publications not listed in *Writer's Market* may accept articles as well. In addition, the websites for many publications contain guidelines for writers.

Websites

Websites provide another outlet for your work. There are literally dozens of websites that specialize in posting lesson plans or teaching tips. Some might be open to accepting ideas from you. Browsing the site will probably give you an idea as to whether outside contributors have prepared any of the material.

The ReadWriteThink.org website at www.readwritethink.org is a great outlet for lesson plans. The site, administered jointly by IRA and the National Council of Teachers of English in partnership with the Verizon Foundation, contains hundreds of peer-reviewed, Web-based lesson plans, many of which are prepared by teachers.

Like print publications, ReadWriteThink.org has specific guidelines for writers to follow. Those guidelines are available through the IRA website (www.reading.org), and you should study them carefully before making a submission. You should also look through the existing lesson plans to see what is being used. As with journal articles, all of the lesson plans that appear on ReadWriteThink.org go through a rigorous peer-review process.

Come Up With Ideas

You know you want to write for publication. You have identified some potential outlets for your work. Now, what will you write about? Again, think about the publication's needs.

Two types of articles commonly found in newspapers and magazines are trend pieces and features. In a nutshell, trend articles provide an overview of a topic or trend that is currently hot. Such an article generally involves interviews with several knowledgeable people and some examples. Why not look for an education trend to write about?

For example, throughout the United States, there is a trend toward the increasing use of reading/literacy coaches in schools. If that is true in your district, you might be able to pitch an article idea on this topic to your local newspaper or a regional magazine. You could offer to interview some coaches and administrators about their experiences on how the program is being implemented.

> "The strokes of the pen need deliberation as much as the sword needs swiftness."
>
> —JULIA WARD HOWE

Features also are a common staple for both newspapers and magazines, and they can be fun to write. Features can focus on a particular person, event, or topic. Almost anything interesting is fair game. Although the writing style for a feature tends to be more free-flowing than for a news article, the key is to find an idea with wide appeal.

As a teacher or teacher educator, there are lots of great ideas swirling around you. Your school may have instituted an innovative program to encourage students to read for pleasure. You may have an interesting method of publishing student writing. You may have a student or teacher in your school whose story is particularly inspiring. You just have to keep your eyes and ears open and think about the needs of your prospective publication.

I am amazed at how often people are surrounded by great ideas and do not realize it. Your school or local reading council may sponsor a wonderful community involvement program or a teacher research group that is especially effective. Your school may have an interesting partnership with another school or council. You may have practical advice to share. If you are a classroom teacher, you may have developed an especially effective method of teaching a particular aspect of reading or writing. You may have a lesson plan on a particular topic that is unique. All these may lead to article ideas.

Present Your Ideas in an Appropriate Manner

Once you determine your target market and select an idea, it is time to work on presenting that idea to an editor. There are many different ways of presenting ideas. Typically, journals prefer to receive completed manuscripts. On the other hand, most trade publications and newspapers, including *Reading Today*, prefer to receive a query letter that provides a brief synopsis of your idea (except for letters to the editor; it is generally easier to simply submit the full text for those). The benefit from the editor's viewpoint is that he or she can tell right away whether the idea has promise for publication. It is much easier to consider a two- or three-paragraph description of an article idea than to wade through a 1,500-word article.

The benefit from your viewpoint is that you do not waste time developing an idea that holds no interest for the editor. I empathize with authors who have obviously spent a lot of time preparing and submitting a complete article for *Reading Today* that just is not appropriate for us.

Queries not only make it easier for editors to evaluate a potential article but also to help shape it. Often, we receive queries at *Reading Today* with ideas that are not quite right for us in their present form. However, with a slightly revised focus or a different approach, they might be perfect. It is much easier to make these changes up front before the article is fully developed. Once the article is completed, it is harder to ask the author to go back and take a different slant.

How should you contact editors? Again, try to find the publication's guidelines, either in print or online. Some editors prefer receiving queries through the mail; others prefer e-mail as we do at *Reading Today*, although we also accept queries submitted by regular mail.

Please note that while e-mail is an immediate medium, you should not expect an immediate response. At *Reading Today*, we try to acknowledge all submissions promptly, but it may be several weeks (or even a couple of months) before we can respond. Our publication cycle is quite demanding, and dealing with freelance article submissions is one of those tasks we do in the tiny windows of time between deadlines.

Please don't call editors with ideas. Depending on where in the production cycle the publication is, editors often do not have time to break away from their schedules to take calls. Often, we are focused on the deadline for our current issue. Once the deadline passes, we have time to think and plan ahead. Furthermore, I personally much prefer seeing an article idea presented in print rather than simply hearing it described over the phone. Sometimes people can tell about an idea much more effectively than they can write about it.

For specific guidelines on submitting material to *Reading Today*, please refer to the information in the chapter appendix beginning on page 95.

GUIDELINE 5

Let Editors Work With You

Editors know what types of articles work best for their audience. Working with them from the earliest stage can help ensure that your article will have the best possible chance of acceptance and of having a real impact on readers.

At *Reading Today*, this means sending us a well-conceived query letter. We will determine if and how an article might meet the needs of our readers. We can help you select the best angle for the article and set a length that will work within our space constraints for coming issues. That way, you do not waste your time developing a 1,500-word article when there is space for only 800 words. You will be sent feedback on the idea, and then it is up to you to develop the article and submit it. After we review the article, one of four things will happen:

1. The article is accepted with only minor editorial and stylistic changes needed. We will make these changes, and your work is done. Congratulations! You have already earned your byline.

2. The article is accepted but some things may need to be changed or some questions need to be answered. If the changes or questions are substantive, you may be asked to do further work. If the changes seem clear-cut, we will make them. Depending on the level of the edit, we may send the manuscript back to you to ensure that we didn't change any meanings.

3. The article is returned to you for revision and resubmission because of major problems. If our guidelines have been followed, such as angle and length, then this should not occur. Indeed, it rarely does.

4. The article may be rejected outright. This almost never happens if the author has sent a query letter and followed our suggestions. It happens frequently when authors submit articles without querying first.

That is our procedure at *Reading Today*, but other publications may have other policies. For instance, many magazines and newspapers never send revised manuscripts or galleys back to authors to review, regardless of the level of editorial work that is done on them. You may want to check with the publication about these policies ahead of time.

GUIDELINE

Take Note of Stylistic Issues

One important thing to remember when writing for magazines and newspapers is that the style is much different than that of journals. Because journal articles are scholarly in nature, sentences tend to be long and often are written in the passive voice. Because the articles are longer, authors can unfold their points over a span of paragraphs or even pages.

For newspapers and magazines, the writing must be punchy and crisp. Authors should use active verbs whenever possible. They must make their points quickly, summing up in a single paragraph the same idea that might take five paragraphs in a journal. Space is tight. Every word has to count.

Writing for *Reading Today*

MaryEllen Vogt, California State University, Long Beach, and President, International Reading Association (2004–2005)

While a high school senior, I was assigned a paper in English literature that required students to host a dinner party for five British authors, decide where to seat them, and create their conversations during dinner. When I received an "A" on that assignment, I felt like a writer for the first time.

Though writing is generally a satisfying endeavor for me, there are times when I reach "writing paralysis." Remember the 20-mile wall described by marathon runners? I've experienced something similar when I have not engaged in "prevision," a step in my writing process that requires me to mull over what I'm going to write, sometimes for hours, days, or weeks. Completing a typical prewriting activity at this point is fruitless because I don't have the ideas to organize.

While writing the President Messages for *Reading Today*, this problem was exacerbated because the deadlines for submitting the pieces came very frequently, providing little time for envisioning what I wanted to say. Also, having to limit a piece to a prescribed number of words is akin to the game of deciding who will remain on a life raft. It is not easy making decisions about which words to cut!

At some point you realize the piece of writing will never be perfect. Just stop and let it go and trust your editor to finalize the process. Effective editors honor your thoughts, if not *all* your words, and once you see your work in print, the feeling you'll experience is like crossing the finish line—there is nothing quite like it!

We have received articles that were quite acceptable except for the fact that they were 2,500 words in length, and our limit for most features is generally half that length. The authors were unable (or unwilling) to pare their article by half, and it would have taken too much time for us to do that sort of major surgery in-house. Had the author queried us first or read our writers' guidelines, the problem could have been avoided.

True news articles typically are written in an inverted pyramid style. This includes the most important information—who, what, when, where, and how—in the first paragraph or two. Subsequent paragraphs provide additional details. Because of editors' issues with space allowances and paging issues, the inverted pyramid style allows editors to cut from the bottom up without sacrificing any of the most important information. On occasion, articles I have written for newspapers or magazines have appeared virtually word for word as I submitted them except the bottom few paragraphs have been lopped off. This shows the importance of using the inverted pyramid style. Incidentally, we do not usually edit that way for *Reading Today*. Although it takes longer, we find it is more effective (and more pleasing to the author) to tighten the text throughout rather than to simply cut large blocks of text. Usually, tightening the wording in an article also makes it stronger. Often, authors do not even realize that the text has been changed. If they do, they often comment that it sounds much better without the extra words.

For feature articles, we advise authors to use a conversational style. That is, write it as though you were telling the story to a friend. That type of simple, straightforward writing generally works well for leading a reader through a story.

IRA style is based on APA style (American Psychological Association, 2001), along with elements from the *Chicago Manual of Style* (University of Chicago Press, 2003). The Association also has a "house style"—for use by the editors across departments to handle specific editorial issues.

GUIDELINE 7

Build on Your Success

Success begets success in any field, including writing. You can build on your successes with a particular publication by sending more articles to that publication. Over time, you become more familiar with the publication's needs and style, and the editors get to know you and your strengths.

Once you have established a working relationship with an editor, keep sending ideas. At *Reading Today*, we appreciate developing ongoing relationships with freelancers. We know what to expect from them, and they know what to expect from us. Because we know their strengths (and their weaknesses), we can plan accordingly. From the writers' viewpoint, they know how we approach certain topics and what kinds of sidebars and photos we tend to use. It is an efficient system because we all can focus better. The writer can focus on pitching ideas that we are likely to use, and we can consider those ideas with the confidence of knowing that the writer can execute them to our satisfaction.

> "I rewrite a great deal. I'm always fiddling, always changing something. I'll write a few words—then I'll change them. I add. I subtract. I work and fiddle and keep working, fiddling, and I only stop at the deadline."
>
> —ELLEN GOODMAN

Does that mean that markets become closed to other writers? Not at all. At *Reading Today*, we are always open to new ideas from new contributors. After all, that may be where our next group of regular freelancers comes from.

Always look for ways to build on what you have done. When I completed my children's book *Daddy Poems* (2000), I thought that was the end of my foray into the realm of poetry. But when my editor invited me to come up with further titles, I decided to try a whole series of family-related poetry books. That led to three more titles published and another in development.

I used the experience of doing the poetry books to branch out into children's biographies. With the poetry books to my credit, other publishers were willing to let me try other types of projects. It is almost a snowball effect.

Obviously, you need at least some talent to successfully write for publication. Over the years, however, I have become convinced that almost as important as writing ability is a sense of what I call "creative assertiveness"—knowing who to pitch, how to pitch, what to pitch, and when to pitch. If you can come up with an original concept that an editor or publisher wants, he or she will be willing to work with you to bring that concept to fruition.

I have been in educational journalism for more than half my life, and I've seen lots of really good (and a fair number of really bad) articles pertaining to reading and reading education. If you follow the guidelines presented here, you can improve your chances of producing articles that fall into the former category.

Closing Thoughts

The rewards of writing are many—some tangible, some not. The tangible rewards, of course, include receiving payment for articles or royalties on books or simply receiving contributors' copies.

The intangible rewards, however, can be even more important. There is nothing quite like the thrill of walking into a bookstore and seeing a book with your name on the cover. Or opening a magazine, journal, or newspaper and seeing your byline—and realizing that thousands of other readers are seeing it, too. Even better are letters or comments from readers indicating that what you wrote taught them something or stirred their emotions.

During the past several years, I have served as a national judge in the Letters About Literature contest. In this annual contest, sponsored by the Center for the Book in the Library of Congress in partnership with Target Stores, young readers in grades 4–12 write letters to the author of a book that has made a difference in their lives. These youngsters have written touching and heartfelt letters to authors such as Dr. Seuss, Lois Lowry, J.K. Rowling, Kate DiCamillo, and Robert Frost about the effect their works have had. These letters serve as a constant reminder to me that the writing we do—whether for children or adults—truly can affect people's lives.

The written word can stimulate the thoughts and emotions of young readers. It can inspire and aid the professional development of fellow educators. You can be part of this process. Give it a try.

REFERENCES

American Psychological Association. (2001). *Publication manual of the American Psychological Association* (5th ed.). Washington, DC: Author.

Micklos, J., Jr. (Ed.). (2000). *Daddy poems*. Ill. R. Casilla. Honesdale, PA: Boyds Mills Press.

University of Chicago Press. (2003). *Chicago manual of style: The essential guide for writers, editors, and publishers* (15th ed.). Chicago: Author.

Appendix: Writers' Guidelines for *Reading Today*

Reading Today invites readers to submit articles on a broad variety of topics relating to reading and reading education. Because *Reading Today* is mailed to all members of the International Reading Association, the newspaper tries to address the needs and interests of an audience involved in education at all levels from pre-K through adult education in 100 countries throughout the world. Therefore, the topics of interest are fairly wide ranging.

General-interest articles appearing in *Reading Today* range from interviews with children's book authors to descriptions of innovative reading programs to coverage of important reading-related conferences. Anything that might help or interest reading professionals is a potential story. Here are some guidelines to consider:

Story Ideas: We welcome story ideas from readers. Perhaps you know of an interesting reading program going on in your community or an issue that everyone is talking about (such as staffing, assessment, funding cuts, or censorship). In some cases, it is easier for the *Reading Today* staff to write about these topics for you, because the information can be linked to similar information already gathered from other places. *Reading Today* has 85,000 readers in 100 countries, which makes for 85,000 sets of eyes and ears to help us hone in on issues that concern all of IRA members.

Length: Remember, this is a newspaper, not a journal. The shorter the article, the greater the chance that it can be used. Articles of 500–800 words are encouraged, while those that run more than 1,000–1,500 words are rarely used. Many times articles are edited to fit the space available.

Style: Keep in mind that newspaper style is quite different from the style of educational journals. Aim for a style that is conversational and light, such as a description or letter to a friend. Try to use active rather than passive verbs. Keep sentences and paragraphs short. However, if the subject matter isn't intrinsically interesting or useful, no amount of reworking will make it so. A straightforward, no-nonsense approach almost always works best.

Some helpful resources for writing an article include *The Elements of Style* by Strunk and White, which is packed with invaluable advice for writers of expository prose, and *The Associated Press Stylebook*, which provides information on hyphens, abbreviations, and other nettlesome small points.

Please note that *Reading Today* articles almost never include lists of references with an article, so if a reference must be cited, work it into the text.

A final word on style: Remember that almost any subject can be fascinating if people are able to really *see* it. This is accomplished by subtracting, not adding—by not adding words or ideas that are not needed. Find the most concise ways to tell the story and ruthlessly cut away everything else.

Leads: For news articles, use the five Ws approach to writing the lead paragraph: who, what, when, where, and why. For feature articles, write a lead that captures the human interest angle of the topic and entices readers to read more. (Focus on the aspect that struck you most when you first encountered the situation you're describing. That's often a good starting point.)

If unsure about how to proceed, especially if new to this type of writing, take a close look at any high-quality newspaper, which will contain scores of articles on which to model your writing. Analyzing at least a few issues of *Reading Today* also will help you become familiar with its style, determine where your article might fit in, and then shape it accordingly.

Remuneration: Most articles are submitted to *Reading Today* from IRA members or from educators in the field who have specific ideas or information they wish to share with other educators. Contributors are remunerated for ideas only in copies of the newspaper. Occasionally, professional writers of feature articles are paid for their contributions. Please advise the editors when submitting your query or article if payment is expected, as payment is reserved for professional writers contributing articles that can't be obtained in another way.

Photos: Photos make an excellent accompaniment to an article. Photos can be sent via e-mail attachment, with black-and-white or color prints also acceptable. Please include either a rough caption or subject identification as appropriate. When submitting photographs of subjects under the age of 18, you will need to provide a signed model release form (available from *Reading Today*). As to composition, try to make the picture tell the story. An image of two or three people actually doing what's described in the story is vastly superior to a group shot of 30 people standing in rows. One simple trick to improve photos: Get close enough so that the image almost fills the viewfinder.

As with articles, *Reading Today* does not usually pay for photos. However, occasionally we use photos by professional photographers, and we do pay for those photos.

Format: In today's busy world, readers like their information to come in bite-sized chunks. For instance, articles that provide lists (e.g., 10 brief tips) or bulleted items are a relatively fast, easy read. Of course, the traditional essay style works better to tell a story or explain a complex concept. Remember that no one approach is right for everything.

Interaction: Always remember to contact the editors for help or assistance. First, send an e-mail providing a brief outline of your proposed idea, which can be used by the editors to help you in finding the best approach to the article before you actually begin to write it. Professional writers and editors do this, because there are many different ways to approach a piece of writing. Writing is far from an exact science; it takes a judgment and compromises. If writers and editors work together at an early stage, everyone saves time and effort.

Readership: Remember that *Reading Today* readers are reading professionals like you. Sometimes people who deal with children all day forget that adults can handle trickier vocabulary and ideas than kids can. They write as if they were talking to a class of children. Just assume that your readers are sophisticated, intelligent professionals and express yourself accordingly.

Editing: Once you have gone through your article and made it as good as you can, it will still be edited here. That doesn't mean that the piece is badly written; it simply reflects an attempt to ensure that every article that appears in *Reading Today* is concise, stylistically consistent, and able to fit the space available.

Deadlines: *Reading Today* is published during the first week of even-numbered months, and the deadline for receiving articles is about six weeks prior to publication (e.g., April 15 for the June/July issue). There is some leeway in those dates to accommodate coverage of late-breaking news, but it is important to submit material as early as possible.

Acceptance and Rejection: The acceptance rate for *Reading Today* is probably a little higher than for a journal, but everything submitted is not necessarily accepted. Further, rejection doesn't necessarily mean that an article is badly written—it could mean that a similar article appeared recently or that the focus was inappropriate for IRA's unique audience. Unfortunately, critiques cannot be done on rejected manuscripts, but writers are encouraged not to give up after one rejection. On occasion, we have accepted later articles from writers whose work was once rejected by *Reading Today*. Even professional writers get rejected sometimes, so don't take it too hard.

Please also bear in mind that *Reading Today* contains up to 100 articles per issue, and as many as 10 of these may have been submitted by outside writers or columnists. Unless an article is especially timely, it may not be used for up to a year after it is accepted. Please be patient.

Special Sections

Reading Today contains several special sections geared to specific purposes. Some of these sections have their own needs and guidelines.

Council and Affiliate News: IRA has more than 1,200 councils and affiliates. This is an area for which we would like to get more submissions, yet we rarely hear from these groups. When we do, it is often a simple rundown of the latest conference or an overview of activities from the past year. These descriptions, while important to the groups involved, do not appeal to a wide audience.

However, many councils and affiliates are doing really interesting and unique activities that other groups could benefit by knowing about. Does your council have an innovative way for involving students, for increasing membership, or for drawing attendance at your meetings? We encourage you to share these ideas with other councils through the Council and Affiliate News section of *Reading Today*.

Many councils are creating fascinating ties with groups in other countries or sponsoring unusual local projects to promote reading and literacy, such as one by a Wisconsin council that provided books and bookcases for a family that had just moved into a Habitat for Humanity house or the Children's Reading Tent activity organized by the Reading Association of Uganda that brought books to youngsters who otherwise might not have access to them.

We invite local, state/provincial, and national IRA groups to submit articles about successful programs they have conducted. These can include community outreach programs, membership recruitment programs, or partnership efforts. Articles should run 800 words or fewer, and photos are welcome.

We especially encourage national affiliates to submit brief reports summarizing interesting or unusual activities. These groups should also let us know the dates for their forthcoming national conferences. State/provincial groups should make sure that they submit their conference information to the Council and Affiliate Services Division at International Reading Association headquarters by the date requested each year. That information provides the basis for the calendar listing in *Reading Today* and on the IRA website.

Ideas for Administrators: For this section, we seek practical ideas that principals or reading supervisors can replicate. Tips on strengthening the schoolwide reading program and ideas for motivating kids to read for pleasure are some of the topics we have covered. Articles may run up to 800 words, and accompanying photographs are welcome. We also welcome very brief (200–400 words) "tip" articles focusing on a single idea relating to reading that administrators might find helpful.

Parents and Reading: This section focuses on practical ideas that parents can use in helping their children with some aspect of reading. Authors should go beyond general advice such as "read to your child." Instead, focus in on a specific topic, such as tips for having a successful parent/teacher conference or getting kids to read over school vacation. Articles may run up to 800 words, and very brief articles of 200–400 words focusing on a single tip are also welcome.

In the Classroom: We welcome brief anecdotes about humorous or heartwarming happenings in the classroom (up to 250 words). We will occasionally consider longer news or feature articles of up to 800 words on interesting or unusual programs in schools or classrooms.

It is important to note that there is a fine line as to what is appropriate for the newspaper and what is more appropriate for a journal. If an activity really needs to be supported by a research base or requires references, it is better suited for a journal. If it requires references, it belongs in a journal. If it cannot be expressed in fewer than 1,000 words (500 is even better), it belongs in a journal.

With that in mind, a detailed article about how best to teach comprehension skills might work better for *The Reading Teacher*. The following are a few examples of recently published practical articles in *Reading Today*, which tend to be more feature based:

- ideas for hosting successful author/illustrator visits in schools;
- suggestions for merging reading and science, using the example of a specific school that created a unit around a family of ducks that lived just outside the school; and
- information about differences between the reading habits or boys and girls, with some specific ideas for encouraging boys to read more. This latter article was based interviews with researchers and educators who have studied this topic.

Forum: For this opinion section, we welcome "Commentaries" of up to 800 words about a topic of interest and importance to reading educators around the world. Don't be afraid to be controversial. We also welcome "Letters to the Editor." These letters run up to 400 words, but the shorter they are, the better the chance that we can use them. Letters are also sometimes shortened to fit the space available.

Send materials to: *Reading Today*, International Reading Association, 800 Barksdale Road, PO Box 8139, Newark, DE 19714-8139, USA. Or call us at 800-336-READ (302-731-1600 outside North America). You can reach editor-in-chief John Micklos, Jr., at extension 250. E-mail jmicklos@reading.org or readingtoday @reading.org.

Writing Books and Edited Volumes

A S YOU LEARNED in Section II, writing for journals, newspapers, and magazines requires a specific focus on a topic that usually must be communicated within a limited number of pages. These outlets are not the place for extensive discussion about a topic or set of related topics. Rather, books—whether they are resource books, teacher guides, course textbooks, strategy books, instructional materials books, how-to books, or research monographs—are the better venue for this level of discussion.

Books, written by one or more authors about a specific topic in literacy, require that the authors have broad and deep knowledge about a topic. This knowledge enables them to convey information clearly and convincingly to the readership. Edited books, developed and organized by one or more editors, require that the editors identify authors who are expert about different facets of a specific topic in literacy and who can write individual chapters. Each type of book has its advantages and disadvantages.

Books present the authors' perspectives about a topic. Authors are responsible for writing the entire text, and they have control over the content and style of writing. Edited books present multiple perspectives, styles, and voices about a topic. Although less writing is required of the editors, they are responsible for coordinating, organizing, and editing chapter authors' writing so the message is coherent and consistent.

This section explains what you should think about if you are interested in writing or editing a book for publication, including idea development, audience, book formats, timelines, and authorship. Each chapter introduces you to the many positive and challenging processes that are involved in the publication of books.

Chapter 7, "Writing Books," provides guidelines for writing different types of books, and how to get from talking about your idea to actually preparing it to send to an editor. This chapter focuses on honing purpose and focus, choosing content wisely and refining audience, and developing a realistic timeline through backward planning approaches.

Chapter 8, "Editing Books: Reflections and Suggestions," discusses how to develop a framework for an edited book, select the most appropriate chapter authors, work effectively with invited authors, and coordinate all the components into a coherent text.

Both of these chapters touch upon the essentials for authoring, coauthoring, editing, and coediting books.

CHAPTER 7

Writing Books

James Flood

Diane Lapp

This chapter focuses on
- establishing the focus and purpose of your book project
- honing purpose, choosing content wisely, and refining audience
- developing a realistic timeline through backward planning approaches

THERE ARE PROBABLY as many different types of books as there are ideas to write about in a book. During our careers, we have written several different kinds of books: research monographs, practitioner guides, teacher resource books, research summary books, and books for children and adolescents. Within each of these five categories, we have written a variety of kinds of books; for example, in the area of teacher resource books, we have written methods course textbooks, teacher manuals that accompany anthologies, strategy activity books, preservice teacher toolbox books, and instructional materials books. There are so many kinds of books that you may write (or that you may have already written) that we have chosen to organize our chapter around guidelines that apply to all books.

Beating the Odds: Getting Published in the Field of Literacy edited by Shelley B. Wepner and Linda B. Gambrell. Copyright © 2006 by the International Reading Association.

Gay Su Pinnell,
Professor Emeritus,
The Ohio State
University

Conversations

I see writing as a way of having an extended conversation with colleagues who love books and love bringing children and books together. As I work in classrooms and talk with teachers, often topics for writing simply emerge, but from there on, the process is not so easy. I have written research articles that involve spending isolated hours analyzing and reporting data, but I think that oral language is the key to the kind of writing I do best. I love sitting with one or two friends and spilling out ideas. My frequent coauthor, Irene Fountas, and I constantly share new books and articles we are reading as well as our observations in classrooms. We frequently watch and rewatch videotaped lessons and discuss them. We talk, build on each other's ideas, and argue.

I acquired a real asset at about age 15—I learned to type very fast. Hardly realizing that I am keyboarding, I can record most of our thinking almost as fast as we can talk. An interesting sideline, though, is that sometimes what I am typing is not what we are saying in our conversation. It's what the conversation is making me think about at the time. After a lot of brainstorming, we bring order and structure to our writing, and we usually create an overall plan for the book. But new writers should know that never once has one of my books been published with the exact same organization I created for the draft. My best advice to emerging writers would be this: Be willing to produce very rough versions of your ideas and make good writing friends in the process.

GUIDELINE 1

Hone Your Purpose: Answer the Blunt Question, What's the Point?

As you start to think about your book, ask yourself again and again, What's the purpose of this book? If it is a methods book intended for preservice teachers, a reader would expect to find some theory and research and a plethora of teaching ideas. If the intended book is for graduate students in a reading research class, the reader would expect to find a great deal of information on research studies that have influenced the field. But rarely are our initial purposes in writing a book so clearly and neatly defined as these two examples suggest. The purpose of your book often begins with a broad emphasis that becomes narrowed and refined once you have begun.

The purpose of a book often evolves as the writing project continues. We always have a primary purpose—to dispense and share information with a specific audience. But we also have secondary and tertiary purposes. We have worldviews that influence our thinking and determine the ways that we see issues.

We have to ask ourselves about our political purposes in writing what we write, and we have to ask ourselves questions about censorship (why we have included particular information and ignored other information).

We have to acknowledge that our own views on literacy and literacy instruction help us to structure our unique views of teaching and learning. Recently, we wrote a book on first-grade literacy learning as part of Donna Ogle and Camille Blachowicz's series on teaching literacy for Guilford Press. As we started talking about our book in the oral-language stage with our coauthors, Kelly Moore and Maria Nichols, we realized that we wanted to write a book that would be very practical for a person who had just been hired for his or her first teaching job. We wanted to make sure that we included enough theory and research to allow for background reading in case there were gaps in knowledge, but we wanted the book to be grounded in the reality of today's first-grade classrooms. We assigned ourselves the task of taking hundreds of pictures in every conceivable type of first-grade classroom to make sure we were capturing contemporary first-grade life.

As we started to design the content of the book, we all acknowledged that we had instructional biases toward reader's/writer's workshop within an effectively managed program. Our approach to first-grade instruction was clearly influenced by our bias, but not limited by it. As we selected and reselected which pictures we would use, we knew we were selecting the pictures that best illustrated our view of the world. This is what honing purpose requires.

GUIDELINE 2

Choose Your Content Wisely: Less Is Often More

Our first and best advice to you on the topic of content is to write lists of ideas and issues that you may want to include in your book. Start with many and then be selective about what really fits. Ask yourself, What is *really* necessary? Before you begin, make sure you have a realistic idea about how many pages your publisher will allow. Then sort your ideas and issues into potential chapters. Remember that these are only placeholders—they need not become your final versions.

> "Published writers still struggle with the writing process."
>
> —LAWRENCE PRINGLE

In our two most recent books, *Teaching Literacy in First Grade* (Lapp, Flood, Moore, & Nichols, 2005) and *Content Area Reading and Learning: Instructional Strategies* (Lapp, Flood, & Farnan, 2006), and in each of our three handbooks (Flood, Heath, & Lapp, 1997; Flood, Jensen, Lapp, & Squire, 1991; Flood, Lapp, Squire, & Jensen, 2002), we had several different tables of contents for each book. We moved information around many, many times until we thought we finally had it right. In fact, we made one more change in the *Content Area Reading and Learning* text once we received the final papers in the collection. We moved one chapter from the front of the book to the end of the book because we believed it clearly captured our intent to produce a comprehensive book on content area reading and learning; it neatly summarized all of the issues included in the book.

Our second bit of advice about content is to pay attention to the adage "less is more." When we first start a book, we instinctively want to include everything that has been written on our topic. It cannot be done; you have to establish criteria for what you will include and what you will exclude. Some criteria might be timeliness, recency, payoff for the reader, state-of-the-art research and practice, and links to other information sources.

Certain topics have to be included in certain textbooks, but other topics may not be so important. When we had to cut more than 300 pages for our second edition of *Teaching Reading to Every Child* (Lapp & Flood, 1983), we sat down and rated every topic in the table of contents. It was clear to us that our chapters on word study, phonics, and comprehension had to stay, but we knew that if we marked every chapter and section as "must stay," we would be heading nowhere. Finally, we got to the appendixes that we loved (lists of Caldecott and Newbery award books, teaching activities, Readers Theatre scripts, words by frequency in English and Spanish), and we knew we had to make cuts. Although we were never happy eliminating this material in the appendixes that seemed so appropriate for a methods book, we accepted the dictum for fewer pages. The moral of our story is to start with everything, then chisel away until you have a match between most important material and number of pages permitted.

GUIDELINE 3

Define, Redefine, and Refine Your Audience

Defining your audience is a tricky business. It has been our experience that the first audience you define for yourself is rarely the refined audience you will come to understand as you eventually publish the book. As you begin thinking about your book, examine other books geared to the same audience that you are considering. Make a list of the common components in those books (e.g., vignettes to open chapters, writing style—whether formal or informal, use of photographs, and summaries to end chapters). Noting these components will help you to plan your book.

We have a personal story about not fully understanding audience. In 1980, we were invited to write a book on literacy for teachers of young children (preschoolers). There had been increased interest in early childhood education during the 1970s, and many educators had begun talking about appropriate literacy methods for preschoolers. We discussed our ideas with other professionals in the field, and we were encouraged to move forward with the book. As we discussed it between ourselves, we decided that the focus of the book should be developing young children's oral language skills. With this emphasis on oral skills, we decided to title the book *Language/Reading Instruction for the Young Child* (Flood & Lapp, 1980). Leading with the word *language* rather than *reading* or *teaching* doomed the book. Our intended audience, teachers of young children, never found our book because they were searching for methods books on teaching reading and prereading skills to young children, not language skills.

The moral of this story is to use a simple title for your book that connects with the specific audience you have in mind. We learned our lesson and gave our subsequent books titles such as the following: *Teaching Reading to Every Child* (Lapp & Flood, 1978, 1983, 1992; Lapp, Flood, Brock, & Fisher, 2006), *Content Area Reading and Learning: Instructional Strategies* (Lapp, Flood, & Farnan, 2006), *Guiding Readers Through Text: A Review of Study Guides* (Wood, Lapp, & Flood, 1992), *Accommodating Differences Among English Language Learners: 75 Literacy Lessons* (Jacobson, Lapp, & Mendez, 2003), *Teaching Writing: Strategies for Developing the 6 + 1 Traits* (Flood, Lapp, & Fisher, 2004), *Vocabulary Strategies Every Teacher Needs to Know* (Brassell & Flood, 2004), and *Language: A User's Guide* (Salus & Flood, 2003).

Sometimes the audience you have in mind is more or less specific and is smaller or larger than the audience your publisher has in mind. You need to talk with your publisher about your vision; it can help tremendously with the overall marketing plan. We have experienced times when the publisher asked us to change a single word in the title, e.g., *children* to *students* in order to broaden the market (in this case from primary grades to primary plus intermediate and upper grades).

GUIDELINE 4

Choose a Format: What Is Best for Your Book?

On rare occasions there is a perfect match between content and format in which the writing of the book flows naturally and positively. Much more frequently there is tension that requires flexibility and compromise. Being part of the team that determines formatting is one of the most rewarding experiences of writing a book; tell your publisher that you want to be involved in formatting, but be prepared for a mildly enthusiastic response (at best). Publishers often think that they are the arbiters of all formatting issues. In general, they are. Most formatting issues involve money and resources; some of your "great" ideas may be beyond the budget set aside for your book. But do not be afraid to express your vision for the book to the publisher.

Formatting issues include everything from layout to photographs to artwork to trim size to cover designs to total number of pages. In general, we deferred to our publishers on these issues throughout our careers. But there were times when we held our ground (and sometimes even won a battle or two). In 1976, we were working on our first methods textbook, *Teaching Reading to Every Child*, and we were fortunate to be working with Lloyd Chilton, a revered editor in college publishing. In fact, he was instrumental in getting us our contract with Macmillan. He advised us through every step and offered recommendations for each of the major formatting issues. When it came to the cover of the book, we were adamant that we wanted a rich, red cover that would stand out among all the other books on an academic's bookshelf.

Lloyd tried to dissuade us, reminding us that academic books traditionally were much more muted in color; he also reminded us that Macmillan was considered to be an "old-fashioned, stuffy" company by some people, and that the "powers that be" might not approve a bright red cover. We stood our ground and the book was published in bright red; we still refer to the book as "Big Red" because it was nearly 1,000 pages. We think it is the prettiest book on our bookshelves—maybe because it was our first. The cover did not deter sales, and the book is currently coming out in a fourth edition.

The publisher frequently controls the number of pages in a book. Tastes and times have changed dramatically since 1978, and methods textbooks are much shorter than they were in 1978. For example, our second edition of *Teaching Reading to Every Child* was 565 pages. The U.S. economy determined these changes, which, in turn, had an impact on decisions about content. With the fourth edition around 400 pages, we joke that we have shrunk to excellence.

GUIDELINE 5

Develop a Realistic Timeline: Backward Book Planning

We always begin with a timeline that provides approximations of when we will need to have each chapter in its draft or final stage. We ask ourselves a series of questions: When will we need to have the entire first draft ready for the publisher? When will we need to write for permissions? How much time will we need to complete a final draft? When will the publisher want our photos, charts, tables, and so forth? We have always referred to this as our "backward book planning" calendar because we begin with the final publication date and move backward to the beginning. It is helpful to do this with the publishers because of their more realistic view of the time it takes to get a book ready for market. Depending on the type of book you are writing, there are more appropriate times than others to introduce it to the general public. Publishers whose primary market is the university community usually want to publish their books by March for September adoption. Publishers whose primary market is practicing teachers have a more flexible schedule; their books are published throughout the year. It is very important to meet all your deadlines in order for publishers to sell the book. Be sure to check off each activity as you complete each task, and do your best to stick to your plan.

Gathering Momentum

**Keith Stanovich,
University of
Toronto, Canada**

The most important rule in my writing life is that I write in large blocks of time rather than small ones—the bigger the blocks, the better. I am not the type of person who can write at all in 30-minute blocks or even in one-hour blocks. I take a very long time to gather momentum, and when I get rolling on my writing I absolutely hate getting interrupted.

Because I value writing so highly, I have tried to arrange my life and schedule so that it fits with my writing style. So, for example, when given the choice between a course that meets three days a week and one that meets two days a week, I always choose the latter; and when given the choice between a course that meets two days a week and one that meets one day a week I again always choose the latter. Once, I arranged my schedule so that I taught two 3 $^1/_2$-hour sessions on the same day (and these were undergraduate lecture courses!). The fewer interruptions in a week, the more likely it is that I will have a couple of big blocks of several hours together—and having these blocks is a great predictor of how productive a writer I will be. You will not be surprised to learn that my most recent book on reading (*Progress in Understanding Reading: Scientific Foundations and New Frontiers*, Guilford Press, 2000) was written entirely on sabbatical, as was my most recent book on thinking and reasoning (*The Robot's Rebellion: Finding Meaning in the Age of Darwin*, University of Chicago Press, 2004).

Writing takes great concentration—sustained concentration. The enemy of writing is the modern world of e-mails, cell calls, faxes, endless committee meetings...and all of the wheels and gears of modern bureaucracies. Ignore these things like the plague. Ten years from now you will not remember any committee meeting you were in, but you will take great pride in the good writing that you accomplished. As the saying goes, do not neglect the important because you are too busy with the merely urgent. Committee meetings and e-mails are merely urgent. Your writing is important.

GUIDELINE

Get Started and Stay With It

As you begin your book, you will have great energy that will propel you to try to do many things (perhaps too many) at once. We suggest you set the stage before you actually start writing. Have your resources readily available (e.g., books, journals, computer files) before you begin. Start with one topic; outline it thoroughly so that you will remember to include all of the appropriate information. Although many writers have idiosyncratic writing styles, ranging from sequential writing to "leapfrog" writing where they jump from topic to topic, we suggest starting with one chapter in your book and working until it is finished. Having a detailed outline will help you to write other chapters or refer to a topic included in a previous chapter. Also, making a folder for each topic and adding any interesting related bits of information, citations, and notes will help you in writing the first and subsequent versions of each chapter. We wrote many of our first editions in longhand on yellow pads of paper. The night before beginning a new chapter we would lay out a fresh pad and many sharpened pencils. We now joke with each other about the volume of work we might have completed if we had computers at the onset of our careers.

Sometimes "sticking with it" means going back to the drawing board. Recently, we worked very diligently on an article that was to be included in a collection of essays. We had discussed with the editors the specifics of the audience for whom the book was intended. When we sent our article to the editors, they phoned us, because somewhere along the line we misunderstood the exact nature of the audience, and the paper that we sent them was inappropriate. Although the publisher invited us to rework the paper, we knew that they were close to their deadline and would not be able to wait for us to do a rewrite. We told the editors to go ahead without our paper, and we would rework it for another journal or collection of essays. We all agreed that this was the best solution.

> "The greatest part of a writer's time is spent in reading, in order to write; a man will turn over half a library to make one book."
>
> —SAMUEL JOHNSON

Although we were initially disappointed, we came to see this experience as an opportunity to rework and match the paper to a more appropriate audience and journal. We believe that the paper is much better now. In fact, after shopping around and deciding on another journal that matched our intent, we are happy to report that our paper has been accepted for publication.

"Sticking with it" also means pausing and reading more. Getting the contract and getting ready to write is very exciting because you feel that you have much to share. As you begin to make detailed outlines and expand your notes, you may feel even more invigorated because you are seeing all of your ideas take shape. A few chapters into it, however, you begin to feel exhausted and overwhelmed. This is natural because writing a book takes a great deal of time and effort. Take a break, do some additional reading, talk it through again with a knowledgeable colleague, and then get yourself back on task. You can never finish what you do not continue.

GUIDELINE 7

Let Your Manuscript Rest and Marinate

Once you have completed a thorough draft of each chapter, take another break. During your break read, read, read about each topic. While your manuscript is marinating, so are you; you are learning more information all the time that you may want to include in your book.

We learned the value of marinating our manuscripts during a long period between editions of our reading methods textbook, *Teaching Reading to Every Child*.

The first edition was published in 1978, the second edition in 1983, the third in 1992, and the fourth in 2006. Thirteen years (between 1992 and 2006) seems like a very long time, which may reflect the fact that we enjoy doing first editions more than revisions, but it also speaks to the marinating issue.

AUTHOR REFLECTIONS

Making Your Writing Interesting

Nell K. Duke, Michigan State University

In writing my first book for teachers, I started chapter after chapter with something along the lines of "Decades of research strongly suggest that...." My editor gently noted that that may not be the most compelling way to begin a chapter, and chapter after chapter, of the book. In the end, we used techniques such as classroom anecdotes, provocative quotations, pieces of student work, and questions to pique interest (e.g., one chapter begins, "Why does Jell-O wobble?") to begin chapters in more engaging, and varied, ways.

We often think about the structure of our writing, its content, who and what we cite, and the like, but perhaps not as often about making our writing interesting. Yet in the long run, "interestingness" may be one of the most important factors in determining who actually reads, and is affected by, what you write.

There are many strategies for making writing interesting, but three have stood out as particularly useful to me. These probably won't come as revelations to you, but perhaps you, like me, will find it worth reminding yourself of them when you write.

A picture is worth a thousand words. Graphs, figures, charts, photos of classrooms, children, children's work—these do so much to both convey information and generate interest. In one piece I cowrote, I thought the text contained fairly compelling arguments, examples, and references, but it is a single Venn diagram (of texts found at home versus at school) in the article that is most commonly referred to when students and others talk with me or write to me about the piece. And some topics—such as creating a rich classroom print environment—are nearly impossible to write about well without photos and pictures.

"For example" is your friend. So often we understand a point much more fully when an illustrative example is provided, and these examples are often both what is interesting, and memorable, about what we read. Major points should always have examples; minor points should whenever possible.

Enlist others to read your work for interest. When others provide feedback on our work, it is often on things like clarity and the soundness of our argument, but I think it is also worth eliciting feedback on interestingness. Others may have excellent insights about how a piece of writing can be made more interesting. And, because they may not share your inherent passion for the topic, they may be able to provide more realistic assessments of interest.

When I think about articles and books in the field that really stay with me, one of the things I see is that the writing is not only clear, rigorous, and well structured, but also full of strategies that generate interest. I look forward to one of these articles coming from you in the future.

Because we always thought of our text as a testimonial to balance, we did not want the publisher influencing us in our particular emphasis or approach. We decided to wait. We marinated, learned a great deal, and decided to keep our emphasis on balance and comprehensiveness. In this case, 13 years was an acceptable amount of time to wait, but we would not recommend it. You should establish a schedule for revisions and try to stick to it. In many instances, the type of book you write will help you to determine the length of time between editions; for example, handbooks of research syntheses usually have the longest time between revisions.

Finish Those Pesky Conclusion/Summary Sections and Clean Up Your Manuscript

Conclusions and summaries of either parts of chapters or whole chapters can be critical to the success of many books. Often they are the most frequently read parts of a book. Therefore, they should not be too long or too short, and, most important, they should not be rushed as you write them. You need to take time to craft your conclusions and summaries. Show them to uninvolved professionals who can give you objective assessments about whether they can stand alone as coherent and single entities. Even though these components are often an afterthought, do not treat them lightly. Many books over the years have been rejected because they did not include summaries and conclusions, or they were so poorly written that they detracted from the overall effectiveness of the book.

Just when you think you are finally finished, it's time to "clean up" your manuscript. This means checking all references and making sure all chapter titles match the wording in the table of contents. You may want to set aside time to read each chapter one more time for content and one more time for editing issues. In these final readings, read like an editor and look for even the smallest grammatical and typographical errors.

Closing Thoughts

Although this volume offers excellent guidelines, they are only guidelines. You will need to personalize them to suit your own style and way of writing. One day you will be writing a book like this, sharing your experiences of what works best for you as an author. We have included advice from our experiences about establishing a purpose, refining our audience, and carefully choosing content to be included in books.

Our thoughts on finishing a book come from our years of character-building experiences. What we have learned is that writing a book is not easy; it is definitely not for the faint of heart. Good luck as you write your book. We are all waiting for it.

REFERENCES

Brassell, D., & Flood, J. (2004). *Vocabulary strategies every teacher needs to know.* San Diego, CA: Academic Professional Development.

Flood, J., Heath, S.B., & Lapp, D. (Eds.). (1997). *Handbook of research on teaching literacy through the communicative and visual arts* (A project of the International Reading Association). New York: Macmillan.

Flood, J., Jensen, J.M., Lapp, D., & Squire, J.R. (Eds.). (1991). *Handbook of research on teaching the English language arts.* New York: Macmillan.

Flood, J., & Lapp, D. (1980). *Language/reading instruction for the young child.* New York: Macmillan.

Flood, J., Lapp, D., & Fisher, D. (2004). *Teaching writing: Strategies for developing the 6 + 1 traits.* San Diego, CA: Academic Professional Development.

Flood, J., Lapp, D., Squire, J.R., & Jensen, J.M. (2002). *Handbook of research on teaching the English language arts* (2nd ed.). Hillsdale, NJ: Erlbaum.

Jacobson, J., Lapp, D., & Mendez, M. (2003). *Accommodating differences among English language learners: 75 literacy lessons.* San Diego, CA: Academic Professional Development.

Lapp, D., & Flood, J. (1978). *Teaching reading to every child.* New York: Macmillan.

Lapp, D., & Flood, J. (1983). *Teaching reading to every child* (2nd ed.). New York: Macmillan.

Lapp, D., & Flood, J. (1992). *Teaching reading to every child* (3rd ed.). New York: Macmillan.

Lapp, D., Flood, J., Brock, C., & Fisher, D. (2006). *Teaching reading to every child* (4th ed.). Mahwah, NJ: Erlbaum.

Lapp, D., Flood, J., & Farnan, N. (Eds.). (2006). *Content area reading and learning: Instructional strategies* (3rd ed.). Mahwah, NJ: Erlbaum.

Lapp, D., Flood, J., Moore, K., & Nichols, M. (2005). *Teaching literacy in first grade.* New York: Guilford Press.

Salus, P.H., & Flood, J. (2003). *Language: A user's guide.* San Diego, CA: Academic Professional Development.

Wood, K.D., Lapp, D., & Flood, J. (1992). *Guiding readers through text: A review of study guides.* Newark, DE: International Reading Association.

CHAPTER 8

Editing Books: Reflections and Suggestions

Cathy Collins Block

John N. Mangieri

This chapter focuses on

- determining whether a book editing project is for you
- considering criteria for inviting chapter authors and how to work with them effectively
- understanding the process of editing a book

This chapter gives us an opportunity to talk about the process of serving as academic editors or coeditors of books on the topic of literacy. Serving as the editors of literacy books has been an important part of our professional careers for over 30 years. Although we have worked hard and received joy from publishing in the literacy outlets described in prior chapters, we have enjoyed and benefited most from editing books. A major reason for editing a book is to provide your audience with many different perspectives and voices about a specific aspect of literacy.

Another good reason for an edited volume is that you learn so much more about a particular aspect of literacy. As an editor, there is a large probability that

---

the chapters you include will present original, up-to-date information and novel outlooks that will expand not only your understanding of the topic but the readers' as well. With each of the eight literacy books that we have edited, we have gained new information and perspectives about the field.

Plato is credited as being the first to say that "thorough, successful planning of any task is the most important determinant for any project's subsequent success." We have found his wisdom to hold true in the development of edited books. Of the 10 guidelines we recommend to you, 5 should occur before the first chapter of your book is written.

Know When You Should Edit a Book

The field of literacy is fortunate to have many well-written books and articles published each year. This plethora of information addresses both general (e.g., comprehension) and specific (e.g., questioning strategies for developing critical comprehension) aspects of literacy. The material is conveyed through both narrative and research presentation formats.

With so much material available, the first question that we always pose before attempting to write a book is, Why should this book be written? The answer helps us to determine whether we should move forward with a project or decide that it is a good idea that has not yet met its time. In order to answer the question, we need to address the two following subquestions: (1) Will this book contribute to the body of professional literacy knowledge in a positive way? and (2) Will it significantly aid teachers in their efforts to provide quality literacy instruction for their students? If neither or only one question elicits a positive response, we will not go forward with the project. If a compelling affirmative answer is made to both questions, we will engage in the next step of our process.

We then ask our next question: What is the best format for this book? We have two choices: (1) a book that we author or (2) a book for which we serve as academic editors, with chapters written by numerous contributors. In deciding between these two options, we ask, Will readers of the proposed book derive more knowledge from a single perspective or from multiple ones? Seeking an answer to this question is both complex and crucial to the success of the book. After all, what purpose is served by editing a book that goes virtually unread?

The advantages and disadvantages of authored versus edited versions of a proposed book need to be carefully delineated and assessed. In so doing, we raise three more questions: (1) What special knowledge about the proposed subject do we (or others) possess? (2) What experiences that are unique and important can we (or others) share with readers? (3) Will the advantages of one writing style (ours) outweigh several different writing styles? Here we must consider the value of the consistency gained through the use of one style as compared to the interest generated from a diversity of styles.

Although the decision is much easier to make when our answers to the preceding questions overwhelmingly indicate whether an authored or edited version is most suitable, in our experience, this rarely occurs. When our answers are less than decisive, we use a weighted response system as a tiebreaker. First, you must establish the weight of each question *before* answering. In the previous example, using three questions, you may decide to give each one an equal value of ⅓ or 33⅓%. Thus, if you decide that the edited version is preferable after answering two of the questions, the edited book would be the best choice.

Alternately, the three questions could be weighted to give them different values. For example, if the first question (What special knowledge about the proposed subject do we and others possess?) is deemed to be the most important issue, it could be given a weight of 60%. The other two questions could each be assigned a weight of 20%. Even if one option received positive responses for questions two and three, we would still go with the option indicated by question one because its score of 60% would be larger than the score of 40% for the other two questions.

If we determined that multiple authors could best speak to the book's proposed topic, we would then discuss our next question—who?

Know Who to Invite as Chapter Authors

Although neither of us has ever served as an ambassador to a foreign country, we view the role of a textbook editor as similar to that of a diplomat. Successful ambassadors must know the current issues that exist within the countries they serve. Their decisions must be carefully considered, and they face many diverse problems that must be solved tactfully and effectively.

In the texts that we have edited, we asked our contributors to share their considerable knowledge and then we delineated the aspects of literacy they would address. When duplication of content occurred in two or more chapters, we had to decide which of them fit best in the flow of the book. And yes, on rare occasions when portions of the submitted chapter missed the mark, we had to share our views with the contributor(s) and identify specific actions that needed to be taken. Although we always sought to conduct these interactions tactfully, we sometimes needed to be somewhat forceful.

> "Of all the needs a book has, the chief need is that it be readable."
> —ANTHONY TROLLOPE

Our experience in inviting and working with chapter authors has been generally very rewarding. We find it helpful *not* to initially discuss with each other the names of potential contributors. Rather, we focus our discussion on the proposed book's objectives and content. The following are illustrative of the questions that we seek to answer individually before we discuss them with each other:

- Who is doing important research in this area?
- Whose professional presentations espouse innovative and practical ideas about this topic?
- Who has her or his finger on the pulse of classroom teachers and can offer doable strategies to help teach literacy skills to students in an exemplary manner?
- Whose message will resonate well with preschool teachers? Primary-grade teachers? Intermediate-grade teachers? Middle school teachers?

After we each compile a list of potential contributors, we meet to discuss the ones we have identified.

The process of deciding who to invite as an author of a book chapter presents both obvious and less-than-obvious choices. Certain professionals are obvious choices when they are doing important research and writing and are making professional presentations about the topic. If you can use your ambassador-like persuasion skills to entice them to take time from their busy schedules to be a part of your writing team, then your book will be much stronger.

It is the not-so-clear choices that engender lively discussions between us. Sometime we find ourselves debating the value of one author versus another as a contributor to the book. It is during these discussions that a different set of questions is raised. Some of these include the following:

- Authors A and B espouse conflicting views about this topic. Do we select A, B, or both? If both, will their contrasting philosophies engage or confuse the reader?
- Author C has written and spoken about this issue for years. Will the contribution made by this individual be "same old, same old" or provide new insights?
- Author D is relatively unknown within the literacy community. Will D's work be interesting to individuals unfamiliar with her or his work?
- If the book is going to be sold in the United States, do the tentatively identified authors present a balance among the regions of the country? Are too many from a single state? Does the authorship team include only university professors? One sex? One race?
- Will there be issues about the amount of compensation paid to the authors by the publisher? For example, given Author E's myriad invitations as a speaker, researcher, and consultant, will he or she agree to write a chapter for this amount of compensation?

In some instances, we also find it necessary to discuss certain human factors. For example, Author F may have the reputation of making commitments and not fulfilling them. How can we determine or ensure that he or she will actually perform the agreed-upon task? Author G may have a reputation for being difficult to work with. How would such an author react to deletions of parts of his or her work or requests to significantly rewrite a section of the chapter? Author H may have a strong reputation as a powerful speaker but does not enjoy writing or excel as a writer. How would you decide whether to invite this author to write alone or to suggest a coauthor that would make it easier to complete the task with greater pleasure and efficiency?

Of all the decisions to be made, the selection of contributors to invite is the most difficult and time-consuming. There is always the temptation to choose contributors primarily on the basis of personal familiarity. We would urge you *not* to make this your selection criterion. Remember that your goal is to produce the best book possible, and to achieve this, you must select the best possible chapter authors. Yes, it is often stressful, but you and your readers will be glad that you spent the time to get it right.

After you have identified the contributors you wish to invite, you are now ready to face the next step in the process.

GUIDELINE 3

Know Who Else to Invite

In the Academy Award–winning movie *The Godfather* (Ruddy & Coppola, 1972), character Tom Hagen tells members of the Corleone family not to take their adversaries' actions personally. He says that what has happened is "strictly business."

We would caution book editors to be prepared for individuals to say no to your invitation to be a contributor in the book. Their reasons will vary (e.g., too many prior writing commitments, a book already in the works). Our initial contributor list has never been the final list.

We wish that we could offer a formula for anticipating when these rejections will occur, but we cannot. Just remember not to take refusals personally or as refutations of the proposed book's worthiness. Rather, plan for these occurrences so that the quality of your book will not suffer. One strategy is to have one or two contributors listed as alternates for each chapter. Thus, when our first choice declines, we have an equally qualified contributor identified as an alternate.

The field of literacy is fortunate to have many knowledgeable contributors upon whom editors can draw. Being familiar with literacy research and attending professional meetings can provide you with a broad and deep bank of individuals who can capably serve as chapter authors. Knowing who these individuals are, and being prepared to call upon a second or even third choice to write a chapter, should not be a source of anguish. In fact, we have had several experiences in which our second and third choices have written chapters that were the most positively received by readers.

Know When and How to Invite Chapter Authors

Previous chapters of this book have presented several points to consider when writing a book proposal. As you write your proposal for an edited volume, develop a table of contents so that you can share with potential chapter authors the exact contribution you want each of them to make.

AUTHOR REFLECTIONS

Laura Smolkin,
University of
Virginia–
Charlottesville

Jacob Wrestling With the Angel

The plain and simple truth is that writing never comes easily for me. I often call to mind, as I sit down at the computer, Jacob wrestling with that angel. I think it is because I always have voices inside my head. They continually prod me with questions and complaints. Some of these voices are potential reviewer voices. They reproach me:

"Well, have you looked at Pinklesmith's (1898) work? I know it is not well known and it is very hard to find a copy, but I can't imagine how you're writing on this topic without it!"

"The ideas in this paper are really good, but the voice seems all wrong. Can't you make your writing sound less academic and more suited to our audience?"

Other voices whisper from my past. There is my high school English teacher: "Can't you see that all these sentences begin the same way? You don't want to bore your readers, do you?" There are my dissertation advisors, dragging out the APA manual or pointing to the *Chicago Manual of Style*. Overcoming these grumbling hordes takes time, effort, resources, and fortitude.

When I am beginning a paper or a chapter for an edited book, I need longer stretches of time to write. I am continually reading to stay as current as possible with the literature in the area. In fact, it often becomes impossible to find my desk. I've got all these books opened to specific chapters; they are piled so high on top of one another that if I add just one more photocopied article the entire mountain will slide off the desk and bury me! And all the time I am reading these resources, I am arguing with the authors, thinking about what my own data has said. These arguments pay off for me when I finally make it to my discussion sections. I know what is new and important in what I've found.

My advice to emerging academic writers? Try things out. Write different types of papers for different types of publications. Learn which papers evolve more easily for you. Success in academic writing involves experimentation, as well as coming to know your writing self.

Some publishers ask that a sample chapter be submitted along with the prospectus for an edited book. You and your coeditors can write this chapter. It can also serve as a model that can be shared with your invited contributors as an example of the guidelines for each chapter, as well as for the style, flow, and voice. Most publishers will not accept a proposal for an edited book unless the editors have received a commitment from each chapter author or set of authors. Once you have established yourself as a successful editor, some publishers will accept your book idea before the chapter authors are invited. In these instances, we have been able to negotiate fees for chapter authors in advance so that we can pass that information on at the same time that we invite them to write with us.

The first time that you contact a chapter author, you can do so by phone or e-mail. We prefer to call, especially if the person is not a personal friend. By calling, you can answer questions and address concerns at once and ensure that the invited person has all the information he or she needs to make the correct decision. After the phone call, we follow our request with an e-mail that specifies in writing the guidelines to follow. We also state that chapter authors are responsible for obtaining their own permissions as needed. These permissions are due to the editors at the same time as the first draft. Always provide contributors with a timeline that includes due dates, such as when they will receive their edited first draft to revise and page or galley proofs. Most editors give chapter authors four to six months to write their chapter.

Finally, when you make first written contact with contributors, ask them (a) to sign an agreement to write the chapter; (b) to provide social security information so they can be paid for their work; and (c) to send you their contact information (addresses, phone numbers, fax numbers, e-mail addresses, and cell phone numbers). Once this information is received, it can be alphabetized by authors' last names. This will provide the required data for you and the publisher to contact the chapter authors during the writing of the book. We also create a contact list in our e-mail address book so that we can easily and rapidly contact all contributors at once as the project continues.

GUIDELINE 5

Decide Who Should Write the Preface, Foreword, Concluding Chapter, Reference Section, and Index

The preface is written to set the tone and purpose of your book. It also tells readers where your topic fits within the body of existing knowledge. Prefaces are best if written by the academic editors or by a leader in the field who has agreed to read all chapters before writing the preface. It should also present the goal for the book, outline key points within individual chapters, and compare similarities and dissimilarities in perspectives that will appear in the book. Book reviewers often quote information in the preface when critiquing or praising an edited volume. Moreover, the preface is the point in an edited volume at which the most important purposes, accomplishments, and benefits of all book chapters are presented as a preview of the content. For all of these reasons, we recommend that you devote considerable time in deciding who will write the preface.

A foreword provides an overview of the book. It should be approximately five to nine paragraphs long and is best written by a known and widely respected person in the literacy field. Whether a foreword is successful can be determined by answering the following questions: After reading the foreword, are you eager to turn the page? Are you convinced that reading the book will inform you in ways that other books could not?

Making the decision to write a concluding chapter is a more difficult one. Although we have edited books for many audiences and many publishers, and were assigned experienced developmental editors to work with us, each editor has had a different view about the value of an overarching, concluding chapter, which was based on the depth and breadth of information contained in individual chapters, page limitations, and the overall purpose of the book. Three books we have edited had concluding chapters; five did not. The conclusion chapters were written by us, the editors. Instead of a concluding chapter you may decide to invite a leader in the field to write what is called an afterword. This leader should not have contributed any other chapter in the book and should have read all chapters in the volume.

Your publisher will tell you whether they want references cited at the end of each chapter or collapsed into a single, end-of-the book reference section. The first option is the one that readers seem to prefer, and we agree that an end-of-chapter reference section is better.

Finally, we recommend that you ask the publisher to hire a professional indexer.

As stated earlier, half of the work of academic editing is completed before the first chapter of the book is written. However, the editors' work does continue during the months in which contributors are writing. Your efforts at this point are vitally important. Sir Frederick Banting, an 18th-century English philosopher and nobleman, stated that every successful project must "begin with an ideal and end with an ideal." We have found that it is during the writing stage of an edited book that many editors lose sight of the book's goal. This occurs because they do not help contributors follow the guidelines created for the book, or they do not carefully edit each chapter. Editors often do not know how to how handle such issues as contributors missing deadlines for submitting chapters. To meet these challenges, we offer the next three guidelines.

Give the Right Amount of Support to Chapter Authors

It is important to be clear with chapter authors about what you expect them to do—the best surprise is no surprise at all. Surprises can be eliminated, or at least minimized to a large degree, through the use of explicit instructions. Providing such instruction will prevent you from receiving a 70-page manuscript when you expected, but did not state, that it was to have been 20 pages. We have learned not to assume anything when working with contributors. Yes, they are bright, well educated, and usually quite experienced in writing for publication. However, their ideas about how a topic should be treated may be dramatically different from your expectations or those of other contributors to the book.

We strongly recommend that all direction be conveyed in writing. The chapter authors with whom you collaborate are busy individuals. They converse with many people—students, other teachers, faculty at their universities, colleagues at other institutions, and members of professional organizations. As such, they will sometimes forget portions of things said over the phone or in person. Hence, they may not recall when their chapter was due, its desired length, or some other salient point that was said when you initially conversed with them. Although such conversations are beneficial in terms of developing a positive relationship with an author, we have found that a follow-up letter that restates the important details of the conversation is particularly helpful. This letter should delineate content as well as format issues about the chapter to be written. Illustrative areas that should be addressed include the following:

- The chapter title—whether identified by you or left up to them.
- Length—the number of typewritten pages; be sure to specify the line spacing, and the font and margin sizes requested by the publisher, as these will affect the length of the first draft of the manuscript. Report this information in terms of typed pages rather than in final book pages.
- The chapter's general content and any specific issues that are to be addressed (e.g., a chapter dealing with vocabulary instruction for the intermediate grades is to also include strategies for English-language learners).
- Bibliography—the style in which references are to be presented.
- Pictures—information to let authors know whether they are to supply photos to be included in their chapters or whether the editors will find ones that match an author's descriptions.
- Copywritten material—a statement to inform the authors that they are to obtain permission and submit the permission on a standardized form provided by the publisher on the date that the first draft of the chapter is due.

- Style of writing—let the authors know, for example, whether they are to write in the first or third person.

- Musts—a list of items that must be included in every chapter, such as an opening vignette or a description of how a real teacher is presently using a strategy described in the chapter.

- Deadline—when the chapter is to be sent to the editor. Underline and boldface this date in the initial letter or e-mail that you send so that chapter authors can easily reference it.

GUIDELINE 7

Try Not to Nag

We adhere to the principle of not interrupting contributors as they reflect on and create the best chapter possible. Because we honor chapter authors' thinking time, we rarely contact them more than three times during the writing stage. After the initial letter of welcome and guidelines have been sent, we have found it helpful to make only two status updates. These are easy to do and quite helpful in keeping surprises to a minimum.

We typically wait two weeks after the first letter has been sent to call the contributors. We ask each chapter author (a) whether he or she received our letter and (b) if he or she has any questions about its content. Contributors typically are quite pleased to receive this call, because despite our best efforts to be clear in our letter, they usually have a few questions. Often, they have delayed beginning their writing because of these questions. Although contributors could have called you within this two-week period to ask their questions, remember that these are busy people. A call to your contributors is a courteous action on your part, and one that is appreciated by them.

The second status update call is typically made about one month before a chapter is due. We remind chapter authors of the publication timeline, and we ask two direct questions: Where are you in the writing of the chapter (e.g., half done, almost finished)? Do you anticipate any difficulty in meeting the submission deadline? As with the other status update call, contributors are pleased to receive this one. Because they are busy professionals, the call sometimes reminds them to move writing of the chapter to their priority list. This call fits with our goal of no surprises. For example, we once had a contributor who had written half the chapter and then fallen ill. We were able to work with the contributor to find a good coauthor. We contacted a potential coauthor, who accepted the invitation to work with the original contributor to complete the chapter, and the deadline was met.

Know How to Deal With a Missed Deadline

Despite all the actions you take to get all chapters turned in on time, and despite authors' assurances that you will receive chapters on time, expect some authors to miss the deadline. Murphy's Law will always come into play at this time of a book project. No matter how dedicated and gifted your chapter authors are and how carefully you have followed the seven guidelines prior to this one, at least one chapter author in every book will either miss the deadline or drop out as author during the final month before first drafts are due.

In the first two books that we edited, we were naive about this phenomenon. As a result, by the time that we finally received the tardy manuscripts, we both had to work long hours to meet our publisher's printing schedules. Moreover, because of the long, late hours without sleep, some of the ideals that we held for the book had to slip. As a result, we missed some overlap of content and omissions of agreed-upon content.

> "The best way to have a good idea is to have lots of them."
> —LINUS PAULING

Some delays can be expected, as circumstances will arise that are difficult to prevent. We would like to share a personal example of the inevitability of Murphy's Law. We have written more than 20 chapters for books that were edited by others. With 19 of these chapters (95% of the time) we met deadlines on or before the due date. The only chapter not received on time was one that we thought had arrived on time but, due to circumstances beyond our control, had not. We tell this story to assure you that no matter how hard you try, sometimes chapters do not reach the editors on time, even with the best of intentions.

We were told by the editors of this book that our first draft was due on March 15. It was submitted by e-mail as an attachment on that date. For some reason, the attachment was noted in the e-mail but not retrievable by either editor. We were certain that we had attached it in our first e-mail, but we were out of town until March 25. It was not until March 26 that we were able to resend our chapter, also e-mailing it to ourselves to ensure that the attachment was present. We could open it ourselves. On March 30, we heard from the editors, who informed us that the chapter was blank as an attachment. At this point, we asked our administrative assistant to resend the chapter from a disk rather than from either of our computer files, thinking that an error was occurring in the document files. This e-mail was sent April 7.

Our e-mail included the attachment, but this time the document could not be opened. None of us could believe it. Such a situation had never happened to us as authors or to the editors. After a week of having a computer technology expert at our university work with the disk, we were finally able to send the document on April 19, a month after the deadline. After these attempts on their end to open the document, the editors told us they were successful. None of these events could have been anticipated. Murphy's Law was alive and well for us as chapter authors for this particular book and it has affected us in some fashion in all eight books we have edited.

When editing, we have learned to allow ourselves adequate time for the review and modifications of late-arriving chapters. To help you avoid this situation, we offer the last two guidelines for this stage of an edited book.

GUIDELINE

Build in a Time Cushion

To ensure that we can perform our responsibilities as editors, we now build in a cushion to allow for an adequate review of *all* chapters. In our reviewing schedule, we initially read the chapters that are received on time. With these chapters, as well as the subsequent ones, we do the following:

1. Read each chapter. This ensures that it meets the standards of a professional book that (a) contributes to the body of professional literacy knowledge in a positive manner and (b) aids teachers in their efforts to provide quality literacy instruction to their students.

2. Find and correct errors. Although the computer has done much to eliminate misspelled words, grammatical errors, and so forth, they still exist. Rewrite unclear sentences and identify any parts of the chapter that need to be fixed.

3. Keep a content log. For example, if two chapters both discuss the same piece of research, record the chapter in which the research will remain and the chapter in which it should be eliminated.

4. Send revisions, questions, and so forth to the author (usually by fax to expedite the process). Establish a mutually convenient time to get together to work through these matters. If the author is to rewrite a portion of the chapter, establish a deadline for when it should be sent to the editors.

This collaborative four-step process has proven successful for almost all of the authors with whom we have worked. Most individuals readily accept recommended changes and agree to have their chapters altered accordingly. In some instances, we found that after conversing with authors, they would agree to slight rewordings rather than major textual revisions.

In the few remaining instances, interactions with authors were neither collaborative nor positive. The authors considered their chapter to be perfect and would not consider revisions. Many times the chapters were not only flawed but arrived after the initial deadline. As editors, faced with a deadline, we had to decide whether to ask someone else to write the chapter, do it ourselves, or use the chapter as written.

In each of these cases, we made the same decision: not to use the chapter. We then explained to the publisher why the deadline was missed and either wrote the chapter ourselves or invited a different author to do it.

Block Off Entire Days to Meet Last-Minute Publisher Requests

We have found that once we receive all the final drafts of chapters, full days of work are required to complete final editing tasks. By scheduling entire days, we can complete a checklist of tasks that need to be done on all chapters and are less likely to be distracted.

For instance, we may find that we have to change manuscript margins, reword subheadings within chapters, write new introductory materials, compose a preface

AUTHOR REFLECTIONS

Two Principles for Writing

Gerald G. Duffy, University of North Carolina–Greensboro

If you are trying to write something, here is my advice—pour yourself a little wine, crank out yet another hard copy, sit in the sun with a sharp pencil, and go through it again, and again, and again, whether it is a chapter in a book or the edited book itself.

For me, that is what writing is. I revise (again, and again, and again)—and it is not until about draft 16 that my message is clear enough. Colleagues who write with me laugh about how my drafts change over time. But it is no mystery to me. Writing is thinking. Early drafts are beginnings; later drafts are better. Through revising I learn what I really want to say and how best to say it.

I am guided by two principles. First, as Dick Burnett, my doctoral advisor, drummed into me: "Tell 'em what you're going to tell 'em; tell 'em; then tell 'em what you told 'em." It is boring, but you can't beat it for clarity. Consequently, I check to see whether what I "told 'em" at the beginning is what I "told 'em" in the end; and then I do the same thing for each section; and then for each subsection; and then, perhaps most important, I make sure my reasoning is the same across sections and subsections.

Second, I remember Tolstoy, who supposedly said, "I'm sorry for writing such a long letter; if I'd had more time, I would have written a shorter one." He knew that prose is tighter (and shorter) after revision. So I mercilessly strike all extraneous words, phrases, sentences, redundancies, asides, and gratuitous statements. In doing so, my premise becomes clearer, my reasoning consistent, and my message coherent.

Maybe it is the wine, maybe it is the sun, but I suspect writing success is due mostly to the sharp pencil and the time invested in tenacious and repeated revising.

or a concluding chapter, create reference sections, renumber tables and figures, reread all chapters to ensure that revisions were made, and oversee or encourage photo shoots if original photos are needed. In addition to the normal tasks, every publisher with whom we have worked has made unique requests of us, including doing additional research. Setting aside full days for completing these editing tasks helps the process of getting the book completed. Great writing is achieved by the selection of the best word for every sentence. As an editor, you will have the responsibility to ensure that every word in your book is the best word.

As summarized in Table 8.1, we have identified 10 guidelines that lead to a successfully edited book, with editors having 10 responsibilities and contributors and publishers each having 2. Thus you, as the editor, are ultimately responsible for the success and potential value of your edited book.

Table 8.1. Checklist to Guide the Creation of an Edited Literacy Book

Task	Person Responsible	Deadline	Comments
1. Ask questions to ensure that the book you envision should be an edited book	Editor(s)	One-month before book prospectus is written	
2. Invite chapter authors	Editor(s)	Before book prospectus is submitted	
3. Create back-up list of contributors in case one or more invited authors cannot complete their chapter	Editor(s)	While book prospectus is being reviewed	
4. Invite chapter authors, obtain personal information, and provide guidelines for chapter authors to follow so book chapters will have consistent, similar features.	Editor(s)	After book prospectus is accepted	
5. Decide who will write the Preface, Foreword, concluding chapter, References, and Index	Editor(s) and publisher	After book prospectus is accepted	
6. Give the right amount of support to chapter authors	Editor(s)		
7. Try not to nag	Editor(s) and contributors		Make only three contacts
8. Anticipate missed deadlines	Editor(s) and contributors		Prepare for Murphy's Law
9. Build in a cushion of time to fully edit all chapters	Editors	One month after chapters are received	
10. Block off full days to meet last-minute publisher requests	Editor(s) and publisher	One month before publisher deadline	

Closing Thoughts

In this chapter, we have shared with you what we have learned as academic editors and described the process that we use in deciding whether to edit a book. These procedures fit both our personalities and working styles. In addition, we discussed the work required of book editors and the satisfaction derived from this form of publication. Editing enables us to work closely with numerous professionals who, over the years, have done much to advance the literacy knowledge base. These chapter authors reinforce our beliefs about some aspects of literacy, cause us to rethink others, and help us to develop new insights about literacy instruction.

We stated that we publish books with two objectives in mind: (1) that the work contributes to the body of professional literacy knowledge in a positive manner and (2) that the book's content significantly aids teachers in providing quality literacy instruction to students. The contributors who have agreed to write the works we have edited have been invaluable assets in the realization of these two objectives.

REFERENCE

Ruddy, A.S. (Producer), & Coppola, F.F. (Director). (1972). *The Godfather* [Motion picture]. United States: Paramount Pictures.

Responding to Revise-and-Resubmit and Rejection Decisions

A S ANY WRITER has come to learn, the review process often brings disappointment. Even after spending many agonizing moments preparing an article or proposal for others to read, we discover that reviewers or editors may find our work unacceptable for a particular publication outlet. War stories abound on the purported unfairness, tardiness, and unkindness of those who evaluate our work. We ask ourselves, What are we supposed to do with so-so reviews in which we are told to revise and resubmit? How should we really handle rejections? This section answers these two questions directly so you are guided to take the next steps in the review process.

Chapter 9, "Responding to Revise-and-Resubmit Invitations," talks about different types of revise-and-resubmit decisions and how to use the editors' recommendations to determine how to proceed. Specific strategies for resubmitting manuscripts for journals and books are discussed at length.

Chapter 10, "Overcoming Rejection," talks about ways to decipher the meaning of the rejection and how to move forward in light of the type and level of rejection. Ideas for finding different journals and publishers are provided.

These two chapters present mechanisms for coping and proceeding with less-than-positive editorial decisions so you can continue to move forward with your writing endeavors.

CHAPTER 9

Responding to Revise-and-Resubmit Invitations

William A. Henk

This chapter focuses on
- viewing revise-and-resubmit invitations in proper perspective
- understanding the factors that need to be considered when revising journal articles, chapters, and books
- using strategies that increase the chances for a favorable review

A SIMPLE YET POWERFUL premise starts this chapter: *Professional writing is largely a matter of revising*. In effect, the premise builds upon Murray's (2000) assertion that writing is essentially rewriting. Even the best writers rarely, if ever, produce initial drafts that are publication quality. Far more commonly, writers labor over their work, engaging in a deeply reflective process of modifying text to improve clarity, completeness, appeal, or impact. Sometimes this rewriting involves modest matters of word choice or grammar, whereas in other instances major changes are required. Typically, major modifications involve retooling, restructuring, and adding or deleting significant portions of text and require a careful rethinking of purpose and a reconsideration of audience (Sommers, 1982). In drafting and reworking this chapter, I have been continually reminded of these revision processes.

A second important premise, specifically tied to writing journal articles and books, is that the ability of authors to respond effectively to revise-and-resubmit invitations is vital to getting published. I honestly believe that, apart from basic

Beating the Odds: Getting Published in the Field of Literacy edited by Shelley B. Wepner and Linda B. Gambrell. Copyright © 2006 by the International Reading Association.

130

writing skill, this ability represents the single most important contributing factor. Such a sweeping claim is certainly debatable, and all I can offer as support are personal experiences and some animated head nodding from fellow writers when I have made the statement. In fact, my strong sense is that most prolific literacy authors, whether they are teachers, school administrators, or college professors, would agree that the art and skill of revision ranks among the foremost explanations for their success with publishing journal articles and books.

Readers should note that I refer to the revise-and-resubmit decisions of editors as *invitations* and to the process of responding to these revisions as an *art*. This positive spin, although not original, is certainly intentional. Too often, authors situate revise-and-resubmit decisions squarely in the realm of gloom and doom, only slightly above rejection. They lament the myopia, bias, and faulty reasoning of editors and reviewers who have perpetrated an injustice upon them. Literacy authors are no exception.

This line of thinking brings me to a third premise: No good can come of dwelling on the negative when it comes to publishing. On the contrary, authors should think of revise-and-resubmit decisions as opportunities to hone their revision skills in ways that will eventually equate to an art form. This perspective is as important to school-based literacy professionals wishing to share their work regularly as it is for higher education professionals who must publish as a condition of their employment.

For experienced authors, the negative reactions to revise-and-resubmit invitations are rooted in the knowledge that the act of rewriting is grueling. Fixing a flawed manuscript is very hard work. However, authors should not lose sight of yet a fourth and final basic premise: When requested revisions are performed in a skillful and artful way, the odds of being published increase significantly. As Dowd and McElveny (1997) state, "At the majority of scholarly journals, publication of a manuscript depends upon its revision. Authors, therefore, should view the revision process not as an obstacle, but as a routine step in the publication process" (p. 47). In fact, Henson (1991) estimates that 75% of revised manuscripts are eventually accepted in education journals, and this success rate almost certainly holds true for literacy-related forums. Although some papers must be revised several times before acceptance occurs, revised manuscripts have $2\frac{1}{2}$ times the chances of being accepted when compared to an original manuscript.

Likewise, effective revision is vital to the chances of a chapter, book proposal, or book manuscript being accepted. If an idea for a chapter or a volume captures the imagination of an editor but is not developed well enough in a proposal, revisions are likely to be invited. Often this retooling involves clarifying, restructuring, or expanding the proposal. If the revisions fail to be compelling, the proposal will be rejected. Of course, once a proposal is accepted, the expectation is that an author will continue to revise the piece until it is ready for publication.

Unlike journal forums, subsequent rejection is somewhat improbable, because the publishing house has committed to the chapter or book. However, terminating a chapter or book project is not out of the question if the author fails to deliver on the expected revisions.

In effect, these four basic premises undergird this chapter. That is, authors are more likely to get published when they fully expect to revise, respond appropriately when invited to do so, approach the task positively, and possess the capacity to make skillful changes. With this backdrop, I first share some personal perceptions of literacy editors and reviewers with the hope of creating a context for better understandings of revise-and-resubmit invitations. Next, I discuss generally how authors might react to these opportunities.

The heart of the chapter, however, includes specific guidelines for revising and resubmitting work to literacy publications. All of the guidelines represent conclusions I have drawn from my experience as an author, a reviewer, an editor, and as chair of the publication committees of both the International Reading Association and the College Reading Association.

AUTHOR REFLECTIONS

When the Discussion Section Disintegrates

Gay Ivey,
James Madison
University

When I review manuscripts for research journals, I get the feeling that not too many people enjoy writing the discussion section, which is where a first draft often disintegrates. When I write up my own research, this is actually my favorite part. For me, this is my own thinking space, the place where I realize what I learned from the study. I start writing the discussion as soon as the research gets underway, on notes in the margins of my data as trends become apparent, during conversations with colleagues over the dining room table, and after memorable exchanges and incidents with kids in the research classroom (usually jotted down on the back of the agenda handed out at one of those infamously long and under-stimulating university faculty meetings). The discussion section turns out to be a record of how I moved from my data to the real world of students and classrooms. I look at the discussion as a way for me to re-enter the conversation on the topic at hand, rejuvenated and ready to change or advance the discourse. It is what I would be dying to share with a roomful of experts in my particular area of study. That is a good measuring stick for powerfulness and usefulness of a discussion. If I get to that point in my manuscript, and I have nothing new to say to people who already know a lot, then I have much more thinking, listening, talking, and writing to do.

A Word About Literacy Editors and Reviewers

In my own efforts to publish in literacy venues, as a schoolteacher and professor, I have experienced both profound disappointment and exhilaration, and everything else in between. Editors' letters usually have been about as constructive in nature as the quality and appropriateness of my work warranted. Actually, I have a large pile of rejection letters as well as several revise-and-resubmit letters, too; most determined authors do.

Although my experiences with editors have been decidedly fair, that has not always been the case with reviewers. Regrettably, the comments of a handful of reviewers over the years have been deeply hurtful and offensive. My advice is to break out your thickest skin when this happens, because it is hard to bear. Early in my career, I was told that reviewers were criticizing my work and not me, so I should not take it personally. It is healthy advice to be sure, but make no mistake—there is almost no other way to take these remarks. So brace yourself, because it is *your* work after all.

Fortunately, the overwhelming majority of reviewers are conscientious and considerate professional volunteers doing their job in the best way they know how. As a result, I have benefited enormously from their comments, even when they were not affirming. In fact, reviews are more valuable when they find legitimate fault. A good reviewer's honest impressions will do an author far more good than sugarcoating ever will. Although an author might retain greater dignity from a soft and polite review, the guidance necessary to make the manuscript better will be lacking. I try unusually hard to keep this notion in mind when reviewers challenge me, and it also crosses my mind when I am let down gently. Far more often than not, reviewers are knowledgeable and skilled, and most of what they recommend turns out to be correct—even though you may not think so at first. That is not to say that the reviewers will agree or be uniformly correct, only that their perceptions ought to be given credence.

In my career as a literacy educator and researcher, editors and reviewers have made my work markedly better. These gatekeepers of the professional literature have stretched me in desirable and often unexpected ways, but only when I was willing to view their feedback through an objective lens. Authors confronted with a revise-and-resubmit decision from journal or book editors need to remember that all literacy venues are obliged to set high standards, and the editor and reviewers must maintain them. The best gatekeepers will advocate for deserving manuscripts and offer recommendations that will make them even better. They will also present formidable obstacles if your work falls short. This state of affairs is exactly as it should be; the field's integrity depends upon it. In this sense, criticism of your work is truly not personal.

Clearly, then, a big part of achieving publication success resides in first getting past the nearly inevitable personal angst that accompanies criticism. Only then can authors attend to the serious business of revising their texts to be more focused and purposeful. Setting aside emotions and hunkering down with the difficult tasks of revision are worth the effort, because there is nothing quite like seeing one's work in print. To this day, I regard letters of acceptance as treasures. And I have come to appreciate masterful revision as the key to achieving the professional gratification that publication allows. After all, as Miller (n.d.) notes, "words worth reading are impossible to create without several drafts" (n.p.).

Reacting to the Revise-and-Resubmit Invitation

Personally, I am not aware of any writers in literacy who welcome the task of making changes to the manuscripts they have submitted for review. On the contrary, they hope that their manuscripts will be accepted outright and require little or no revision. This desire is not especially realistic, but neither is it altogether without foundation. Accomplished writers know better than to submit their work before it is as finely crafted as possible. Consequently, when an editor's disposition letter arrives with an invitation to revise and resubmit, most authors experience at least some amount of disappointment. When the rewriting figures to be extensive, nearly all authors will dread it. Instead of viewing the editor's invitation as an opportunity, they regard the newly requested work as daunting.

This fear makes sense. Weaving the ideas and concerns of others into the tapestry of a beloved piece of writing is no small or comfortable feat. First of all, it is painstaking. Authors find it objectionable to alter manuscripts they have literally agonized over. The recommendations of editors and reviewers almost always intrude upon a writer's work in ways that cause varying levels of resentment, anger, and defensiveness. For experienced authors who have navigated these seas before, these feelings tend to be less enduring. They understand that a revise-and-resubmit decision represents an encouraging result overall. These authors wisely operate on the assumption that revisions, when properly executed, greatly increase their chances of publishing success, even when the scope of work is substantial.

Before proceeding, readers should note that the following guidelines will not enhance the fundamental quality of one's basic writing skills. Nor will the guidelines ensure the acceptance of one's work. Becoming a better writer comes only with experience, practice, and the resolve to spend long hours intensely scrutinizing and elevating one's writing—always with an audience in mind. Becoming a *published* writer, however, takes all that and much more. It requires making prudent choices about literacy topics and forums, dispensing with ego, sizing up the scope of revision, rewriting strategically, communicating your progress, and most of all, aspiring to perfection. The guidelines that follow provide suggestions that will help guide the revision process whether you are working on a journal article, edited volume, or book. Whereas some guidelines focus more on issues related to journal submissions, the suggestions also apply to the process of revising professional writing in general.

Be Grateful for Revise-and-Resubmit Decisions

Few authors receive immediate and unconditional acceptance of the work they submit to professional forums (Huth, 1982). In fact, the probability of a journal article, edited volume, or book being accepted without an accompanying request for modification is rare. Only 5% to 10% of the manuscripts that are submitted to scholarly journals are accepted outright. This acceptance rate may be even more stringent for premier literacy journals such as *Reading Research Quarterly* and the *Journal of Literacy Research*. Even conditionally accepted papers are not assured publication space in these elite journals, although editors will work in earnest with authors to bring these papers to closure.

When first-tier literacy forums offer revise-and-resubmit invitations, it is expected that at least one and perhaps two or more significant revisions must be made before a paper will be approved for publication. One indicator of the rigor of the review process is found at the end of articles in some literacy journals and all American Psychological Association (APA) journals. These forums note a manuscript's first date of receipt, the dates each resubmission was made, and the final date that the work was accepted. Journals of lesser stature, including some in the field of literacy, will exhibit higher immediate acceptance rates and a greater number of acceptances overall. In academic circles, greater prestige is associated with smaller acceptance rates (Nagata & Trierweiler, 1996).

The type of revise-and-resubmit decisions that you receive from book editors depends on how you came to submit your manuscript for review and the type of review process used. If you were invited to write a chapter or book manuscript on a specific topic, book editors probably will look for ways to help you revise and resubmit your work so that it meets preconceived standards. However, if it is not written as expected, book editors will not let it be published. If you sent your work to publishers without a prior invitation, book editors of publishing houses who invite you to revise and resubmit obviously are less invested in your work from the outset but see potential for publication.

Perhaps the most compelling reason for you to be encouraged by any type of revise-and-resubmit decision is that the manuscript has not been rejected. Although this statement might seem obvious, keep in mind that the overwhelming majority of adjudication decisions are one of two types, either reject or revise and resubmit. In a game of percentages, having your paper fall into the revise-and-resubmit category means avoiding rejection, the other most frequent judgment. It is important to keep in mind that a primary reason why manuscripts are not published is because authors do not revise and resubmit them (Dowd & McElveny, 1997).

Do Not Be Discouraged

**Lawrence Sipe,
University of
Pennsylvania**

The first time I submitted something to a literacy journal, the response was "Accept with minor revisions." As I continued to submit manuscripts to journals, I realized that this is indeed a very rare response. In most cases, some substantive revisions are necessary, and the editors ask that the manuscript be revised and sent in for another round of reviews. I think my major piece of advice to those who are new to academic publishing is not to be discouraged if the response to your manuscript is "Revise and resubmit." This should be taken very positively: It means that the editors (and reviewers) are truly interested in your piece and think that it is worth your time (as well as their time) for you to revise it and send it in again. Some related advice is to read the editors' letter very carefully, with attention to what they would like you to do in the revisions, and make sure that you address every one of their points in your revised manuscript.

Recognize That There Are Different Types of Revise-and-Resubmit Decisions

Invitations to revise and resubmit vary along a wide continuum. At one end is the safe bet. It carries a near but not absolute certainty that publication will occur. These decisions are marked by letters or e-mails from an editor that ask for relatively minor changes—more than merely polishing or tidying up a paper, but nothing truly substantial. It would be premature to celebrate upon receipt of such a communication, but putting some champagne on order, as opposed to on ice, is not out of the question either. The safe-bet communication will sound like the following:

> There are numerous commendable aspects to your manuscript, and despite some minor disagreement about its publication potential among the reviewers, the editorial team sees definite promise in it. Please note that the chief obstacle to publication is that the case examples you use are not tied closely enough to your literature review. We also ask that you address Reviewer #2's concerns about tense and compliance with APA style.

At the other end of the continuum is the extreme long shot. In this instance, the manuscript just barely escaped being rejected. Yet there is some redeeming value in it that has caused the editor to see a glimmer of hope. The topic might be timely or unique, the approach might have been unusually rigorous or creative, or perhaps the content or recommendations are truly interesting or have far-reaching practical value. These revise-and-resubmit decisions carry the expectation that a major and perhaps monumental rewrite will be necessary to make the manuscript publishable. Authors who decide to tackle the extensive revise-and-resubmit work that is required should do so with the knowledge that the manuscript probably will not get published. The extreme long-shot communication will sound like the following:

> While all of the reviewers and the editorial team felt that your topic was important and timely, several noteworthy aspects of the paper were identified as problematic. Given the nature and magnitude of these concerns, which are outlined below, we are honestly not sure whether the manuscript, however promising, can be revised sufficiently well to warrant publication. Still, we felt that the invitation to resubmit was technically appropriate on the basis of the reviewers' recommendation.

In my various publication-related roles, I rarely have seen this type of manuscript make it into print, but it can, in fact, occur. Be careful, though, because this type of revise-and-resubmit decision could be the sign of a weak editor who should have rejected the manuscript in the first place. When the editor's message is code for "You can try if you want, but do not expect much, if anything," you should strongly consider sending your work to another literacy outlet. In doing so, it would still behoove you to use the feedback from the original forum to revise your manuscript.

As it turns out, most revise-and-resubmit decisions fall between these two extremes. Accordingly, a key for authors is recognizing where along the continuum their revise-and-resubmit decision falls. If papers hover near the "extreme long shot," revision efforts will need to be extraordinary. On the other hand, if papers hover near the "safe bet," authors can anticipate an easier time of rewriting. Even so, a safe-bet manuscript has fallen sufficiently short of acceptance that significant work remains.

With extreme long shots and safe bets as anchors, a horse race seems to be a useful metaphor to differentiate revise-and-resubmit decisions. The range could extend from nags to thoroughbreds with the horses in the middle of the pack carrying varying odds or probabilities of succeeding. Authors need to know the caliber of the horses they are riding and gauge realistically whether revision will position them for the winner's circle. Slow horses with overweight jockeys on a wet track should enter a different race.

> "You must often make erasures if you mean to write what is worthy of being read a second time."
> —Horace

Put another way, there are often alternative literacy outlets for which an author's work might be placed. When the odds for a successful revision are exceedingly long, you should contemplate submitting your manuscript elsewhere. By contrast, you should embrace the challenge of revision when the editor's communication (a) is sufficiently encouraging, (b) provides clear direction, (c) requests revisions that are both feasible and reasonable, and (d) provides for adequate time to make the changes.

Revise and Resubmit When the Changes Will Not Compromise the Integrity of the Work or Your Professional Principles

Sometimes revise-and-resubmit invitations carry with them a set of requested revisions that could fundamentally change the character of the work. The changes might be manageable enough, but they may require conceding closely held beliefs, adding extraneous concepts or analyses as appeasements, shifting research emphases, or reinterpreting valid results. In these instances, revision is not merely a matter of compliance; it becomes a matter of principle. Although these accommodations might satisfy the concerns of editors and reviewers, they represent a dubious surrendering of values or standards. Authors need to resist such temptations. Acceptance is a seductive goal, but never worth it. Once published, a manuscript endures forever, and authors must ask themselves if they can live with a lifelong specter of questionable motivation.

In offering this caution against revising and resubmitting, I am not at all suggesting that either editors or reviewers purposely ask authors to act unethically or irresponsibly. Rather, these gatekeepers may (a) misunderstand the work and its underpinnings, (b) seek a preferred but unwarranted shift of ideology, (c) mistake rigor for overkill, or (d) simply not grasp the magnitude or implications of what they are asking authors to do.

When these situations occur, you must decide whether to forgo resubmitting to the forum altogether or to rework the manuscript in ways that are personally agreeable before trying the forum again. If making the revisions represents too much of a stretch, then you should seek another home for your work. This approach is advisable for both noble and pragmatic reasons. In the first and most important case, sending the manuscript elsewhere allows your professional and personal principles to be upheld. The appropriateness of doing so cannot be overstated. Moreover, making the seemingly manageable revisions will probably render your paper susceptible to a whole new set of criticisms. In the end, forced fits and inauthenticity do not play well in the publishing game.

If you decide to revise and resubmit your work, then do so within the limits of your beliefs, ideologies, and paradigms, and explain your rationale in the letter that accompanies the new version of your manuscript. These arguments are not easy to make, but done properly, they can sometimes achieve their desired effect. Fortunately, the best editors are open to well-reasoned, compelling justifications, even when they run counter to their own predispositions.

Imagined Dialogues With Potential Reviewers: A Personal Reflection

Zhihui Fang,
The University
of Florida

Writing for literacy publications in the United States is, for me, both a cultural struggle and a professional dialogue. It is a struggle in the sense that every time I start the composing process, I feel the need to assume, albeit uncomfortably at times, a new identity, one that is diametrically different from my old Chinese self. Born and educated in China for over 20 years, I've developed a Chinese way of thinking and writing, one that requires me to be humble and to follow the logic of circular/spiral thought processes. In essence, my Chinese upbringing taught me that my voice does not really matter in scholarly work—it is the words of authority figures that count, and I should let the words speak for themselves without showing emotion and subjectivity. Having spent a decade in the U.S. academe, I have come to realize that writing for literacy publications necessitates the adoption of a U.S. self, one that is confident, assertive, and not afraid to foreground my own views. I have learned that my voice does count and is valued in literacy research. I have learned that personal vignettes can be both relevant and significant in scholarly work. I have learned that my Chinese logic of beating around bushes has to give way to a more linear Western approach, one that values openness, directness, and succinctness.

In writing for literacy publications, I also find myself entering into imagined dialogues with potential reviewers. One thing that I have learned over the years is that I need to develop a keen awareness of the values and concerns of members of other discourse communities. All reviewers come with their own perspectives based on their experiences, and each has things that they feel strongly about. As a writer, I have to anticipate, as well as address, questions and issues that might be raised by people with different theoretical and methodological orientations.

Because of my training in applied linguistics, I have a tendency to speak in linguistics jargon. When writing for literacy publications, I have to learn to recontextualize my linguistics discourse for the literacy audience. I have to be sure to define terms that linguists often take for granted and be careful to avoid terms that may evoke overreaction from reviewers. Moreover, I have to predict what reviewers are likely to say and then incorporate statements that acknowledge my sensitivity to their concerns.

Over the years, I have become more attuned to the nuances and complexities involved in writing for publications. As I get more accustomed to the new American identity and become more sensitive to the values of other discourse communities, I have found writing a more exciting and enjoyable adventure.

GUIDELINE

Remember That You Get Limited Chances to Make the Manuscript Near Publication Quality

An invitation to revise and resubmit is the equivalent of a gift. It carries the expectation that authors will do their utmost to remedy all major concerns and raise the caliber of the manuscript to publication standards. There is a limit to how many chances authors receive, though, particularly when journals are the intended forum. In those cases, the number of opportunities to revise depends to a large extent on the degree of improvement each new version of the manuscript demonstrates. If editors note truly significant improvement in a paper, they will generally afford authors additional tries. Conversely, if any resubmitted version fails to show ample progress, the review process will cease at that point, and the paper will be rejected. For both journals and books, editors and reviewers simply do not have the time to contend with multiple resubmissions, particularly when manuscripts hit an apparent plateau.

For this reason, it is incumbent on you to set perfection as your goal with each attempt at revision. Each version should be written as though it will be the manuscript's final chance. Every concern of the editor should be addressed or explained. The manuscript should flow logically and seamlessly. Its style should be clear and consistent, as well as fully appropriate for the audience. The appearance of the manuscript should be meticulous, and it should conform completely to the required style form. No spelling, typographical, or punctuation errors should exist. The checklist in Table 9.1 details a wide range of criteria that you can use to monitor and advance the quest for writing perfection.

You can also use the checklist to estimate your odds of being successful with a revision. If you find that several of these points are cited in your letter from the editor and the reviewers' comments, then your manuscript is closer to being considered an extreme long shot than a safe bet. This is particularly true if key aspects of your manuscript have been questioned, such as its match with the outlet, the timeliness or importance of your topic, the appropriateness of your literature review, the integrity of your approach, or your organization.

Revise-and-resubmit considerations for a chapter in an edited volume are somewhat different. Scholars who publish in journals also often publish in edited volumes dedicated to particular topics, with the editors of these volumes often selecting authors on the basis of their journal publications (e.g., an editor of a volume on comprehension instruction invites the authors of recent journal articles on the topic to participate in the volume). Typically, the invitation to write a chapter is clear about the purpose of the volume, including its intended audience as well as its expected length. The editor might also suggest a particular aspect of a topic for the author. An author should do everything possible to meet the requirements of the invitation with the first submission, which should be written with the goal of providing the editor with a polished draft—ideally, a final draft. Failure to meet the requirements of the original invitation, however, will almost certainly result in a request to revise and resubmit to conform with the original invitation. Failure to provide a polished draft will result in a frustrated editor

Table 9.1.   Checklist for Writing for Publication

Initial Considerations
_____ Important and timely topic
_____ Informative and engaging title
_____ Crisp, informative abstract if appropriate

Introduction/Content
_____ Appropriate lead-in (general to specific thesis statement, done efficiently)
_____ Relevant literature shared in sufficient, rather than excessive, detail
_____ Need for the manuscript argued persuasively
_____ Explicit purposes for the manuscript established

Body/Content
_____ Accurate, up-to-date content
_____ Properly geared toward sophistication level of the audience
_____ Ideas flow logically within body of the manuscript
_____ Adheres to expectations for genre
_____ All redundancies are deliberate and purposeful
_____ Thorough (yet economical) coverage of material

Internal Conventions
_____ Desirable word choice/style (e.g., accurate, clear, and aptly descriptive; active tense)
_____ Straightforward sentence structures
_____ Appropriate variety of sentence types represented
_____ Ideas flow logically within paragraphs
_____ Smooth and well-reasoned transitions between paragraphs

Conclusion/Content
_____ Purposes restated
_____ Previous ideas pulled together meaningfully
_____ Author's unique voice/interpretation evident
_____ Significance/application explained
_____ Limitations acknowledged and qualified, as appropriate
_____ Future directions discussed

Overall Organization
_____ Structure made overt to readers through early enumeration
_____ Thoughtful use of headings and subheadings
_____ Effective transitions between major sections

Professional Appropriateness
_____ Appropriate number and type of references
_____ Judicious presentation of nontext information
_____ Absolute adherence to professional style form (e.g., APA 5th edition)
_____ Perfect spelling, punctuation, and typing

Overall Impact
_____ Thought-provoking and/or useful
_____ Provides unique/fresh perspective
_____ Makes quality contribution to the field

Forum/Submission Considerations
_____ Topic is thematically aligned with the venue
_____ Nature and depth of work matches the journal, volume, or publisher
_____ Style of language closely resembles typical forum contents
_____ Length parameters observed
_____ Manuscript is formatted specifically for particular forum (i.e., headings, graphics, etc.)
_____ Manuscript is consistent with audience expectations

who is likely to make clear that the writing must improve considerably before the chapter can appear in the volume.

Even a polished first submission that is consistent with the invitation is likely to come back with revision suggestions. Just as in journal article writing, the best practice in book chapter writing is to attempt to improve the manuscript as much as possible based on the comments. Chapters typically get better with such revision. Because the editor was clear in the original invitation about what was wanted for the chapter, and because the editor knows the stance of an author invited to submit for a book, it would be unusual, indeed, for an editor to demand revision that would fundamentally alter the author's message in the original submission. If an editor makes such a suggestion, how (and even whether) to respond to it deserves especially careful consideration.

As an author working in the area, you have already gone on the record in the professional literature with respect to many of the messages in the chapter. You should not write anything in a chapter that contradicts those notions. If you detect that it would be necessary to do so to meet the editor's requirements, contact the editor to make certain you are interpreting the editor's message correctly and that the editor recognizes the implications of the editorial request. Often, such an informal discussion can result in a clarification that is tantamount to a revision request you can meet without altering your message. If the editor really is asking you to say something you do not believe (or at least contradicts a public stance you have already made), then you have to confront the possibility that it might be better not to publish in this particular volume.

Most of the time, however, the revisions requested for edited volumes and books do not compromise your basic beliefs about a topic but rather challenge you to use different frameworks or styles to communicate your knowledge and understandings. Some edited volumes and books become prominent resources that are seen and read by many, and every effort should be made to benefit as much as possible from revision comments that are provided.

GUIDELINE 5

Use the Ideas and Recommendations From the Editor to Help Strengthen Your Manuscript

In sizing up the scope and nature of the requested revisions for a journal article, chapter, or book, pay particular attention to the editor's cover letter. Although the reviewers' comments are certainly important to revising and have probably driven the editor's decision to a large extent, their conclusions are secondary. In fact, the editor's considered opinion definitely trumps the comments of the individual reviewers about what you must do. Do not lose sight of the fact that the final decision belongs to the editor, not the reviewers (Roediger, 1987).

Unfortunately, some editors rely too heavily on reviewers, and their revise-and-resubmit letters amount to saying, "Do what the reviewers want and send it back." Again, this is the mark of a weak or lazy editor, so beware. For all intents and purposes, you have received a form letter. Consequently, there is no telling how your paper will fare in the next round of review regardless of how well you address the reviewers' concerns. Follow through with the revisions, but only if all of the following apply: (a) the forum has a good reputation, (b) the forum reaches your most coveted audience, (c) the reviewers' comments are reasonable, (d) the revisions are manageable, and (e) the forum is a nearly ideal home for your paper. Otherwise, submit elsewhere. This advice holds especially true if the reviewers' comments are numerous and elaborate. In effect, your manuscript is an extreme long shot, despite the editor not portraying it as such.

Thankfully, almost all literacy editors function far more responsibly. The best of them give manuscripts several careful readings and make every attempt to reconcile and synthesize their perceptions with those of the reviewers. This task is always extremely difficult, because reviews can vary widely in perspective, accuracy, relevance, completeness, and objectivity. Editors must look for patterns among the gatekeepers' opinions, weigh the merit of the conclusions that are drawn, recognize bias and trivialities, and consolidate a mass of data into a coherent letter that can tactically guide authors in revising their manuscripts.

An explicit, thoughtful, and thorough letter from an editor is an author's best friend when it comes to framing and executing a rewrite. In fact, the most helpful letters not only tell you what to do, but also what *not* to do. When editors do not make mention of particular points made by reviewers, there is a fair chance that they do not feel the issue is important enough to demand your effort. Occasionally, they may go so far as to instruct an author not to make certain changes recommended by a reviewer. Whatever it is that good editors suggest—whether directly, indirectly, or by omission—their goal is the same: making the journal article, chapter, or book the best that it can be.

GUIDELINE 6

Identify Which Reviewers You Most Need to Satisfy and Address Their Concerns First

Most of the time it is not difficult to determine the reviewers who most require your attention. Read the reviews several times, noting their logic, depth, and tone. Clearly, some commentaries will be more on point and substantial than others. Some reviews might disagree completely (Fiske & Fogg, 1990). Pay special attention to any reviews that suggest your manuscript is fatally flawed. You will have to craft a counterargument and either incorporate your reasoning into the body of the paper, include it in the resubmission letter, or do both. The good news is that if the editor truly felt the manuscript was beyond hope, you would not have received the invitation to resubmit.

If you cannot discern the key reviewers by virtue of their remarks, the editor's letter will typically clarify whose comments matter most. Editors will cite the reviewers with whom they most agree more often, and in greater detail. In fact, you might get the sense from the editor's letter that if a single key reviewer can be appeased, the work will be accepted. Be aware that the key reviewers will likely receive your revised paper, and they will specifically look to see if you have addressed their concerns. Expect a thumbs-down verdict if you have not.

Satisfying the key reviewers does not mean that you can completely dismiss the concerns of the other reviewers whose reviews may not rate as the editor's favorite; some of their points might still be essential ones. Although their remarks might not be frequently cited in the editor's letter, the few that surface must either be dealt with or explained in your resubmission letter, because these reviewers might also receive your revised manuscript. Like the key reviewers, they would not be pleased to see their concerns ignored.

Still, authors do need to draw a line on deciding which reviewers' points do not merit effort. Trying to address every single comment regardless of its importance is probably futile, and it will net you very little return on your investment. Although outlier comments can be ignored, if more than one reviewer points to a problem in your manuscript, then it must be addressed no matter how small (Day, 1983). By all means, address these points. A good general rule of thumb, borrowed from the Nike corporation, is that if reviewers are right, "Just do it." If not, incorporate all of the suggested changes that you can reasonably accept, and address the ones to which you take exception.

One other point about successive reviews needs to be made. Even though revised papers commonly go back to some or all of the original reviewers, this is not always the case. Depending on how editors handle this situation, your paper could be sent to a majority of new reviewers or to all new reviewers. Editors use new reviewers when some or all original reviewers could never be placated or when original reviewers were not available. Although it is true that fresh reviewers could conceivably increase your odds of success, they could also be more critical or raise new concerns. With new reviewers, you could lose ground, finding yourself back at square one. There is no way to anticipate how to please one or more new reviewers, so all an author can do is aim for a level of excellence that might hold up under nearly any reader's scrutiny.

GUIDELINE 7

Carefully Frame Your Letter of Resubmission

There is no question that reviews can be very different because the viewpoints of reviewers are different. Reviews can vary in insightfulness, helpfulness, depth, and fairness. Consequently, some reviews deserve more reflection and effort than others when making revisions. However, some degree of attention needs to be paid to each one when crafting your letter of resubmission, not only because the same reviewers might receive the revised manuscript.

In my experience, even seemingly meager and misguided reviews have something to offer. It might be a subtle point or nuance, a grain of truth, a pet peeve. The point is that other readers of the forum may make the same slight distinction. Again, this does not mean that every reviewer concern needs to be remedied. What it does mean is that even shallow and wrong-minded reviews may include some valuable points that you should incorporate into the revised manuscript.

One of the most crucial elements in a successful revise-and-resubmit attempt is the letter that accompanies the resubmitted manuscript. When crafted expertly,

AUTHOR REFLECTIONS

The Value of Feedback From Reviewers

Rita M. Bean, University of Pittsburgh

When I talk with graduate students about writing for publication, I often share the story of my first experience submitting a manuscript for publication. A colleague of mine and I had done some action research in the school where we taught, developing a tutoring program in which high school students who had reading difficulties worked with struggling readers at the elementary level. We were so delighted with the intervention that we decided to write about it. Our submission to a literacy journal came back with much constructive criticism. It was also rejected. At first, we experienced acute disappointment and a feeling of inadequacy. But perhaps because we were novices, we decided to try again. We discussed every suggestion made by the reviewers and revised the article. We then sent it to *The Reading Teacher*. And, to our delight, the article was accepted in that well-respected and widely read literacy journal. Moreover, there were few or no changes to be made.

Lessons learned? First, the reviews one receives are really important, and in my view, provide important and constructive feedback. I tell beginning writers that they should think carefully about what reviewers say, what problems they identify, and suggestions they make that would improve the document.

Second, I share my writing with my colleagues, including my graduate students, before submitting any manuscript for publication. Often, my initial responses to their feedback are defensive (e.g., I think I did a good job of making that point! Why don't they understand what I'm trying to say?). But, when I take the time to reflect, I realize that the readers have made good points. And I am reminded again of the value of the feedback from the reviewers of that initial manuscript.

So my one best tip is that emerging writers should always share their work with others before sending it out for publication. Getting feedback from colleagues may limit the criticisms of reviewers and increase the possibility of "accept with minimal revisions."

this letter can strongly influence the extent to which your revised paper will be reviewed favorably. It can serve as an accounting of all the ways you have worked to address the gatekeepers' concerns. Equally important, it should note and explain each key point that you chose not to address. The letter also should indicate any inventive ways in which you attempted to make the paper better. The resubmission letter is your final opportunity to advocate for your work, and, perhaps, not only with the editor. Often, editors will share your resubmission letter with the reviewers of your revised manuscript, along with the new version of the paper and the previous reviews. To any new reviewers, the letter will be especially instructive because they will be working without the benefit of having seen the original manuscript.

In writing these letters, it is best to use the editor's disposition letter as a framework for crafting your own. Presumably, the editor has laid out the concerns in their order of importance. Issues noted at the beginning of the editor's letter must either be addressed satisfactorily in the revised manuscript or explained sufficiently well in the letter you write. Points made near the end of the editor's letter may not be as pivotal, but if they merited mention, the editor must want something done with them.

When contesting the editor's or reviewers' perceptions, it is important to be respectful. Your arguments about the issues can be forceful, but use courteous language that allows for fair-minded disagreement. Adjectives and adverbs used in the letter will set the emotional tone, and there is no quicker way to take your paper out of contention than by antagonizing the editor or reviewers. Labeling their judgments as naive, prejudiced, or flawed invites negative commentaries, something an author can ill afford. To predispose the gatekeepers to your revised manuscript, temper your language and exercise proper deference.

At the beginning of your letter, thank the editor and reviewers for their feedback, and if appropriate, comment that their remarks have made for a better, more thoughtful paper. Then, carefully and specifically detail how you have addressed the editor's and reviewers' concerns. Go point by point according to the hierarchy you perceive in the editor's letter. In showing your progress or explaining your points, note reviewer numbers, as well as the page numbers, on any changes you have made in the revised manuscript. This is the time to point out to the editor any contradictory reviews and to describe how you have reconciled the different perspectives. Conclude the letter by again expressing gratitude for the opportunity to revise your work and offering to make additional changes if necessary. Indicate that you are looking forward to hearing about the status of the paper. If your letter effectively and truthfully documents that you have done everything asked of you, then your paper stands a good chance of moving forward.

If the editor has requested the revised manuscript by a certain date, do everything possible to meet the deadline. By failing to do so, you surrender any right to additional consideration of your work. In effect, the editor has sufficient grounds for dismissing the manuscript altogether. Editors have their own deadlines and schedules and do not appreciate authors who fail to follow through in a timely manner. In particular, to ensure timeliness, forfeiture of a publication will be a near certainty if you fail to meet the revision deadline for a themed journal issue or edited book.

In a dynamic field such as literacy, certain topics can become passé rather quickly, and especially with journals, it is possible for similar papers to be submitted at the same time. Should this happen, the editor could decide to print only the piece that reaches publication quality first. Space in literacy journals is normally so precious that an editor may be precluded from running two pieces on the same topic, even if both are high quality.

Another reason not to delay revising your work centers on preparedness to write. If you wait too long to revise, you risk losing your edge in expert knowledge, resulting in forgetting to include information that would normally be at your fingertips. When your edge dissipates, it then becomes necessary to reeducate yourself about the topic, and revisiting the topic usually requires hours of rereading, which will set you back even further. The possibility of a vicious downward spiral looms large in this case. Simply put, delays beget delays.

GUIDELINE 8

Do Not Be Afraid to Communicate With the Editor

Although rejected authors might feel otherwise, editors are indeed human. Their jobs are inherently complex, and the list of attendant responsibilities is vast. They must shoulder hefty editorial duties, while juggling all aspects of their professional and personal lives. Journal editorships, in particular, are high-stake, volunteer positions that leave a person open to all types of criticism and verbal assault, even though their work is predicated upon a sense of duty to the profession. Although their primary function is to adjudicate manuscripts, journal editors are regularly called upon to encourage and solicit papers, select review board members, communicate with authors, and be accountable to their sponsoring organizations and the field.

Interestingly, revise-and-resubmit decisions encourage more interaction with editors than either rejections or acceptances. Authors may not entirely understand what they should do in revising their manuscripts, so a follow-up query is not inappropriate. A central point to keep in mind is that editors want to publish the best work they receive. If your paper holds that promise, they will normally give generously of their time and energies. In receiving a revise-and-resubmit invitation, you have already consumed a significant block of time and attention. Without question, the amount of editorial effort associated with a revise-and-resubmit decision outstrips acceptance and rejection decisions by a sizeable margin. Revise-and-resubmit invitations represent the most extensive and thorough pieces of author correspondence. Pointing out what is patently wrong or stellar is not nearly as difficult as giving an author direct, insightful, and thorough guidance on how to frame a successful revision. Editors want authors to be successful; they do not relish rejecting manuscripts, especially ones that have been revised and resubmitted.

As stated previously, the primary rule in communicating with editors is to always be respectful. Be mindful of the tone you use in speaking or writing to them, and be sensitive to the fact that they are busy people. Your manuscript will be one of dozens in their pipeline, and although it might be the most important thing in your world, it will not and cannot hold that status in theirs. Editors tend to welcome well-intentioned, thoughtful queries, and they will attempt to respond to them in a timely and useful manner. Use discretion when interacting with them, though, so as not to become a nuisance. Generally, editors are quite approachable, but like anyone else, they do not like to be harangued or bullied. Crossing this line can jeopardize the status of your manuscript.

> "Revision is very important to me. I just can't abide some things that I write. I look at them the next day and they're terrible. They don't make sense, or they're not to the point—so I have to revise, cut, shape. Sometimes I throw the whole thing away and start from scratch."
> —WILLIAM KENNEDY

Closing Thoughts

It seems fitting to end this chapter by revisiting one of its initial premises. Near the outset, I claimed that skillful and artful revisions significantly increase the chances of publication. Of course, in some respects, this assertion only makes sense. But on a deeper level, the statement is profound in a way that belies its straightforward appearance. As authors, we always hope that our work will be judged worthy of acceptance. However, we tend to operate from a defensive posture, one that assumes rejection is the norm and that our chances for success are slim. Our fears are fueled by the fact that the locus of control resides with others whose beliefs, training, and ways of thinking may differ markedly from our own.

Although it is true that we surrender the fate of our work to others, there is much we can do as authors to brighten our prospects. All of the stakeholders of literacy forums share the same goal—the inclusion of timely, valid, useful, interesting, and well-written content. Manuscripts that meet those standards will be given serious consideration, and the majority of them should make it to the publication stage. Ultimately, it is up to the teachers, school administrators, professors, and researchers who submit the work to meet the standards.

Being a successful literacy contributor requires the following: the ability to identify appealing topics and appropriate forums, a grasp of genres and methodologies, well-developed writing skills, attention to detail, and perhaps most of all, an abundance of perseverance. If you are fortunate enough to receive an invitation to revise and resubmit, you may have the chance to see your work in print. Although some chances are better than others, if you think your work has a reasonable chance, you should go for it.

The bottom line is that if you can defend your article, chapter, or book, most of your resubmitted manuscripts can become published. The worst thing you can do is to mire yourself in self-pity and not revise at all. Without revision, your paper is going to sit in a file or desk drawer and never be published. At a minimum, submit a revised version of the paper to another forum. Give it your best and take your chances. Good manuscripts that go unpublished do nothing to advance the field of literacy. You owe it to yourself and to the literacy profession to try.

REFERENCES

Day, R.A. (1983). *How to write and publish a scientific paper* (2nd ed.). Philadelphia: ISI Press.

Dowd, S.B., & McElveny, C. (1997). Revision of manuscripts for scholarly publication. *Radiologic Technology, 69*(1), 47–54. Available: http://www.asrt.org/media/pdf/R09_97DowdMcElveny.pdf

Fiske, D.W., & Fogg, L. (1990). But the reviewers are making different criticisms of my paper! Diversity and uniqueness in reviewer comments. *American Psychologist, 45,* 591–598.

Henson, K.T. (1991). *The art of writing for publication.* Boston: Allyn & Bacon.

Huth, E.J. (1982). *How to write and publish papers in the medical sciences.* Philadelphia: ISI Press.

Miller, R.L. (n.d.). *Writing, revising, and writing again: Preparing a manuscript for publication.* Retrieved February 1, 2005, from http://www.psichi.org/pubs/articles/article_305.asp

Murray, D. (2000). *The craft of revision.* Fort Worth, TX: Dryden Press.

Nagata, D.K., & Trierweiler, S.J. (1996). Revising a research manuscript. In F.T.L. Leong & J.T. Austin (Eds.), *The psychology research handbook* (pp. 291–300). Thousand Oaks, CA: Sage.

Roediger, H.L., III. (1987). The role of journal editors in the scientific process. In D.N. Jackson & J.P. Rushton (Eds.), *Scientific excellence: Origins and assessment* (pp. 222–252). Thousand Oaks, CA: Sage.

Sommers, N. (1982). *Revision strategies of student writers and experienced adult writers.* Washington, DC: National Institute of Education. (ERIC Document Reproduction Service No. ED220839)

CHAPTER 10

Overcoming Rejection

Michael
Pressley

> This chapter focuses on
> - responding to letters of rejection with a positive mindset
> - using criticism constructively
> - finding new outlets for your work
> - effective tactics for overcoming rejection

This chapter is about overcoming rejection but mostly about overcoming rejection of a piece that you have written for a journal or a book. Just so you know you are not alone in having to think about rejection, in my career as an author submitting to journals, I have had about 1% of my manuscripts accepted without revision on the first submission and, in my 14 years as a journal editor, I do not recall accepting a single article on initial submission. This means that the overwhelming majority of the time, an initial submission either is rejected or the author is asked to revise and resubmit for additional consideration. However, a revision invitation carries no guarantee of eventual acceptance, and I have had my share of revisions eventually not make it to publication. I also have had my share of outright rejections. Some rejection is just a fact of life for those aspiring to publish.

Read the Action Letter Carefully: Is This a Rejection or an Invitation to Revise and Resubmit?

As soon as you read the action letter from the editor, the most likely scenario is that you will be disappointed: Your manuscript has not been accepted for publication. The key question is whether this is a complete rejection—meaning that the editor does not feel the manuscript can be revised to the point of acceptability— or an invitation to revise and resubmit based on the comments of the external reviewers (and more important, the editor's summary of the reviewers' comments). You might have to read the letter several times to be certain what is implied.

Excellent editors make it very clear when they want a revision and resubmission. They do so by saying something like, "I invite you to revise by attending to the concerns raised in the reviews and then resubmit your revision." Other editors are more subtle, perhaps offering the invitation in this fashion: "It is possible that a significantly revised version of this paper, one responsive to the reviewers' concerns, would fare more favorably in another round of review." Still, others are downright vague, as illustrated by this possible wording: "I cannot gauge whether your paper could be revised to the point of acceptability at this journal but invite you to reflect on the points raised by the reviewers as you consider this possibility."

Over the years, I have had several dozen meetings with new authors who are trying to decipher whether they have received an invitation to revise and resubmit or a rejection from a journal. So one strong piece of advice I have for you is that, if you are not sure what an editorial letter says, seek the advice of a veteran author, who can read the letter based on experience and perhaps do so a little more dispassionately than you can. Face it, you may really want to see good news in the letter, or alternatively, you may be convinced that it can only be bad news.

Although revise-and-resubmit invitations are addressed in the previous chapter, I would like to add that some revise-and-resubmit invitations are so noncommittal that they are, in fact, rejections. As chapter 9 explains, even if you do make a good faith effort to revise, there is only a small chance of success with the journal. How do you figure out if your revise-and-resubmit letter is more likely a rejection? It's tricky. One way to find out is by asking a veteran author who has dealt with the particular journal to appraise the letter with respect to your odds for success. For example, a veteran author might know something about the editor or the outlet—whether either has a reputation for inviting more resubmissions than the number of acceptances that can be offered. Another way is to e-mail or call the editor and ask questions directly: First, explain that getting published in a timely fashion is important for your advancement. Then, ask about the chances of acceptance by attending to the issues raised by the reviewers.

Responsible editors will take you seriously and attempt to respond fairly. Moreover, if they indicate that there is a good chance of eventual acceptance, they might keep working with you if your first resubmission is not quite sufficient. If, however, the editor makes clear in an e-mail or phone call that the odds of eventual acceptance are low, my advice is to treat the revise-and-resubmit invitation as a rejection and move on to another journal.

Fortunately, clear rejections are easier to spot in the editor's letter. Typically, the news comes in the first paragraph of the letter, often in the first line of the letter. The phrasing varies little, from, "I reject..." to "I regret that I cannot accept...." Such letters are often short, only going on to point out the selectivity of the journal and wishing you well as you continue to work with your manuscript. Such boilerplate responses, generally, are not helpful. What is helpful is for the editor to provide feedback about why the paper is being rejected, beyond simply stating that the enclosed reviews recommend against publication. Sometimes editors will provide a few lines or a few paragraphs about shortcomings, and these should be heeded carefully, as well as the reviewers' reasons for rejection. That leads us to the next topic, which has to do with understanding the reasons for rejection and responding constructively to those reasons.

GUIDELINE 2

Process the Reviewer Comments Until You Understand Them Completely

A manuscript is most likely to move from the rejected to accepted category if you make substantial improvements in the paper. An initial rejection almost always includes substantial feedback about aspects of the submission that cause reason for concern. Understanding such feedback is the first step in responding to the rejection in ways that improve the manuscript. We have already mentioned the first source of such feedback in guideline 1, the editor's letter. That letter is almost always accompanied by reviews provided by scholars with expertise in the problem you are studying, with those reviews typically including much more detail than the editor's brief comments in her or his letter to you. Such reviews should be studied closely.

The first reading of a rejection and the accompanying reviews is often overwhelming and discouraging. Rarely is it meant to be, either by the editor writing the letter or the reviewers, but rather any comments are intended to be helpful. Editors and most involved reviewers recognize that the process should be constructive and that it should assist colleagues in improving their work. Even with that in mind, you still are likely to be discouraged and overwhelmed by the first reading of the reviews.

Keep reading the reviews until they do not seem so overwhelming and until the larger themes become apparent. The reason is that certain themes common-

Jonda McNair,
Clemson
University

Reject Rejection

Some years ago at my sister's college graduation ceremony the commencement speaker presented a speech entitled "Reject Rejection." This speaker advised the college graduates about the importance of learning how to "reject rejection" as they entered a new phase of their lives. This phrase, "reject rejection," has become one that I have learned to embrace as a literacy scholar, and I have found it to be particularly helpful in dealing with rejection and "revise-and-resubmit" notices that I receive from leading literacy publications. When I received my first rejection notice from a well-respected language arts practitioner journal, I was so devastated and infuriated by the reviewer comments that I immediately deleted the e-mail. Since that time I have found several effective ways to deal with rejection and "revise-and-resubmit" notices, which at times can be as painful to read as rejection notices.

The first thing I have done is to learn from my mistakes in order to decrease the chances of having my manuscripts rejected. For example, now before I submit a manuscript for review, I ask at least one or two colleagues, oftentimes ones with perspectives and identity markers (e.g. race, class, and gender) that are different from my own, to read it and provide valuable feedback. I also make careful decisions about which journals to submit my manuscripts to for possible publication. For example, if my manuscript is one that is progressive, I send it to a journal that has previously published this kind of work.

In spite of taking these precautions, it is impossible to completely avoid receiving rejection notices, so I have learned to deal with them specifically in several ways. First of all, I read the reviewer comments once or twice (but no more), and then I put them away and give myself time to think about the suggestions and criticisms. Once, to keep from reading pointed reviewer comments repeatedly, I forwarded the e-mail to a friend with directions to save it for sending to me at a later date. Then I deleted the e-mail and asked for the comments about a month later. Usually, after some time has passed, the comments don't seem as overwhelming as they did initially. I have also learned to try not to perceive the reviewers' comments as personal attacks against me. This is often difficult because I consider my writing to be a reflection of who I am. Lastly, I try and put my struggles with handling constructive criticism and my experiences with rejection in perspective by acknowledging that rejection is a normal part of the publishing process. In fact, while taking a course as a doctoral student at The Ohio State University with Gay Su Pinnell, she described how difficult it was for her to receive criticism from Jeanne Chall and Marie Clay. I figure that if Gay Su Pinnell and other prolific literacy scholars whom I admire such as Violet Harris and Rebecca Rogers have learned how to "reject rejection," then I can, too!

ly come up in editors' and reviewers' remarks. Within these themes, the commentators make specific remarks relevant to your manuscript. Although the devil is in these details, it is helpful to organize the comments in the action letter and the reviewers' comments into the various themes. In the following guidelines 3–7, I address some of the most common themes that are encountered in editorial correspondence and ways to respond to these likely comments.

Before beginning, ask why you should revise your manuscript in light of the feedback received from the rejecting journal, because that particular journal will not see the paper again. However, addressing at least a few points made by the editor or reviewers can improve your paper in ways that will make it more attractive to any publishing outlet.

Once you carefully read the reviews received from the rejecting journal, outline (at least in your head) the themes raised in the reviews and the specific points raised under each theme, you are ready to respond. Often, once you have spent time with the reviews, the situation will look much more manageable. Further, if your paper is in relatively good shape, there may be only a few themes touched on by the reviews, calling for relatively little revision before resubmitting to another outlet. Even so, there are times when the conclusion is that the situation is not manageable.

GUIDELINE 3

If the Rejecting Outlet Was Inappropriate, Find a More Appropriate Outlet

It is not at all uncommon for an editor to reject a paper because it is not appropriate for the outlet or for the publishing house, a reason often mentioned by reviewers as well. This can be because of a topical mismatch (e.g., you have a study of oral communications in the literacy classroom, and this outlet publishes mostly on reading and writing). It can be because of a genre mismatch (e.g., you have submitted a review paper to an outlet that only publishes individual studies). It can be because of a mismatch in length (e.g., the manuscript of your book is 600 pages and the publishing house you have submitted it to typically publishes books in the range of 250–300 pages).

If the only problem cited in the reviews is mismatch, you are in a very good situation. Your job boils down to finding an outlet better matched to your manuscript. If the editor suggests potential outlets, look at those carefully. In addition, this is often a situation in which veteran authors can be very helpful. After a decade or so in the literacy field, most published writers have knowledge of a wide range of outlets and the types of manuscripts they are likely to consider seriously. Gather information about potential outlets, and then look at them yourself, with an eye for determining which seems best matched to the manuscript you have written. You might want to consider other factors, such as the relative prestige of the journals or the publishing house you are considering, but I urge weighing heavily the following considerations: whether the outlet regularly publishes articles or books in the content area of your paper, has a high proportion of papers or books in the genre of your article, and is willing to allocate space for a manuscript or book as short or lengthy as yours. If the only issue is appropriateness, all that may be required is to make additional copies of your original manuscript, submit it with a letter to the editor of the new outlet, and place it in the mail (or submit electronically, depending on the outlet).

If Reviewers Signal There Is an Insufficient Advance in Knowledge for the Rejecting Outlet, Send the Paper to a Lesser Journal or Revise to Make the Advance in Knowledge More Obvious

Some excellent journals often have a high standard with respect to the novelty of a finding, so it is not unusual for a paper to be rejected because there is not sufficient advance in knowledge produced by the paper. Perhaps your study is a replication of a previous effort, or the findings are too similar to other efforts. Although top journals may reject such papers, they are largely the bread and butter of many of the second-tier journals, ones that are refereed and selective, just not as selective as the best outlets. Sometimes in rejecting a paper for this reason, the editor will point to potential alternative outlets. Again, such recommendations should be taken seriously. This is also a situation in which published authors can be helpful if you are not aware of the hierarchy of journals in the field in which you aspire to publish. If the only problem with the paper is that there is not enough of an advance in knowledge for the top-tier outlet, you may have little revision to do before resubmitting.

> "Everywhere I go I'm asked if I think the university stifles writers. My opinion is that they don't stifle enough of them."
>
> —FLANNERY O'CONNOR

On the other hand, the verdict of "insufficient advance of knowledge" may prompt you to rewrite your manuscript to clarify the advance made by your paper. In fact, I would advise looking hard at this issue whenever an editor concludes that there was not enough advance in knowledge to justify publication, to see if it is possible to make more obvious what is unique about your paper. Did you perhaps study the problem with a new population or with materials that are more relevant than classroom materials in previous studies of the problem? Or did you study the problem more completely, using more appropriate dependent measures? It might help for you to review previously published papers pertaining to the topic and map out what is different about your study and make the differences clear in your revisions before submitting to another journal.

Of course, you might conclude after such a revision that there was more significance to the paper than you made obvious in the initial version, perhaps enough to justify another look by the originally rejecting journal. I urge you to raise this possibility with that editor via e-mail or a phone conversation, asking that the editor look at just the issue of whether a significant enough advance is now more obvious in light of your revisions. If the editor's mind is changed, then there is likely to be additional review at the original, first-choice outlet. If not, do not be disappointed, but rather proceed to another journal, perhaps using the conversation with the original editor as an occasion to ask for her or his advisement about where you might submit the paper. Editors at top journals, which are likely to render a verdict of insufficient advance in knowledge, are accustomed to thinking about the competition for their journal. Moreover, most senior editors I know want to be helpful, and asking for guidance about another potential home for a paper permits the editor to help you find an appropriate outlet for your manuscript.

Finally, there is another possibility you should consider if your paper is not deemed a significant enough advance. Sometimes a study is divided into shorter papers, with authors taking one aspect of the design and data for one paper and another aspect of the design and data for another paper. Often, this results in several small advances rather than the somewhat larger advance that would be permitted by showing and reflecting on the entire design and all of the data. However, if you have taken this tactic and are receiving feedback on one or more of the papers that there is insufficient advance to warrant publication, you should think hard about putting the design and data back together into a new, more ambitious paper, one that could be submitted even to the journal that rejected your original paper. If you decide to combine and resubmit to a journal that previously rejected the smaller piece, honesty is the best policy with the editor: Write a cover letter explaining exactly what you did. Invariably, the editor will treat it as a new manuscript and start the review process again.

GUIDELINE 5

If There Are Concerns About the Writing, Rewrite Your Paper or Book

If the article or book is written well enough, writing problems cited by the reviewers should be quite specific. Most commonly, they are issues of completeness of content. If the introduction does not cover important, relevant literature, excellent reviewers will provide good clues about the literature that is missing, either citing particular topics or authors that deserve citation and discussion. Look at this literature and determine how it can be meaningfully assimilated into a revised introductory section for your manuscript. If the methods section is not sufficiently detailed, and does not cover all that is expected according to the *Publication Manual of the American Psychological Association* (American Psychological Association, 2001) or whatever style guide is required by the outlet, excellent reviewers will signal the most critical methodological points that are missing. In addition, you should use the style manual to inventory what is expect-ed in a methods section and make certain that you have included all items on the inventory, at least briefly. If the results or discussion section does not take up important aspects of the data, perhaps include how the data relate to issues in the introduction that presumably motivated the study: Once again, excellent reviewers will point to issues that need more attention. You should, however, make certain that, at a minimum, your results and discussion appropriately bring closure to the paper, making clear how the study provided answers to the ques-tions raised in the introduction.

One quite specific writing problem that comes up often is that the manu-script is too long relative to the contribution it makes. When you receive this crit-icism from a rejecting journal or book publisher, there are several things to consider with respect to revision. You probably should attempt to shorten the manuscript somewhat; however, you do not want to shorten so much that the manuscript does not clearly convey its message to the next outlet that will re-view it. If that outlet is interested in the manuscript, the editor is likely to work with you on the issue of length. Whether you shorten before submitting to a new outlet does not seem that critical, although you should probably go through the manuscript carefully, making sure sentences are as concise as possible and grossly tangential material is deleted. Chances are, however, that once you are successful in getting a positive response from an outlet, you will have another op-portunity to address the length of the paper.

Often, reviewers will flag writing problems that are easily managed. For ex-ample, they may cite sentences that do not make sense or typos or incorrect word choices. All of these should be addressed and revised before sending the paper to another journal. On the other hand, if reviewers point out numerous typos or grammatical errors or some other frequent mechanical problem, this calls for harder editing, sometimes even the use of a professional editor or a coauthor who has good editing skills, as was suggested in chapter 3. Such problems will have to be resolved, and you should resolve them as soon as they are brought to your attention.

After you have resolved the writing issues, it helps to have others read your manuscript and provide comments. Again, this is an occasion to call on senior colleagues. Often, they can spot exactly the types of writing problems that might be found by a reviewer. (After all, your senior colleagues are often journal and book reviewers themselves.) Get their input and revise additionally based on it.

In my own career, there have been quite a few papers that I rewrote exten-sively before resubmitting. Although attending to writing problems is often painful and time-consuming, publishing outlets demand good writing. Take maximum advantage of specific input about how to improve your writing to max-imize the likelihood that your ideas will be published.

If There Are Concerns About Your Analyses, Take a Hard Look and Perhaps Analyze Differently

For those who submit research papers, reviewers will often point out data that need to analyzed differently. Again, the more specific they are about this issue, the better. For example, a reviewer may question the appropriateness of a statis-

AUTHOR REFLECTIONS

The Challenges and Rewards of Writing for an International Audience

Riitta-Liisa
Korkeamaki,
University of
Oulu, Finland

I had never dreamed about writing and publishing for an international audience until I found myself sitting in a graduate class at the University of Maryland, College Park. The aim of the class was to write and publish a paper. To me, it was more than a challenge to write about reading instruction in my home country, Finland. The Finnish language is quite unique and spoken by about five million people. Therefore, I had several problems such as writing in a second language and describing the Finnish educational system and instructional background. The paper I developed in that graduate class was finally published in a well-respected journal, after much revising and mentoring from my adviser, Professor Jean Dreher, who made me strictly control every word in the paper! I have learned that writing is a disciplined exercise. Writing that paper with Jean Dreher made us not only coauthors, but also friends and colleagues. So we have continued writing together about Finnish literacy education.

I still continue to have struggles with writing, just as I did the first time. I feel the same way, even as I write this brief piece about my writing experiences. I must make sure the reader will understand the context and the background in which my writing is grounded. It is often hard to find matching terms across the Finnish and English languages. But it is even more difficult to make cross-cultural papers interesting to international readers. For example, what will English-speaking readers learn from a study of teaching spelling in Finnish, a language with strong sound–symbol relationships?

Because of the challenges of writing across languages and cultures, it is a great privilege to have international colleagues. Often, in my own writing, when I have solved the problem of the content and the point of the paper, there are still problems with writing in the English language. This is where my international colleagues are often very helpful.

I remember writing my second paper and how I struggled with the English language. I thought that my paper would be regarded as "too simple" or even naive because I was not able to use sophisticated words and phrases. However, much to my surprise, one of the reviewers of a prominent journal to which I submitted the paper wrote, "Only very rarely do we get a paper so well written as this." In fact, I'm still in shock. Writing for an international audience can be extremely demanding but worth the effort. And it is especially rewarding if you have international colleagues who share your research interests and like to collaborate.

tical test you used versus another possible test. Such an issue can be dealt with directly, with careful reflection on the approach recommended by the reviewer versus the approach you took. If you are not very savvy with statistics or do not feel comfortable in your own judgments about the relative merits of statistical tests, it makes sense to seek out the advice of a statistician, who often can help sort out the issues, perhaps leading you to a test that will be more compelling. Alternatively, the statistician may approve the approach you took.

As you consider comments raised about analyses, keep in mind that there are many different ways to analyze any data. That said, there are some decidedly wrong ways. If the reviewer points out a wrong way—and your methodologist can help you decide whether that is the case—you should do all that is possible to move from a wrong analysis to a more defensible analysis. Wrong analysis decisions are likely to be held against you in future reviews at other journals. If, on the other hand, the approach you have selected is defensible, construct a good defense, perhaps with professional methodological advisement. Perhaps you should add a few lines to the manuscript about why you chose to analyze as you did, but it should not be so lengthy a defense that it seems overly defensive. Other times, it might be better not to add anything to the manuscript, especially if the professional methodologist is certain that your approach is defensible and would be so recognized by many readers. A lot can be gained by getting advice from more knowledgeable people, specifically, by asking a statistician whether additional comments need to be added to the manuscript to justify your approach.

This point about responding to suggestions about analyses makes the more general point that revisions should not be made only because a reviewer said so but should be made only after reflecting on the reviewers' comments and discerning the strengths and weaknesses of the suggestions. In doing so, you probably should convince yourself that most comments have at least some merit and will warrant some response, but that response should not come until you understand why you are responding—and if it will improve the manuscript.

GUIDELINE 7

Adjust Your Interpretations So They Do Not Exceed Claims Possible Based on Your Design

As with guideline 6, this guideline addresses research-based manuscripts. If an editor or reviewer asserts that the design you are using cannot answer the questions you are posing, this is a serious charge. Your first task is to determine whether the reviewer is correct. Of course, your first resource for doing so is your knowledge of your own design and what you are concluding based on it. If you are, in fact, going beyond what your data reveals, you have to back off (e.g., if you have correlational data and are attempting to make causal claims). Often, all that is required with respect to criticisms of design shortcomings is to make certain that your claims do not exceed the limits of claims permitted by the research design you have chosen.

A classic example that comes to mind is a qualitative design that can be a source of causal hypotheses but cannot be a test of causality. In my own qualitative work, my colleagues were able to specify in great detail that the qualities of primary-grade classrooms in engagement during language arts was high, as was achievement (see Pressley et al., 2003). This permitted us to advance the hypothesis that the teaching behaviors used by engaging teachers (which were very different from those used by less engaging teachers) caused the engagement and achievement observed, but it did not permit us to draw a causal conclusion. Such a conclusion would require a true experimental design, a study in which the behaviors of teachers were controlled (i.e., some would teach as engaging teachers taught in our study; others would teach as less engaging teachers taught in our qualitative study). My colleagues and I succeeded in publishing our findings largely because we greatly respected that boundary between hypotheses and claims of causality. You should know your design and what it can reveal, and do not state that you have found more than can logically follow from that design. If you overstated the case in the submission to the original journal, make certain not to overstate the case in the submission to the next journal.

There are multiple reasons for the rejection of a manuscript. One reaction would be simply to submit to another outlet without adjusting the manuscript at all. I have very much urged other ways of thinking about rejection. Authors of rejected papers should treat the input they receive very seriously, responding almost as if they are going to resubmit it to the rejecting outlet. Editors and reviewers do try to be helpful even when rejecting a paper. It would be to your benefit to take advantage of suggestions that will strengthen your manuscript.

What is implied here is that often much will need to be addressed before a manuscript should be submitted to another outlet—or at least it will seem like much to do as you sit with your categorizing of the various suggestions from the rejecting editor and reviewers. I urge resisting thinking that the task is overwhelming. Dive into the revision as quickly as possible after receiving feedback. Procrastinating will not improve the manuscript. Only serious reflection on the revision and revising will do that. If the reviewers cared enough to provide detailed feedback, it probably is because they can envision that your paper can be published somewhere. Join them in that vision by doing your part, by responding to their input with a better manuscript.

GUIDELINE 8

Make Major Revisions in Response to Devastating Journal Reviews (or Move On)

Occasionally, a rejection will carry the message—either explicitly or implicitly—that the journal manuscript is not ready for publication and not really close enough to encourage submission elsewhere. There are sometimes problems that cannot be resolved simply by extensive rewriting; for example, the journal reviewers make the case that the design and data collection are not nearly substantial enough to investigate the questions you want to address in your paper. Thus, if you want to test a cause-and-effect question, you cannot do it with an uncontrolled pretest to posttest design. If you want to test possible subtle effects of an intervention, it cannot be done with only a handful of participants in each condition of an ANOVA-type design. If you want to develop a theory about how middle school reading clubs work, you probably cannot do that by observing one reading club. What you need to do in each of these cases is to collect more data. Respectively, you might need to design and carry out a controlled pretest–posttest study, add a substantial number of participants to the ANOVA design, or study a half-dozen middle school reading clubs rather than just one, using cross-case analyses rather than a single-case-study design.

Another problem that can be as devastating is that the design is adequate to the problem, and there is more than enough data, but the data conflict so that there is no clear interpretation in the minds of the reviewers and certainly not the interpretation you are favoring in your discussion section. One tactic is to rewrite the paper, being blatantly honest that what emerged from your analyses was anything but a clear picture. Although such messages seldom make it into top-tier journals, they can sometimes get published in second-tier outlets. Another possibility is to continue doing research on the problem, clarifying the research using more data. For young scholars, who often are on short tenure, I do not recommend this tactic, because such scholars often can move on to other problems with a higher probability of payoff.

In summary, rather than be devastated by a very critical review, respond to it in one of two ways: Either resolve to do the very substantial work required to remedy the situation, such as running an additional study or doing substantial rewriting or, alternatively, cut your losses, especially if it is not clear that a large investment of effort will result in any better situation. It is better to spend time on something that provides more promise of payoff. Definitely do not persist in advancing indefensible conclusions; such advocacy can be seen as indicative of scholarly weakness. Rather, move on to another study or problem with greater potential to yield defensible outcomes.

Expect Feedback on Invited Contributions and Respond to It Appropriately

Being invited to write chapters for books edited by highly regarded scholars in the field is an indication of the recognition of your work; however, such an invitation is not a guarantee that your manuscript will be published. In anticipation that some invited authors will drop out of such projects or fail to produce acceptable papers, editors often will invite more chapters or articles than they actually could include. In that case, you might receive a letter informing you that your chapter or article cannot be included because of space limitations, even though it was admirable in many ways. My suggestion is simply to accept such a verdict, although I think it is fair to let the editor know that you did not appreciate an invitation being rescinded. Any time I have tried to negotiate a paper into such an invited source after receiving a "sorry, no space" letter, I have never succeeded.

What can you do with a manuscript that was invited but is not going to make it into the originally invited source? Save it. Basically, because invitations are always in areas in which you have expertise, you will be invited to write about the same or a very similar problem for another book or special issue, often sooner than you think. There are many edited books being published. In fact, if you learn about one in which your chapter might fit, try contacting the organizing editor. You will be far ahead of other potential contributors if you show the editor a draft of your manuscript. In addition, sometimes such chapters or articles can be reworked for submission to archival journals, which you should consider if such an outlet would make sense for your piece. In fact, if you succeed in placing the paper in an archival, refereed journal, you may be much further ahead than if you had placed it in the invited outlet. For example, one of my most cited articles, on the topic of transactional instruction of reading comprehension strategies (Pressley et al., 1992), started as an invited book chapter that was ultimately rejected by the editor. My colleagues and I worked with the paper until it could be submitted to a very good journal, and I have benefited from that original rejection for a dozen years. I am certain that the paper would have never been as visible in the invited book that rejected it as it was in the refereed journal that published it.

GUIDELINE 10

Shop the Publishers After Rejection of an Authored Book

Before writing a book, most authors negotiate a contract with a publisher based on a book prospectus, which basically outlines the purpose of the book, its intended audience and market, and projected contents. Most authors send their prospectus to a number of potential publishers, with a subset of these willing to talk further, and a smaller subset actually willing to offer a contract for the book. That is, landing a contract with a publisher often occurs in a flurry of rejections, with more publishers turning down a prospectus than accepting it. Thus, in book publishing, rejection often occurs before a single word of the book is written. The only way to land a book contract based on a prospectus is to try a number of pub-

The Pains and Pleasures of Writing

Susan Neuman,
Michigan State
University

When I look back at my beginnings in educational publishing, I think about its pains as well as its pleasures. Writing is difficult: Moreover, it is personal. There is simply no way to divorce one's feelings from one's writing. And like so many other assistant professors, very aware of the tenure clock, I knew I had to publish—and publish quickly. But exactly what to publish, especially when my dissertation had rather dismal findings, was the problem.

I remember having a discussion with my husband when I had just taken my first job at Yale University. I gave him an elaborate story about the data I was about to collect—I would request lots and lots of journals from children and their families—that would certainly lead to a rich repository of future articles. He skeptically listened to my account and then quietly asked, "But what's your theory? Don't you need a theory before you collect data?" "Who has time for a theory?" I asked, and abruptly ended that conversation.

During that first year, I wrote six articles for publication. And I dutifully sent them off to editors, holding my breath that they'd be accepted. None of them was. In fact, I remember vividly how I felt when I received two rejections in the mail on the same day. Like Alexander in *Alexander and the Terrible, Horrible, No-Good, Very Bad Day* by Judith Viorst (Simon & Schuster, 1972), I really wished I could have run off to Australia.

Once again I turned to my husband, not for advice but for solace. Being an academic himself, however, advice is what he gave me. "Most people give up after one rejection. Don't give up."

And so I kept at it, reading comments from the reviewers so many times that I could memorize their lines. At the same time, I found wonderful mentors in editors such as John Readence, David Pearson, Jeanne Chall, and Dick Anderson, who would read my work and help me to get over the scary feelings that come with rejection and revision. I owe these people a wonderful debt of thanks for their kindness and integrity.

Since those early years, I have come to enjoy writing more, knowing that my task in academic writing is not only to report the data, but also to convey what I've learned about the participants who were involved in my studies. I want to give them voice and help those who wish to study early literacy for high-poverty children to better understand my passion and commitment to this work.

lishers until one is interested in offering a contract. Before proceeding with any one of those publishers, however, I urge you to talk with authors whom the publisher has already published. Find out what their experiences were with the publisher, both with respect to the editorial process but then also with the marketing of their books once completed. If you are fortunate enough to have more than one publisher vying for your book, sign with the one with authors who reported the best experiences. Their experiences will soon be your experiences.

Securing a contract is no guarantee the book will be published, however. About all that it does guarantee to the author is that the prospective book will be published once it is acceptable to the publisher. There are many books that get written (or at least partially written) that do not get published for various reasons that have little to do with how well the book is written. For example, a common reason for rejection of a manuscript in progress in recent decades has been that the original, signing publisher has been sold to another publisher, who does not see how the contracted volume would work well on its list.

The good news is that many completed or partially completed books will be picked up by other publishers. A first step in moving on to those other publishers is to obtain a release from the publisher holding the first contract. This may be very difficult, and the details and specifics of this process go well beyond this chapter. First, a publisher might not be willing to tell you that the book will not move forward but, rather, serves up an impossible number of revision suggestions or an overarching revision suggestion that would mean an entirely different book (e.g., requesting that you turn your volume-length critical analysis of the National Reading Panel report into a volume about how reading educators can work within the conclusions of the National Reading Panel). Second, a publisher may have many layers of bureaucracy that need to be cleared before your book is released. Unfortunately, the most efficient way to deal with this situation is to employ an intellectual property attorney to negotiate the release for you. That can be expensive, but it is unlikely that another publisher would take on a book without a contractual release from the original signing publisher. Having an attorney when the contract is originally drafted makes getting a release at this stage easier, because the original contract will have been redrafted before acceptance by your attorney to create more favorable terms for you, including a provision for when the publisher decides not to move forward with your book. Therefore, getting an intellectual property attorney involved sooner rather than later may make sense for book authors.

Once your book is released, it is time to begin shopping other publishers. Approaches to other publishers will occur when you have much more than a prospectus—you may have a few chapters written for the book. Thus, conversations with publishers can be advanced further and faster than they were at the prospectus stage. In fact, potential publishers may be willing to get external reviews of the chapters to inform their decision making, which should permit them to make a more informed decision about whether your book belongs on their list. Once you receive a new contract, take it to your intellectual property attorney for review. At this point, being more informed about the process, you will know more about what you want in that contract, and having an attorney will increase the likelihood of getting the best terms. There is very good reason to be optimistic that the second deal for a book can be a better deal than the first deal that went sour.

There are many publishers that are anxious to sign promising young authors, especially authors with books that match the publisher's vision of what they want to publish. Do not jump at the first offer but rather explore widely. Find the publisher whose vision accurately matches what you are writing or want to write. As you do so, you will learn a lot about the book publishing process.

Closing Thoughts

A few years ago, some students and I asked editors what qualities they were looking for in a manuscript for it to be published at their journal (Lounds et al., 2002). Basically, their answer was, "Everything had to be good." The paper needed to be well written, the design sound relative to the questions posed and issues addressed, and the statistics and analyses appropriate. Therefore, the charge for authors aspiring to be published is to get their paper to that level of good. One way for this to occur is by learning from feedback that comes with rejection and then moving on in the ways suggested in this chapter. Be assured that if you make the paper as good as it can be by attending to and addressing critical concerns, you will have a much better paper than the one you originally wrote, hopefully, a paper that is good enough to be published.

> "Really, in the end, the only thing that can make you a writer is the person that you are, the intensity of your feeling, the honesty of your vision, the unsentimental acknowledgement of the endless interest of the life around and within you."
>
> —SANTHA RAMA RAU

I note as well that sometimes multiple rounds of rejection and attempts at different journals or outlets are required before a piece finds a home. So long as the paper or book receives some positive remarks from reviewers, I urge you to persist. Every successful scholar's vita contains publications that were turned down one or more times before they were accepted for publication. Every successful scholar's vita also contains publications that benefited enormously from feedback provided as part of the publication process, including feedback accompanying rejection letters.

REFERENCES

American Psychological Association. (2001). *Publication manual of the American Psychological Association* (5th ed.). Washington, DC: Author.

Lounds, J., Oakar, M., Knecht, K., Moran, M., Gibney, M., & Pressley, M. (2002). Journal editors' views on the criteria a paper must meet to be publishable. *Contemporary Educational Psychology*, 27, 338–347.

Pressley, M., El-Dinary, P.B., Gaskins, I., Schuder, T., Bergman, J.L., & Almasi, J., et al. (1992). Beyond direct explanation: Transactional instruction of reading comprehension strategies. *The Elementary School Journal*, 92, 511–554.

Pressley, M., Roehrig, A., Raphael, L., Dolezal, S., Bohn, K., & Mohan, L., et al. (2003). Teaching processes in elementary and secondary education. In W.M. Reynolds & G.J. Miller (Eds.), *Handbook of psychology* (Vol. 7: Educational psychology; pp. 153–175). New York: John Wiley & Sons.

Top 10 Ideas for Getting Published

This epilogue highlights and extends the authors' messages about writing for literacy publication. Eighty-nine guidelines were provided across the 10 chapters in this book. Not surprisingly, although the guidelines are different in the way they are expressed for each chapter, common themes are conveyed. These same themes emerged when we asked the authors to write down their top 10 thoughts (or pearls of wisdom) about writing for publication.

We identified key topics from their statements and counted the number of times that a topic was mentioned. For example, the idea to *set aside time and conditions for writing* came from comments such as "leave blocks of time for writing," "write in a spot you like with lots of light and a comfortable chair," "make time to write," and "schedule writing time daily or weekly." We then developed 10 big ideas to consider as you develop your own methods for getting published.

In the spirit of David Letterman, host of the *Late Show* in New York City, we present the *top 10* ideas for getting published, from the least frequently mentioned to the most frequently mentioned. But it is up to you to decide when and how to use each idea to strengthen your own potential for success for beating the odds of getting published in the field of literacy.

Number 10: Write About Something You Really Care About

The best writing comes from something you really care about. You cannot fake interest in a topic because your depth of knowledge, level of research, and commitment to the topic is communicated through your writing. You are better served if you spend time identifying topics of interest that you can pursue with a passion rather than writing superficially about topics that are only marginally appealing to you.

Do not pursue a topic because it is someone else's passion. Find your own niche and your own voice, and you will have many more good years of writing about an area that touches your soul.

Number 9: Collaborate

If you see yourself as someone who takes pleasure in sharing ideas and working with others, think about collaborating. Teamwork can make writing more enjoyable and productive. Find people you enjoy and respect, and who complement your own interests and work patterns. Try collaborating once or twice, and if it helps you become more productive and successful, look to collaborate on other projects.

Number 8: Let the Piece Rest for a Time Without Working on It, and Before Doing the Final Draft and Submission

When we take breaks from our writing, especially after writing a thorough draft, we can learn more about our topic. Allowing a piece of writing to rest for a period of time also helps us to have a fresh perspective and develop a more critical editing eye. Lapp and Flood call this rest period *marinating* because we are giving our minds time to soak up additional ideas that we may want to include in our writing. The length of this "wait time" depends on the deadlines that you face, your other professional and personal responsibilities, and your own ability to process additional ideas and information.

Number 7: Remember That Patience and Persistence Are Crucial in Getting Published

Many authors in this book believe that *the* most important quality needed for getting published is persistence. Nothing else matters because, if you are persistent, you can transcend those discouraging moments and operate with the assumption that eventually you will succeed. Patience with the process also is crucial because it can take two to three years to see your manuscript published. But it definitely is worth the wait!

Number 6: Don't Minimize That Writing Is Often Difficult, Painful, and Discouraging

As Red Smith said, "Writing is easy. You just sit at the typewriter and open a vein." Although we use computers today instead of typewriters, we still give blood, sweat, and tears. Writing is hard work, and it takes lots of time and effort to say something worthwhile in a way that is organized, clear, accurate, and engaging and advances the audience's knowledge base. Authors find different ways of coping with the challenge of writing. If you are like the late Paula Danziger, who cleaned every closet before she could write a word, so be it.

Number 5: Remind Yourself That Writing Is Wonderfully Rewarding

Writing is wonderfully rewarding, whether you like to write or not. Having written means that you have contributed to the profession and to your own professional development. It means that you have the ability to communicate to your peers that you have enough knowledge and ideas about a topic, and enough confidence in yourself, to record something permanently for others to read and use. As Henry Miller said, "Writing, like life itself, is a voyage of discovery."

Number 4: Know Your Audience (or Publication Outlet) Thoroughly

Nothing is more aggravating to editors than to receive manuscripts that do not fit the purpose of the publication or the audience for which the publication is written. For instance, it does not make sense to send an article about helping middle school students with basic skills to a journal that focuses on early childhood education. It does not make sense to send a chatty piece about an at-home reading project to a major research publication. Do a thorough search of possible outlets. If you want to publish in journals or newsletters, get to know those in your area of expertise to better understand their focus, style of writing, and voice. See chapters 2, 4, and 5 and Appendixes A and B for information about journals and newsletters. If you want to publish a book, study the types of books advertised by specific publishers. Study the common components of the books, such as style of writing and organizational formats, to fully understand the audience.

Number 3: Set Aside Time and Conditions for Writing

Whether you set aside time every Monday morning, every Sunday, two hours each day, or three hours every Tuesday evening, you need to carve out time to write, and you need to honor your own schedule. Guilt about responding to other pressures in your life—whether it is returning phone calls, responding to e-mail, helping a student, spending time with your family, or cleaning the kitchen—needs to be set aside so that you have time to focus on your writing. You need blocks of time, too. A good piece of writing needs time to develop and simmer in just the right environment.

Decide the best conditions for your own writing and follow them. If you need to be at home in a quiet room surrounded by your computer and books, make sure that is where you go to write. If you find that the library is the only place that does not distract you, find your spot and try to keep it. If you need to have your entire house in order before you sit down to write, do it. If you need to bake cookies to have by your side as you write, do that. Determine the best conditions for you to write (no matter what anyone else says), and follow through in maintaining those conditions.

Number 2: Get Feedback of All Kinds, Even When the Piece Is Not Yet Finished

If you agree with Ernest Hemingway that first drafts are not worth very much, you understand the importance of receiving some type of feedback before your writing is ready to submit for review. Feedback comes in many forms. Peer conferencing helps you get feedback from others who also are interested in writing. Professional associations, such as the International Reading Association, may have workshops at annual conferences where those experienced with writing give feedback to those with less experience. Informal committees with colleagues can be established and used to get feedback as needed. Take advantage of those editors who you know will give feedback to prospective authors before your work is actually submitted.

Family and friends can be an excellent source for feedback, especially if they have an interest in your topic or are excellent writers themselves. We have depended on our family and friends to bring out their thick red pens through the years to help us express our thoughts more clearly and concisely. We found that although we did not always smile at the many red marks on each page, we were grateful for the feedback and help before we embarrassed ourselves with prospective editors. This leads to the most frequent and "number one" thought that the authors shared about being a productive writer.

Number 1: Don't Take Personally Rejections and Criticisms—Instead, Use Them to Improve Your Writing

As you read in the preface, the contributors for this book have published widely. In very broad strokes, and as an average, each author for this book has published at least 60 articles and five books. Yet these authors can share vivid moments in their publishing careers when they experienced profound disappointment from letters of rejection and severe criticism from reviewers. To say that they did not take it personally would not be quite honest. However, after an appropriate cooling-off period, they used the rejections and reviews as opportunities to rethink, rewrite, and revise.

We actually believe that the way you handle rejection and criticism is an indicator of your long-term ability to be successful in writing for publication. As Michael Pressley said, "rejection is a fact of life for those aspiring to publish...."

The key is to understand reasons why your manuscript has been rejected or criticized, and use the feedback to respond constructively. Outright rejection means that another publication outlet needs to be found. You can submit to other outlets immediately without even changing a word. You can make major changes before submitting again, or you can find other authors to help conceptualize ideas differently and rewrite entire parts of the manuscript.

Recommendations to revise and resubmit require different decisions because, although the criticism might be disheartening, the editors and reviewers are giving you a chance to get published. And although some chances are better than others in ultimately getting accepted, you owe it to yourself to at least try to respond to the recommendations.

If you are reading this book, you have at least some interest in getting published. As we can appreciate, "Beauty is in the eye of the holder." One person's masterpiece is another person's pile of scrap. If you can put your emotions aside, it is just a matter of time and rewrites until you find an editor or publisher who is interested in accepting your work to share with other literacy professionals. Eventually, and with your own accumulation of publishing war stories, you will find yourself published over and over again in different literacy outlets.

U.S. and International Literacy and Literacy-Related Organizations

Associations/Organizations	Journals	Newspapers and Newsletters
American Association of Colleges for Teacher Education 1307 New York Ave., NW Suite 300 Washington, DC 20005-4701 202-293-2450 www.aacte.org	*Journal of Teacher Education*	*AACTE Briefs*
American Educational Research Association 1230 Seventeenth St., NW Washington, DC 20036-3078 202-223-9485 www.aera.net	*American Educational Research Journal* *Educational Evaluation and Policy Analysis* *Educational Researcher* *Journal of Educational and Behavioral Statistics* *Review of Educational Research* *Review of Research in Education*	DIVISION K: *Teaching and Teacher Education*
American Reading Forum www.americanreadingforum.org	Yearbook	

Associations/Organizations	Journals	Newspapers and Newsletters
Association for Childhood Education International 17904 Georgia Ave, Suite 215 Olney, MD 20832 301-570-2111 www.acei.org	*Childhood Education* *Journal of Research in Childhood Education*	*Professional Focus Quarterlies*
Association of Supervision and Curriculum Development 1703 N. Beauregard St. Alexandria, VA 22311-1714 800-933-2723 www.ascd.org	*Journal of Curriculum and Development*	*ASCD SmartBrief* *Classroom Leadership* *EDPolicy Update* *Infobrief* *ResearchBrief*
Association of Teacher Educators 1900 Association Drive, Suite ATE Reston, VA 20191-1502 703-620-3110 www.ate1.org	*Action in Teacher Education*	*ATE Newsletter*
College Reading Association www.collegereadingassociation.org	*Reading Research and Instruction*	*The Reading News*
Council for Exceptional Children 1110 North Glebe Road Suite 300 Arlington, VA 22201 888-CEC-SPED www.cec.sped.org	*Exceptional Students* *TEACHING Exceptional Children* *TEC Plus Online*	*CEC SmartBrief* *CEC Today*
International Reading Association 800 Barksdale Rd. PO Box 8139 Newark, DE 19714-8139 800-336-READ (800-336-7323) www.reading.org	*Journal of Adolescent & Adult Literacy* *Lectura y Vida* *Reading Online* *The Reading Teacher* *Reading Research Quarterly*	*Reading Today*
National Association for the Education of Young Children 1313 L Street NW, Suite 500 Washington, DC 20005 202-232-8777/800-424-2460 www.naeyc.org	*Young Children* *Beyond the Journal* *Early Childhood Research Quarterly*	*Early Years Are Learning Years*

Associations/Organizations	Journals	Newspapers and Newsletters
National Council of Teachers of English 1111 W. Kenyon Road Urbana, IL 61801-1096 217-328-3870/877-369-6283 www.ncte.org	*Classroom Notes* *College Composition and Communications* *College English* *English Journal* *English Leadership Quarterly* *Language Arts* *Research in the Teaching of English* *School Talk* *Talking Points* *Teaching in the Two-Year College* *Voices From the Middle*	*NCTE Inbox* (E-Newsletter) *The Council Chronicle*
National Reading Conference 7044 South 13th St. Oak Creek, WI 53154 414-908-4924 www.nrconline.org	*Journal of Literacy Research* Yearbook	Newsletter
Phi Delta Kappa International 408 N. Union St. PO Box 789 Bloomington, IN 47402-0789 800-766-1156 www.pdkintl.org	*Phi Delta Kappan*	*PDK Connection*

State Literacy Associations and Their Journals and Newsletters

State Literacy Association*	Journals	Newsletters
Alabama Reading Association www.alabama-reading.org		*Lines*
Alaska State Literacy Association www.alaskareading.org		*ASLA Newsletter*
Aloha State Council	*The Reading Circle*	*KHH Newsletter*
Arizona Reading Association www.azreadingassoc.com		*Arizona Reading Journal*
Arkansas Reading Association www.arareading.org	*The Reader*	*Arkansas Reader*
California Reading Association www.californiareads.org	*The Book Club*	*The California Reader*
Colorado Council International Reading Association www.ccira.org	*Colorado Reading Council Journal*	
Connecticut Reading Association www.ctreading.org	*CONNections*	*CRA Newsletter Newspaper in Education (NIE)*
Diamond State Reading Association www.doe.state.de.us/dsra		*DSRA Reader*

State Literacy Association*	Journals	Newsletters
Florida Reading Association www.flreads.org	*Florida Reading Quarterly*	FRA Newsletter
Georgia Reading Association http://georgiareading.org	*Georgia Journal of Reading*	*FOCUS Quarterly Newsletter*
Idaho Council www.idahoreads.org	*The Portals Journal*	*Reading Matter in Idaho*
Illinois Reading Council www.illinoisreadingcouncil.org	*Illinois Reading Council Journal*	*Illinois Reader*
Indiana State Reading Association www.indianareads.org	*Indiana Reading Journal*	*Connection Newsletter*
Iowa Reading Association www.iowareading.org		*Iowa Quarterly Newsletter*
Kansas Reading Association www.kansasread.org	*Kansas Journal of Reading*	KRA Newsletter
Kentucky Reading Association www.kyreading.org	*Kentucky Reading Journal*	*Reading Next: A Vision for Action and Research in Middle and High School Literacy*
Keystone State Reading Association (Pennsylvania) www.ksra.org	*Pennsylvania Reads: Journal of the Keystone State Reading Association*	*The Keystone Reader*
Louisiana Reading Association www.lareading.org	*Exploration and Discovery*	*Newspaper in Education*
State of Maryland International Reading Association Council www.somirac.org	*SoMIRAC Journal*	*SoMIRAC Newsletter*
Massachusetts Reading Association www.massreading.org	*Massachusetts Primer*	*The Connection*
Michigan Reading Association www.michiganreading.org	*A View Inside Linking-Developing Strategic Readers and Writers in the Primary Classroom*	*International Reading Association News and Views on Reading*

State Literacy Association*	Journals	Newsletters
	Michigan Reading Journal	
	Writing to Learn Handbooks for Social Studies, Sciences, and Math	
	Kaleidoscope	
Minnesota Reading Association www.mnreading.org		*(Highlights) MRA Newsletter*
Mississippi Reading Association www.msreading.org	*Mississippi Reading Journal*	*MRA Newsletter*
Missouri State Council www.missourireading.org	*The Missouri Reader*	*MSC/IRA Newsletter*
Montana State Reading Council www.montanareads.org	*Montana State Reading Journal*	*Range Reader Newsletter*
Nebraska State Reading Association www.nereads.org		*The Nebraska Reader*
Nevada Silver State Reading Association www.nevadastatereading.org		*Quicksilver SSRA Newsletter*
New Hampshire Granite State Council www.granitestatecouncil.org		*The Granite State Newsletter*
New Jersey Reading Association www.njreading.org	*The Reading Instruction Journal*	*The NJRA Newsletter*
New York State Reading Association www.nysreading.org	*The Language and Literary Spectrum*	*ReAD The Reading Scene*
North Carolina Reading Association www.ncreading.org		*NCRA Newsletter*
North Dakota Reading Association http://ndreadon.utma.com		*The Prairie Reader*

State Literacy Association*	Journals	Newsletters
Ohio Council of the International Reading Association www.ocira.org	*The Ohio Reading Teacher*	OCIRA Newsletter
Oklahoma Reading Association www.oktagagent.com/ora	*The Oklahoma Reader*	*The ORA Newsletter*
Oregon Reading Association www.oregonread.org	*Teachers as Readers Northwest Reading Journal*	*The ORAcle Newspaper in Education Week*
South Carolina State Council of the International Reading Association www.scira.org	*Reading Matters*	*SCIRA SPEAKS Newsletter*
South Dakota Reading Council of the International Reading Association www.sdrc.dsu.edu	*South Dakota Reading Journal*	
Tennessee Reading Association http://plato.ess.tntech.edu/tra	*Tennessee Reading Teacher*	*Reading Matters*
Texas State Reading Association www.tsra.us	*The State of Reading*	*The Texas Reading Report Newsletter*
Utah Council of the International Reading Association www.utahreading.org	*The Utah Journal of Reading and Literacy*	*The Reading Connection*
Vermont Council on Reading www.vermontcouncil onreading.com	*The Vermont Council on Reading (VCR)*	
Virginia State Reading Association www.vsra.org	*Reading in Virginia*	*VSRA Newsletter*
Washington Organization for Reading Development http://wordreading.org		*The WORD*
West Virginia Reading Association www.wvreading.com		*WVRA Interchange*

State Literacy Association*	Journals	Newsletters
Wisconsin State Reading Association http://wsra.org	*WSRA Journal*	*WSRA Update*
Wyoming State Reading Council http://read.1wyo.net	*Wyoming Journal of Literacy*	

* All state literacy associations are affiliates of the International Reading Association.

Literacy Book Publishers in the United States

Academic Therapy Publications
20 Commercial Boulevard
Novato, CA 94949
800-422-7249
www.academictherapy.com

Allyn & Bacon/Longman Publishers
75 Arlington Street, Suite 300
Boston, MA 02116
617-848-6000
www.ablongman.com

Association of Supervision
    and Curriculum Development
1703 N. Beauregard Street
Alexandria, VA 22311
800-933-2723/703-578-9600
www.ascd.org

Brookes Publishing
PO Box 10624
Baltimore, MD 21285
800-638-3775/410-337-9580
www.brookespublishing.com

Christopher-Gordon Publishers
1502 Providence Highway, Suite 12
Norwood, MA 02062
800-934-8322/781-762-5577
www.christopher-gordon.com

Corwin Press/Sage Publications
2455 Teller Road
Thousand Oaks, CA 91320
800-818-7243/805-499-9774
www.corwinpress.com

Eye on Education
6 Depot Way West
Larchmont, NY 10538
888-299-5350
www.eyeoneducation.com

Guilford Publications
72 Spring Street
New York, NY 10012
800-365-7006/212-431-9800
www.guilford.com

Harcourt
6277 Sea Harbor Drive
Orlando, FL 32887
407-345-2000
www.harcourt.com

HarperCollins
10 East 53rd Street
New York, NY 10022
212-207-7000
www.harpercollins.com

Heinemann
361 Hanover Street
Portsmouth, NH 03801
800-225-5800
www.heinemann.com

Houghton Mifflin
222 Berkeley Street
Boston, MA 02116
617-351-5000
www.hmco.com

International Reading Association
800 Barksdale Road, PO Box 8139
Newark, DE 19714-8139
800-336-7323/302-731-1600
www.reading.org

Jossey-Bass
989 Market Street
San Francisco, CA 94103
www.josseybass.com

Kendall/Hunt Publishing
4050 Westmark Drive, PO Box 1840
Dubuque, IA 52004
800-228-0810
www.kendallhunt.com

Lawrence Erlbaum Associates
10 Industrial Avenue
Mahwah, NJ 07430
800-9-BOOKS-9/201-258-2200
www.erlbaum.com

Mid-Continent Research for Education
  and Learning
4601 DTC Boulevard, Suite 500
Denver, CO 80237
303-337-0990
www.mcrel.org

The National Academies Press
500 Fifth Street NW, Lockbox 285
Washington, DC 20055
888-624-8373/202-334-3313
www.nap.edu

National Association for the Education
  of Young Children
1313 L Street NW, Suite 500
Washington, DC 20005
800-424-2460/202-232-8777
www.naeyc.org

National Council of Teachers of English
1111 W. Kenyon Road
Urbana, IL 61801
877-369-6283/217-328-3870
www.ncte.org

Pearson Education
One Lake Street
Upper Saddle River, NJ 07458
201-236-7000
www.pearsoned.com

Scholastic
557 Broadway
New York, NY 10012
800-724-6527/212-343-6100
www.scholastic.com

Stenhouse
480 Congress Street
Portland, ME 04101
800-988-9812
www.stenhouse.com

Teachers College Press
1234 Amsterdam Avenue
New York, NY 10027
212-678-3929
www.teacherscollegepress.com

Books on Writing for Publication

Author	Title	Date/Publisher	Annotation
Cantor, Jeffrey	*A Guide to Academic Writing*	1993 Praeger Publishers Greenwood Publishing Group 88 Post Road West Westport, CT 06881 203-226-3571 webmaster@ greenwood.com	A handbook giving basic information on getting into academic print using service-based accomplishments (consultation and speeches) and classroom contributions as well as research. Gives specific strategies, discusses mechanics of producing for scholarly journals, conference papers, and successful grant writing.
Casanave, Christine Pearson, and Vandrich, Stephanie (Eds.)	*Writing for Scholarly Publication: Behind the Scenes in Language Education*	2003 Lawrence Erlbaum Associates 10 Industrial Avenue Mahwah, NJ 07430 201-258-2200	A collection of first-person essays by established authors provides support and insights for new and experienced academic writers in language education and multicultural studies, covering a range of practical, political, and personal issues.

Author	Title	Date/Publisher	Annotation
Germano, William P.	*Getting It Published: A Guide for Scholars and Anyone Else Serious About Serious Books*	2001 University of Chicago Press 1427 E. 60th St Chicago, IL 60637 773-702-7700 Marketing@press. uchicago.edu	This is a guide to academic publishing and how to make it work for the reader.
Glatthorn, Allan	*Publish or Perish: The Educator's Imperative*	2002 Corwin Press/ Sage Publications 2455 Teller Road Thousand Oaks, CA 91320 800-818-7243 webmaster@sage pub.com	The author offers tools to create and enhance professional submissions in a conversational tone.
Henson, Kenneth T.	*A Brief Guide to Writing for Professional Publications*	1998 Phi Delta Kappa Educational Foundation 408 N. Union Bloomington, IN 47408 800-766-1156 orders@pdkintl.org	This short pamphlet for new and experienced writers covers preparing and submitting a manuscript and setting up a productive framework for writing.
Huff, Anne Sigismund	*Writing for Scholarly Publication*	1998 Sage Publications 2455 Teller Road Thousand Oaks, CA 91320 800-818-7245 webmaster@sage pub.com	This step-by-step guide includes choosing a subject, developing content, and submitting a manuscript based on the idea that the publication should follow the rules of a good conversation among scholars. Includes exercises, checklists, useful appendixes, and bibliography.

Author	Title	Date/Publisher	Annotation
Jalongo, Mary Renck	*Writing for Publication: A Practical Guide for Educators*	2001 Christopher-Gordon Publishers 1502 Providence Highway Norwood, MA 02062 800-934-8322 cgpublish@christopher-gordon.com	Advice on publication of topics such as class-room experience, confer-ence presentations, or research projects with practical strategies, concrete examples, recommended resources, and lessons for learning to work with editors and reviewers.
Miller, Sharon K., and Richards, Janet C.	*Doing Academic Writing in Education: Connecting the Personal and the Professional*	2005 Lawrence Erlbaum Associates 10 Industrial Avenue Mahwah, NJ 07430 201-258-2200	Intended to help readers gain confidence and competence in academic writing. Encourages reflection on how the professional connects to the personal.
Moxley, Joseph H.	*Publish, Don't Perish: The Scholar's Guide to Academic Writing and Publishing*	1992 Praeger Publishers Greenwood Publishing Group 88 Post Road West Westport, CT 06881 203-226-3571 webmaster@green wood.com	Intended to help professors thrive as writers, this book provides the support for scholarship that can ease tension between teaching and writing.
Powell, Walter W.	*Getting Into Print: The Decision-Making Process in Scholarly Publishing*	1985 University of Chicago Press 1427 E. 60th St Chicago, IL 60637 773-702-7700 Marketing@press. uchicago.edu	Offers insights into the internal politics and the external networks that influence the decisions made by organizations that publish scholarly discourse.
Silverman, Franklin H.	*Publishing for Tenure and Beyond*	1999 Praeger Publishers Greenwood Publishing Group 88 Post Road West Westport, CT 06881 203-226-3571 webmaster@green wood.com	This guide compares successful writing/ publishing to a game with specific rules and strategies to achieve success for tenure and periodic reviews.

AUTHOR INDEX

SUBJECT INDEX

Note. Page numbers followed by *t* indicate tables.

L

LANGUAGE ARTS, 60t
LEARNING DISABILITIES RESEARCH AND PRACTICE, 61t
LECTURA Y VIDA, 60t
LETTERS: cover, 18–19; query, 90–91; resubmission, 143–147
LINE OF INQUIRY: reputation for, 82
LITERACY AND LITERACY-RELATED ORGANIZATIONS, 173–175
LITERATURE REVIEW: in professional journals, 62
LITERATURE SEARCHES: and topic selection, 4
LONG-SHOT REVISE-AND-RESUBMIT LETTER, 136–137

M

MAGAZINES: style of, 91–93; teacher, 88
MANUSCRIPT(S): cleaning up, 112; preparation, for professional journals, 62–66; resting, 110–112, 168; revisions to, chances for, 139–142; submission guidelines, 18
MARKET: study of, 86–87
MCNAIR, JONDA, 153
METHODOLOGY: in research journal manuscripts, 80–81; selection of, 9–11
MEYER, PAUL, 4
MILLER, HENRY, 169
MINDSET: for writing for publication, 2–23
MOORE, DAVID, 27
MORROW, LESLEY, 26
MOTIVATION, 58

N

NATIONAL ASSOCIATION FOR THE EDUCATION OF YOUNG CHILDREN, 174
NATIONAL COUNCIL FOR TEACHERS OF ENGLISH, 175; journals of, 60t
NATIONAL READING CONFERENCE, 175
NEUMAN, SUSAN, 163
NEWSLETTERS, 88
NEWSPAPERS: as outlets, 87; style of, 91–93; writing for, 85–99
NICOLSON, HAROLD, 59

O

O'CONNOR, FLANNERY, 155
OPENNESS: in collaboration, 50–51
ORAL LANGUAGE: prewriting, 32; versus writing, 72
OUTLETS: appropriate presentation for, 89–90; evaluation of, 30–32; and idea development, 14–17; literacy and literacy-related organizations, 173–175; other, 85–99; questions on, 15; for rejected work, 137, 154–155, 162–165; for research journal manuscripts, 77–78
OUTLINES: and focus, 14; timing of, 34–36

P

PAGE LIMITS: and pruning, 14
PASSION: in writing, 11–13, 167
PATIENCE, 168; in collaboration, 50–51
PAULING, LINUS, 124
PEARSON, P. DAVID, 29
PEER REVIEW, 17
PERCY, WALKER, 33
PERFECTION: versus quality, 82
PERIODICALS: writing for, 55–99
PERMISSIONS, 122
PERSISTENCE, 168; in writing, 110
PHI DELTA KAPPA, 175
PICTURES: in edited volume, 122; for interest, 111
PINNELL, GAY SU, 104, 153
PLANS: for publishing in professional journals, 57–58
POLYA, GEORGE, 27
POWER: writing with, 25
PRECISION: in research journal manuscripts, 76–77
PREFACE, 120–121
PRESSLEY, MICHAEL, 170
PREWRITING ORAL LANGUAGE, 32
PRINCIPLES: and revise-and-resubmit decisions, 138
PRINGLE, LAWRENCE, 105
PROCEDURES: for professional journal manuscripts, 64
PROCRASTINATION: versus collaboration, 47–48
PROFESSIONAL ACTIVITIES: as topics, 39–40
PROFESSIONAL JOURNALS, 56–71; audience of, 57–59; types of, 60, 60t–61t
PRUNING, 14
PUBLICATION OUTLETS. See outlets
PUBLISHING ETIQUETTE, 18–19
PUBLISHING HOUSES, 30–31, 181–182; homework on, 31–32; requests from, 126–128
PUBLISHING PROCESS: beginning, 1–53; learning about, 17–19

Q

QUALITY: versus perfection, 82
QUERY LETTERS, 90–91
QUESTIONS: on publication outlets, 15; research, statement of, 80

R

RAU, SANTHAT RAMA, 165
READERS: of research journal, 77–78
READING: about scholarly publication, 74–75, 75t; and book writing, 110; and topic selection, 5–6
READING AND WRITING QUARTERLY, 61t
READING HORIZONS, 61t
READING PSYCHOLOGY, 61t